Praise for *The Growth Drivers*

"Clear, insightful and pragmatic. It clarifies the unique contribution that effective marketing and marketers can make to driving business growth – just as relevant to the digital world as to more conventional markets."
Dan Cobley, VP Marketing, Northern and Central Europe, Google

"A provocative, insightful book that drives deep into the marketing function. It highlights the strategic contribution of marketing and is full of practical advice on how to build marketing capabilities to encourage growth."
Sir Roy Gardner, Chairman of Compass Group plc

"Skillfully blending concepts and frameworks with case studies and first person accounts, this highly readable, practical book is a must-read for all those interested in taking their marketing and business performance to the highest level."
Kevin Lane Keller, E.B. Osborn Professor of Marketing at Tuck School of Business, Dartmouth, USA

"Redefines the role of marketing. A must read for any business leader who wants to better understand the role marketing can play in driving business growth, particularly in today's matrix'ed environment – and puts them in a position to do something about it."
Simon Lowden, CMO, Pepsi Beverages, North America

"A great book that is both easy to read and well worth the effort. A 'big picture' guide to what marketing involves in practice and to the invaluable role capability development plays in driving growth."
Jill McDonald, UK Chief Executive and President Northern Europe Division, McDonald's

"Unlike most marketing books, this is a great read. It is replete with practical points, each of which is supported by examples from world class companies. I urge everyone in marketing, be it practitioner, academic or student, to buy it, read it and act on it."
Professor Malcolm McDonald MA(Oxon) MSc PhD DLitt, Emeritus Professor Cranfield University School of Management

"Undoubtedly the defining work in the field. Each page is built on deep, deep experience of the realities of turning the ambition of powerful marketing into its reality, and putting marketing and the marketing director at the very centre of a company's success. Reading it could dramatically improve your career path."
Adam Morgan, Founder, Eatbigfish

"This is an excellent book. It explains how marketers can set a more strategic 'growth-driving' vision, engage the whole organization with a customer-centric agenda and then help deliver tangible results. I recommend it as a must read for all global marketing and business leaders."
Steve Radcliffe, Partner, Steve Radcliffe Associates

"An excellent guide to the unique contribution that marketing makes to driving business growth. Underpins the strategic value of marketing capability development as a key driver of growth."
Russ Shaw, former Vice President and General Manager-Mobile Division and Europe, Middle East and Africa, Skype

"Mhairi and Andy practise what they preach. They perfectly epitomise the growth driver principles outlined in this book. Their own marketing consultancy has grown explosively in size and stature. They service a wide range of blue chip marketing clients and they run a happy ship, stuffed full of talented marketing people. This book distils their knowledge and packages it in a useful and readable way."
Cilla Snowball CBE, Group Chairman and Group CEO, Abbott Mead Vickers BBDO

"Brand Learning are the best in the business when it comes to building marketing capability. And this book is a great way to get the inside line on their approach."
David Taylor, Founder and Managing Partner, the brandgym

"An excellent, accessible guide to the crucial role that strategic marketing plays in driving business growth and the practical ways in which business leaders can build stronger marketing capabilities in their organizations. Andy and Mhairi always have a lot to offer and it is great to see so many insights captured in this book."
Keith Weed, Chief Marketing and Communications Manager, Unilever plc

THE
GROWTH
DRIVERS

THE GROWTH DRIVERS

The Definitive Guide to Transforming Marketing Capabilities

ANDY BIRD AND MHAIRI McEWAN

A John Wiley & Sons, Ltd., Publication

This edition first published 2012
© 2012 Andy Bird and Mhairi McEwan

Registered office

John Wiley & Sons Ltd, The Atrium, Southern Gate, Chichester, West Sussex, PO19 8SQ, United Kingdom

For details of our global editorial offices, for customer services and for information about how to apply for permission to reuse the copyright material in this book please see our website at www.wiley.com.

Wiley publishes in a variety of print and electronic formats and by print-on-demand. Some material included with standard print versions of this book may not be included in e-books or in print-on-demand. If this book refers to media such as a CD or DVD that is not included in the version you purchased, you may download this material at http://booksupport.wiley.com. For more information about Wiley products, visit www.wiley.com.

Designations used by companies to distinguish their products are often claimed as trademarks. All brand names and product names used in this book are trade names, service marks, trademarks or registered trademarks of their respective owners. The Brand Learning Partners Limited owns all rights relating to the following trade marks, which are reproduced with its kind permission:

Brand Learning
The Brand Learning Logo
Brand Learning Radar

All rights in relation to the title and content of this work, including the registered trade mark 'The Growth Drivers', are owned by Andy Bird and Mhairi McEwan. The Authors also own all rights in relation to the cover and jacket design of this work, save the 'blue blurred sparkler' image used under license from iStockphoto © Andy Bird and Mhairi McEwan, 2011.

The publisher is not associated with any product or vendor mentioned in this book. This publication is designed to provide accurate and authoritative information in regard to the subject matter covered. It is sold on the understanding that the publisher is not engaged in rendering professional services. If professional advice or other expert assistance is required, the services of a competent professional should be sought.

Library of Congress Cataloging-in-Publication Data

Bird, Andy.
   The growth drivers : the definitive guide to transforming marketing capabilities / Andy Bird and Mhairi McEwan.
      p. cm.
   Includes bibliographical references and index.
   ISBN 978-1-119-95331-9 (hardback)
  1. Market segmentation.   2. Economic development.   3. Investments.   I. McEwan, Mhairi.   II. Title.
   HF5415.127.B57 2011
   658.8'02—dc23

                                                                                    2011034158

A catalogue record for this book is available from the British Library.

ISBN 978-1-119-95331-9 (hardback) ISBN 978-1-119-96118-5 (ebk)
ISBN 978-1-119-96119-2 (ebk)   ISBN 978-1-119-96120-8 (ebk)

Set in 10/14.5 pt FF Scala by Toppan Best-set Premedia Limited, Hong Kong
Printed in Great Britain by TJ International Ltd, Padstow, Cornwall, UK

A special dedication to our friends and colleagues at
Brand Learning.
Without your unswerving passion, commitment to excellence, collaboration and
support, this book would never have been written.

"He who learns but does not think, is lost.
He who thinks but does not learn is in great danger."
Confucius 551–479 BC

CONTENTS

FOREWORD

It gives me great pleasure to write this short foreword to *The Growth Drivers*. The task of driving sustainable, profitable growth is of critical importance to organizations of all shapes and sizes across the globe and I believe this book will undoubtedly make a contribution to meeting that challenge.

Our world is changing before our eyes. Technology is evolving at a rapid rate and as a result, the availability, speed and impact of data are at levels never previously seen. Indeed, the accessibility of information is empowering people as never before. In turn, the demands on business are ever increasing as previously dormant economies become the new global growth engines and a fresh source of competitive challenge.

The need to deliver sustainable growth for the benefit of shareholders, customers and employees alike, demands that business must relentlessly strive to build competitive edge. Marketing is not the only source of growth but it is an important one. Without respect and responsiveness to its customer needs, any organization is running on borrowed time.

In this book, the authors argue that effective marketing has a vital role to play in this mission – and they are right. It is a critical role and it is also a weighty responsibility – one that cannot be ignored.

Customer expectations of brands and of organizations are higher than ever. To fulfil such demands, innovation must be balanced with consistency, quality with value, choice with responsibility and sustainability with growth. But whilst there are enormous challenges and complexities to be addressed, there are also unparalleled opportunities for those organizations equipped for change.

The Growth Drivers is a practical guide to what organizations can do to transform themselves to meet those challenges – how they can develop their marketing capabilities to build strong and distinctive brands that create better customer value and help drive sustainable, profitable, demand-led growth. It explains the role that effective marketing should play in enabling organizations to drive that growth, clarifies what 'world-class marketing' really means and explores how effective marketing should work in practice – highlighting the key role played by marketing, by marketers and by marketing capability development in driving growth.

The Growth Drivers is filled with deep insight and the grounded, practical experience of international business leaders who are all grappling daily with growth challenges. Its message is an optimistic one – that any organization with the right focus and effort can build stronger marketing capabilities to help drive demand-led growth. The organizations with the foresight to recognize that fact, and to act on it, will be the ones who best succeed in driving that growth – and they will deserve it.

Sir Roger Carr

Sir Roger Carr is Chairman of Centrica plc and President of the CBI

INTRODUCTION – OUR STORY

"Think for a moment of the long chain of iron or gold, of thorns or flowers, that would never have bound you, but for the formation of the first link on one memorable day."
Charles Dickens *Great Expectations*

We owe our deep passion for marketing to the extraordinary commitment to marketing excellence shown at Unilever – one of the world's leading suppliers of consumer packaged goods. Unilever took us both on from university in the mid-1980s as marketing trainees and over many years the people we worked with taught us to understand and respect, in equal measure, the discipline of marketing.

Andy's career took him through foods marketing roles in the UK, Singapore and India before he moved on to scope and set up the global Unilever Marketing Academy. He led this group for several years, introducing new thinking, process tools and learning programmes that were cascaded globally to all business units and geographies.

Meanwhile, Mhairi's career in Unilever's Home & Personal Care business included international marketing and sales roles based in the UK, France and Egypt. She then moved on to head up marketing for PepsiCo Europe and Walkers Snack Foods, before becoming a consultant to Burger King, Guinness and Unilever and supporting for several years the development of content materials for the global 'Diageo Way of Brand Building'.

As we moved on in our careers, we began to appreciate the much wider context in which marketing operates in different companies, cultures and industries. In our combined 50 years of marketing experience working with global, regional and local teams across the world, we have each experienced, first hand, the power and potential for marketing to drive brand and business growth.

However, as we looked across these businesses, we also began to appreciate the extent of the challenges facing marketers – global brands, specialized roles, increasing channel complexity, high staff turnover, return on investment pressures and enormous changes in the legal, regulatory and digital landscape.

There was widespread confusion and misunderstanding about the scope and role of marketing. There was no established terminology, few practical tools, poorly defined processes and inadequate training. Moreover, the responsibility for marketing capabilities was unclear and fell within two functions – the Marketing and HR teams.

It was for this reason that, in July 2000, we set up Brand Learning, joined initially by a third director, Mark Simmonds, who a few months later stepped out into an independent consultancy role. Brand Learning was established around a unique passion to build the marketing capabilities and commercial performance of people, teams and organizations across the world. What first started as an idea then became a shared vision to shake up the world of marketing "training" and to establish a whole new category – that of *marketing capability development* – to help re-engineer the way marketing works.

We were soon joined by other marketing professionals who made essential personal contributions to that mission along the way, most notably by our four board partners – Jill Hughes, Michele McGrath, Ana Maria Santos, and Nevine El-Warraky. Each in their turn brought deep expertise in marketing and consultancy with leading organizations such as Colgate, Reckitt Benckiser, PepsiCo, Unilever, PricewaterhouseCoopers (PwC) and the Added Value Group.

Our experience since then, with our world-class clients and colleagues at Brand Learning, has shaped where we are today and why we wrote *The Growth Drivers*. Our aim is to clarify the role of marketing and its important contribution to growth, to highlight the unique growth contribution made by marketers, and to share our experience of how to build the marketing capabilities needed to help create better customer value and drive growth.

We are inspired by two passions. First, by the role that strong brands and propositions – fuelled by effective marketing – can play in helping *organiza-*

tions grow. And second, by the impact that learning can have on the growth of *people* – by building their marketing skills, changing their attitudes and building their capabilities and confidence to become more effective in their work and in their lives more generally.

There are many people who have strong credentials in the sphere of marketing. However, their focus is usually on doing the job itself, rather than on explaining to others *what* they do and *how* they do it. We have a unique perspective that comes from being experienced marketing practitioners. We have also been able to look at marketing through the wide lens of international consultancy and we have worked passionately over the past 10 years and more, to pioneer the category of marketing capability development.

Together with our team at Brand Learning, we have worked in every global continent, in over 60 countries, with more than 100 multinational organizations in almost every sector. Our collective experience ranges from consumer packaged goods, retail, technology, financial services, telecommunications, leisure and media to pharmaceuticals, oils and gas, chemicals, household white goods and consumer electronics, in both the public and private sectors and the not-for-profit sector.

We have seen these many different organizations struggling with the same issues and striving to address the same challenges. Over and over we have heard the same pleas – we need to grow faster yet we lack the capabilities; we need to be 'world class' at marketing but we don't know how to get there, or even how we rank compared to our peers.

So we have written this book to share what we have learned. We offer it not only as a practical guide to building marketing capabilities, but also with the belief that marketers around the world will benefit from their organizations meeting some of the challenges we set – helping to establish marketing, marketers and marketing capability development as valuable *growth drivers*.

Thank you

• • ● • •

We are very grateful to *all* those who have helped *The Growth Drivers* itself "grow" from an idea and a somewhat daunting task several years ago, into this book. We'd also like to thank some very special people, without whose help both the book and Brand Learning itself would not be the same.

First, a huge thank you to all the senior business and marketing leaders who, despite the pressures of very busy jobs, have given so freely of their time, experience and learnings and for the many valuable insights they have shared throughout this book. A list of all the contributors is provided overleaf.

Our heartfelt thanks and appreciation to our fellow board directors, partners and to every member of the Brand Learning team. We are honoured to be on this journey of growth with you. Thank you for your confidence in us, for your professionalism, passion and unswerving commitment in growing Brand Learning over the past 11 years. And for all the many ways in which your deep expertise and experience has contributed to the exciting new category of marketing capability development that we have opened up together.

Thank you to our researcher Elen Lewis – a respected writer for The Marketing Society and author in her own right, and a source of fantastic inspiration and support over the past three years. Thank you also to Claire Plimmer and to our publishers Wiley, who first approached us many years ago to ask us to put some of our ideas into writing and who have shown incredible patience!

Thank you to Jane Boydell and Lisa Thomas, our PAs, for their good humour, indefatigable commitment and practical skills; to Stuart Tucker for his support on images and visuals; to Lisa Schaverien and ArtHaus for concept and cover design; to Lee Waters for keeping the IT system operational; to Susan Sochart, Sorcha Hunter and Tonia Cassandro for marketing support; and to Graham Viles and James Mitchell for their support on the commercial and legal aspects of producing this book.

A big thanks must go to everyone who read and gave feedback on our draft text – our board partners, also Sam Ellis, Linda Miller and Bruce Levi for patiently reading, reviewing and critiquing the content and structure, and to Emma Jenkins for her research and support on marketing developments in digital and social media. We are immensely grateful for all your contributions.

And finally . . . a very personal and heartfelt thank you to our partners Jacqui and Phil, our kids Susanna, Jonnie, Naomi and Guy, our parents Derek, Ann, Eddie and Rose and to all our friends for their amazing support, belief, patience and encouragement. We only hope we can now find more time to spend enjoying your company!

CONTRIBUTORS

We are deeply indebted to all of the following business and marketing leaders for generously sharing their insights, experiences and examples with us as we wrote *The Growth Drivers*:

- **AkzoNobel**
  Karen Jeffery, Global Marketing Capability Leader
- **Alliance Boots**
  Torvald de Coverly Veale, International Brands Development Director
- **AstraZeneca**
  Andrew Bailey, Vice President, World Class Marketing
  Tim Bailey, Head of Marketing Academy
- **Aviva**
  Jan Gooding, Global Marketing Director
  Amanda Mackenzie, Chief Marketing Officer
- **Barclaycard**
  Nina Bibby, Global Chief Marketing Officer
  Jon Harding, Head of Organization Development
- **British Gas**
  Phil Bentley, Managing Director
  Chris Jansen, Managing Director, Services & Commercial
- **BT**
  Lesley Wilson, Head of BT Marketing Community and Brand Operations

- **Bupa**
  Martin George, Managing Director for Group Development
  Fiona McAnena, Global Brand Director
- **Carlsberg**
  Julie Blou, Senior Manager, Carlsberg GroupWay
- **Diageo**
  Paul Walsh, Chief Executive
  Nick Rose, former Chief Financial Officer
- **FrieslandCampina**
  Franc Reefman, Marketing Director
- **Google**
  Dan Cobley, VP Marketing, Northern and Central Europe
- **Honda Motor Europe**
  Ian Armstrong, European Communications Director
- **HP Imaging and Printing Group**
  Philip Darnell, VP of Marketing
  Kevin Kussman, Director Learning & Development
- **HP Snapfish**
  Barry Herstein, Chief Marketing Officer
- **Ideal Standard**
  David Hamill, Chairman
  Kerris Bright, Chief Marketing Officer
- **IHG**
  Tom Seddon, EVP and Chief Marketing Officer
- **Kellogg**
  Mark Baynes, Global Chief Marketing Officer
- **Kerry Foods**
  Phil Chapman, Group Marketing Director
- **Novartis Pharmaceuticals**
  Huw Jones, Senior Director, Global Commercial Excellence
  Cathy Strizzi, Director, Learning and Capability Development
- **PepsiCo (Pepsi Beverages)**
  Simon Lowden, Chief Marketing Officer, North America

- **Pfizer Europe**
  Craig Scott, former Head of Specialty Analytics
- **Reckitt Benckiser**
  Victoria Coe, Global Brand Marketing Manager
- **Rolls-Royce**
  Steven Dyke, Head of Global Early Career and UK Recruitment
- **SABMiller**
  Nick Fell, Group Marketing Director
- **Sara Lee**
  Nilgun Langenberg, former VP Talent Development and Learning
- **Shell**
  Navjot Singh, Global Marketing Manager, Recruitment and HR Communications
- **Shell UK Oil Products**
  Mel Lane, General Manager, UK Retail
- **Shell Bitumen and Shell Sulphur Solutions**
  Richard Davies, Global Marketing Manager
- **Unilever**
  Ros Walker, VP Marketing Capability
  Helen Lewis, Consumer Insight and Marketing Strategy Director, Unilever Marketing Academy
- **Virgin**
  Mark Gilmour, Brand Director, South East Asia

We are also very grateful to all those whose own work we have quoted in small extracts – may we thank you and accredit your thinking and contributions.

In *The Growth Drivers* we aim to help organizations and business leaders reach a deeper appreciation of the strategic value of marketing, of marketers and of marketing capability development in driving sustainable, profitable growth. It can be read from start to finish or readers can feel free to dip into the most relevant chapters reflecting their interest and experience. For ease of reading we have divided the book into three main sections:

Part 1: Understanding the Growth Drivers

- **Chapter 1 – The Growth Challenge** (page 7) explains what growth involves, the role of marketing as a discipline, what we mean by *The Growth Drivers* and why marketing capability development is so important to drive growth.

- **Chapter 2 – How Marketing Drives Growth** (page 37) examines in more detail the role of the marketing function and the specific tasks and activities that are involved in driving growth through marketing. We introduce a powerful new model called *The Growth Propeller* to explain the core marketing capabilities needed to drive growth.

- **Chapter 3 – Transforming Marketing Capabilities** (page 71) focuses on the challenges of marketing capability development, explaining what it is and overturning the common misunderstanding that "capability building" is just training. We introduce another useful tool, *The Brand Learning Wheel*, which defines a more holistic approach to capability development.

Part 2: How to Transform Marketing Capabilities to Drive Growth

- **Chapter 4 – Defining a Marketing Capability Strategy** (page 103) explains how to kick off a marketing capability development programme by defining the key issues facing the organization and creating an inspiring marketing capability vision, strategy and plan.

- **Chapter 5 – Developing Solutions (Processes and Skills)** (page 133) guides readers through the detailed process of developing marketing capability programmes focused on the capability drivers in the "top half" of *The Brand Learning Wheel*, i.e. marketing processes, tools and their integration with skill development initiatives.

- **Chapter 6 – Developing Solutions (Organization, People and Culture)** (page 165) continues the development stage, covering initiatives that focus on the capability drivers in the "bottom half" of *The Brand Learning Wheel*, i.e. organization structure and roles, people and talent management, and company culture.

- **Chapter 7 – Driving Embedding** (page 199) covers the challenge of launching and embedding capability development programmes in an engaging, inspiring way that changes the way people work to deliver business growth in practice.

Part 3: Sustaining Growth in Practice

- **Chapter 8 – Measuring Impact** (page 229) examines the challenge of measuring the effectiveness both of marketing and of marketing capability programmes. Here, we review some of the main approaches used to measure the tangible impact of marketing and of capability development.

- **Chapter 9 – Mobilizing Capability Resources** (page 255) covers insights and practical advice on a range of ways to organize marketing capability development, for those with limited resources right up to those looking to establish a dedicated in-house marketing academy or marketing excellence team.

- **Chapter 10 – The Future Growth Journey** (page 277) concludes by looking forward to some of the future opportunities and challenges facing marketing and provides a practical *Fit for Growth* tool with 15 simple questions to help readers assess the status of marketing and marketing capabilities in their own business.

Part 1
Understanding the Growth Drivers

Chapter 1

The world is changing fast. The breathtaking pace of technological advances and the advent of social media have prompted an unprecedented growth in "people power". In parallel, the urgency of achieving environmental sustainability, the shift in economic power to emerging markets and the cultural implications of globalization are transforming the world in which we live.

The speed and scale of these changes are having a major impact on all organizations. Yet, as businesses everywhere strive to keep pace with these challenges, they remain under more pressure than ever to drive profitable, sustainable growth and deliver shareholder value – creating a significant *growth challenge*.

As organizations strive to weather the storms of economic recession, the focus for many is on the financial drivers of shareholder value, on cost reduction, efficiencies, staff severance and budget restrictions. But costs can only be cut so far.

There is now a growing recognition of the need to embrace new market opportunities, to create value in new ways and to drive growth in a more proactive and sustainable way that addresses and balances the needs of all stakeholders – customers, shareholders, employees and society as a whole.

But what do we mean by growth? What is the role of marketing and marketers in driving growth? And how can you build the marketing capabilities to drive that growth in practice? These are some of the important questions we will answer in *The Growth Drivers*.

Types of growth

Organic business growth, as opposed to growth from mergers and acquisitions or other financial activities, is best driven by increasing customer demand. To avoid confusion, we use the term customer here and throughout *The Growth Drivers* to mean the people or organizations that buy an organization's products or services – which may include consumers, shoppers, channel partners, businesses or public bodies.

Demand-led growth is driven, at its core, by more customers choosing to buy those products and services, buying them more frequently, buying greater quantities of them or being prepared to pay more for them. So, to drive demand-led growth, organizations have to be able to *consistently create better value* for their customers – this task is the core role of marketing.

What is Marketing?

We believe that the most urgent priority facing all organizations striving to drive growth today is to pay as much attention to the *marketing* drivers of performance as they have traditionally paid to the *financial* ones.

This raises a fundamental issue that needs to be overcome. Many organizations and their leaders do not fully understand what marketing is all about, its role as a business function and its potential to drive growth. They therefore lack the marketing capabilities they need to create value and deliver demand-led growth on a sustainable basis.

At one level, many people in an organization could be considered "marketers" because they contribute towards "creating customer value" – such as sales, customer service teams, research and development, etc. This is one reason why the role of the marketing function is widely misunderstood and undervalued.

Another reason is that marketing gets relegated to only one

> *A lot of companies have chosen to downsize, and maybe that was the right thing for them. We chose a different path. Our belief was that if we kept putting great products in front of customers, they would continue to open their wallets.*[1]
>
> Steve Jobs, *CEO, Apple*

dimension of its role – that of brand communication, promotion or sales support. Or, alternatively, it gets merged into sales roles or into an amorphous "commercial" role, where its true purpose gets obscured, or becomes the responsibility of general managers who may lack any specialist marketing expertise.

In our view, marketers have a critical functional contribution to make as the *growth drivers* of an organization. Their *unique* role is to drive growth and create better customer value by building salient brands and innovative propositions that customers find relevant, appealing and distinctive. This creates the crucial demand or *pull* that drives sustainable, profitable growth throughout the system.

> ### The Role of the Marketing Function
> The unique role of the marketing function is to create better value for customers, by building salient brands and innovative propositions that people find relevant, appealing and distinctive, to drive sustainable, profitable, demand-led growth.

The Marketing Capability Challenge

Overview

As we will demonstrate, there has never been a more challenging time to be in marketing, but neither has there been a more exciting time. Marketing has never been more important, but greater appreciation is needed of the *growth-driving* capabilities related to its role, such as insight generation, market segmentation and portfolio planning, innovative proposition and brand development. The power and impact of key enabling skills such as creativity, inspiration, cross-functional leadership and engagement are also often underestimated by executives with too strong a financial or commercial focus.

The marketing capabilities required to drive growth in today's intensely competitive world extend further than the skills of individual marketers,

Figure 1.1: *The Growth Drivers*
Three key drivers of sustainable, profitable, demand-led growth

further even than the skills of marketing teams. The capabilities needed may require reorienting the entire organization, starting with the marketing function, to enable it to operate passionately and continuously in a customer-centric way.

In *The Growth Drivers*, we aim to help business and marketing leaders reach a new, deeper appreciation of the role of three key, inter-related *drivers* of sustainable, profitable, demand-led growth (see Figure 1.1).

- **Marketing:** the *discipline and practices* of marketing, which enable companies to create better value for their customers and thereby drive sustainable, profitable, demand-led growth.

- **Marketers:** the *people* who are responsible for specialist marketing tasks and activities – however these are defined in any specific organization.

- **Marketing capabilities:** the *abilities* of people, teams and organizations as a whole to manage the marketing activities needed to create better customer value and drive demand-led growth.

Where will we focus?

There are many experts pioneering new thinking in *individual* aspects of marketing such as insight, digital marketing etc, and this is also at the heart of our own consultancy work with those at the leading edge of marketing. However, *The Growth Drivers* has a different aim. It will give the 'big picture' on marketing and address all three drivers of demand-led growth, but our primary focus will be on exploring the last one – *how to build the marketing capabilities needed to drive growth.* It is here that, over ten years ago, we identified both a gaping hole and a significant opportunity for organizations to be more proactive and take practical steps to improve their ability to drive growth.

In *The Growth Drivers* we will share our practical experience based on working in international marketing and building marketing capabilities with thousands of marketers across over 100 multinational clients in over 60 countries globally. We are also privileged to be able to share the direct experiences and honest reflections of over 40 senior international business and marketing executives, as we examine the role and impact of the *growth drivers* in their organizations.

Our agenda is forward-looking, positive and optimistic and one that we hope will inspire businesses and their leaders to develop and sustain more customer-centric, growth-oriented strategies. And the practical set of tools, principles and case studies we provide will equip readers with a leading-edge, proven way to approach the task of *building marketing capabilities* and commercial performance in practice.

According to Interbrand's "Best Global Brands Survey 2010", the fastest growing global brands were Apple (up 37% to $21 billion), Google (up 36% to $43 billion) and Blackberry (up 32% to $6.7 billion). Their growth stories to date demonstrate an impressive blend of customer focus, technological innovation and speed of action. But brands in other industries can also successfully drive their growth by becoming more customer-focused, as the following ICI/AkzoNobel case study illustrates.

 ## The ICI Growth Story

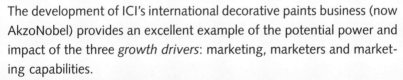

The development of ICI's international decorative paints business (now AkzoNobel) provides an excellent example of the potential power and impact of the three *growth drivers*: marketing, marketers and marketing capabilities.

What was the burning platform?

Going back to 2004, the ICI paints business was facing some big commercial challenges. Although its brands were market leaders in a

number of countries around the world, its market shares were coming under increasing pressure. ICI's brands were being squeezed from below by economy and retailer private label brands and from above by premium competitors positioning themselves as style leaders. The only growth the company was able to achieve was unprofitable, and in the UK, a key market, its primary retail customer was losing patience with ICI's lack of category leadership. Pressure was growing on retail listings and prices and the situation was heading to a crisis point.

The new CEO, David Hamill, and Kerris Bright, UK Marketing Director and later CMO, were clear where the root cause of the problems lay – a lack of strategic marketing. Hamill had been brought on board from Philips to lead a turnaround in ICI's performance and was firm about what the marketing function needed to achieve. *"All businesses must deliver profitable growth if they are to succeed in the longer term, and ICI was no different"*, reflects Hamill. *"The key priority was to create robust brand and product portfolio strategies that would enable us to create competitive advantage and fulfil our commercial potential as a business."*

Kerris Bright adds her perspective, *"David single-mindedly recognized that without strategic marketing thinking we wouldn't win. When I joined the company and talked to our sales colleagues, they also felt that marketing was not creating a sense of direction. There was no clarity on what our future strategy was going to be or where our future growth and profits were going to come from."*

Both Hamill and Bright realized that in order to transform ICI, they first needed to overhaul and develop the marketing capabilities within the company. At the heart of their approach was a drive to upgrade the professionalism, skills and attitudes of the global marketing community so that they were capable of creating the portfolio strategies, brand building innovations and communications so essential to the company's future success.

What was the impact of building marketing capabilities?

Over the coming years, ICI launched a coordinated, worldwide programme of award-winning capability building initiatives. This included an ongoing global audit of its marketing processes and practices, the creation of a common ICI language and a bespoke set of best practice marketing tools. These were launched and cascaded via a series of "live-action learning" programmes for marketing teams focused on helping them

understand the "ICI Way", build their skills, address current marketing challenges and develop proactive business solutions.

The impact was significant and fast. Across the world, ICI focused its marketing efforts behind a lead brand in each market and reduced the complexity in its portfolio. Differentiated positioning was established that played to the company's strengths and new products and award-winning brand communications were soon brought to market.

By 2008, the results were impressive. Hamill's three-year commercial targets to turn round decline and deliver growth in excess of 4% per annum with significantly improved profitability were exceeded. Sizeable share growth had been achieved around the world in key markets such as China, India, Brazil, Poland, and Indonesia. And in the UK, ICI and its flagship Dulux paints brand were awarded the Grand Prix for Marketing Excellence in the prestigious Marketing Society Awards.

ICI's business has since been acquired by AkzoNobel and its "Advance" marketing capability development programme has been adopted across the wider business globally.

As AkzoNobel's Global Marketing Capability Leader, Karen Jeffery, explains, "*In addition to providing people with key skills, tools and processes, Advance continues to play a pivotal role in helping people to understand our strategy and to contextualize their role in building our brands and business. At its core, the Academy's central mission is all about building connectivity, both across the marketing community as well as with our customers.*"

Further investment in capability building has delivered a more integrated, global approach to brand development and an inspiring new brand idea of "adding colour to people's lives" is providing fresh inspiration and purpose across the company. The continued benefits of the strategy are evident in AkzoNobel's performance, with 2010 sales revenue in its decorative paints business up 9% and profits up 13%.

"*The impact of the marketing capability pro-gramme was very significant. We grew the business beyond the normal level of growth in a very slow moving market. We saw a much stronger interaction and way of working between marketing and technical innovation, which created a very healthy pipeline of new products. We saw our brands strengthen and we saw an enormous amount of enthusiasm created in a lot of people, because there was a growing recognition that people's role in the marketing function was important. And I guess the most important thing was that we saw a very, very healthy improvement in the bottom line of the busi-ness. At the end of the day, there has to be clarity of return on invest-ment and we certainly saw that in ICI.***"*

David Hamill, *former CEO, ICI/AkzoNobel*
(now Chairman, Ideal Standard)

A timely call to action

ICI's growth story demonstrates the critical role that marketing, marketers and marketing capability development can play as the *growth drivers* within a business.

For companies to succeed and flourish, investment in building the mar-keting capabilities of their people, teams and the organization as a whole needs to be an important strategic priority. At a time when many organiza-tions are facing unprecedented challenges in driving growth in today's global networked markets, this call to action has never been more timely nor more important to commercial success.

Let's now move on to explore these points in more detail and to understand why growth is so important to organizations. In doing so, we will examine the role of marketing as a discipline, the role of marketers themselves and finally the role of building marketing capabilities in driving sustainable, profitable, demand-led growth.

66 We live in an environment that is changing hugely. Competition is continuously more challenging, the fusion of media and technology is transforming the relationships between brands and consumers, and there is a need for brands to possess a social integrity beyond their economic intent. So it is critical, if we are to continue to deliver results and win in our categories, that we build up stronger specialist marketing capabilities across the organisation. 99

Mark Baynes, *Global Chief Marketing Officer, Kellogg*

Why Growth Matters

Driving shareholder value

Growth is a core driver of shareholder value. In technical terms, shareholder value measures the capital gains of a stock plus the dividends received. It is best correlated to the expected level, timing, duration and risk of future cash flows and the capital employed to generate these cash flows. In the short to medium term, these cash flows can be improved by cutting costs and through acquisition of other businesses, but there is a limit as to how far these strategies can be leveraged. Ultimately, the most sustainable way to create shareholder value in the long term is to enhance customer demand-led growth.

"What many executives have not understood," said Peter Doyle in his book *Value-Based Marketing, "is that shareholder value is more about growth and grasping new market opportunities than reducing expenses . . . the companies that have created the greatest value for shareholders have generally been market-led, high-growth companies."* Doyle went on to conclude that, *"Marketing strategy lies at the heart of value creation. It is the platform on which are based growth, profitability and return on investment."*[2]

DIAGEO Driving Shareholder Value

Diageo, the guardian of iconic brands like Guinness and Johnnie Walker, understands more than most the crucial role that brands and marketing play in driving growth. Nick Rose, previously Diageo's Chief Financial Officer, explains, *"The best way to gain value for shareholders is to get top line growth as it feeds straight through to the bottom line and generates cash."* He goes on to say, *"the more we understand about our brands and the drivers of their success, the more we have seen that brand innovation is a key part of getting that top line growth."*

Driving stakeholder value

However, the importance of growth doesn't begin and end with shareholders. Indeed, relying too heavily on the concept of shareholder value can result in companies focusing excessively on short-term financial gains to the detriment of longer-term brand building and neglecting other influential stakeholders like customers, employees and even society as a whole, all of which have a major influence on sustained commercial success.

We believe that the key growth challenge is to ensure that the needs and demands of all stakeholders are assessed, balanced and reconciled. This imperative will become

❝The job of a leader is to deliver commitments in the short-term while investing in the long-term health of the business. Employees will benefit from job security and better rewards. Customers will benefit from better products and services. Communities will benefit because successful companies and their employees give back. And obviously shareholders will benefit because they can count on companies who will deliver on both their short-term commitments and long-term vision. ❞

Jack Welch, *former CEO of GE.*[3]

Growth brings tangible benefits for all key stakeholders

- Provides more products and services of value to **customers**

- Generates jobs, security and career development opportunities for **employees**

- Creates superior returns for **shareholders**

- Creates commercial benefits for **trade customers, partners and suppliers**

- Improves overall economic prosperity and welfare for **social communities**

ever more important as the world addresses the needs for environmental sustainability, greater social equality and corporate social responsibility.

Driving sustainable growth

Not all growth may be good growth. When brought to task over a serious safety problem with sticky accelerators that led to the recall of over 8.5 million vehicles globally, Akio Toyoda, the chief executive of Toyota, revealed in his written testimony to the US House Oversight Committee: "*I fear the pace at which we have grown may have been too quick. We pursued growth over the speed at which we were able to develop our people and our organization and we should be sincerely mindful of that.*"[4]

By positioning marketers as *growth drivers*, we are not suggesting they should pursue growth at any cost. In addition to the *commercial* sustainability considerations illustrated by Toyota's experience, marketers are increasingly embracing their responsibility to develop more sustainable brand and business opportunities that help alleviate *social* and *environmental* problems, not exacerbate them. But sustainability is not at odds with driving profitable growth.

Paul Polman, CEO of Unilever, sees no conflict between Unilever achieving its sustainability goals and growing its business: *"We are already finding that tackling sustainability challenges provides new opportunities for sustainable growth: it creates preference for our brands, builds business with our retail customers, drives our innovation, grows our markets and, in many cases, generates cost savings."*[5]

 **The "Plan A" Initiative**

Marks and Spencer launched its "Plan A" eco and environmental initiative in 2007 and subsequently targeted the goal of becoming the world's most sustainable major retailer by 2015. As explained on its website, *"Through Plan A we are working with our suppliers to combat climate change, reduce waste, use sustainable raw materials, trade ethically and help our customers lead healthier lifestyles."*[6]

Initially 100 commitments were made within five years, 62 of which have already been completed. Highlights have included reducing CO_2 emissions by 50,000 tonnes, 20,000 tonnes of waste diverted from landfill and 1.8 million clothing garments being recycled via Oxfam. Mike Barry, head of sustainable business at M&S, explains, *"We believe there is more traction to be had with the consumer by engaging them in activities like clothing recycling with Oxfam. It makes a much greater difference to the consumer to be participating in the Plan A journey rather than being told about it by us."*[7]

Marks and Spencer has succeeded in translating social and environmental needs into propositions that have relevance and appeal to customers as well as commercial potential for its business. In 2010, it reported that £50 million additional profit had been generated by "Plan A" which was invested back into the business.[8]

The Role of Marketing

Having established earlier in this chapter what we mean by marketing and by sustainable, profitable growth, let's now move on to explore further the role of marketing, as a discipline and as a business function, in driving that growth. We will start by explaining the role and importance of *brands* in that task.

> *" In marketing we are the growth engines . . . people are either brand developers or brand builders. And the whole business is dependent on our establishing consumer preference for our brands. "*
>
> **Helen Lewis, *Consumer Insight and Marketing Strategy Director, Unilever Marketing Academy***

Over time, brands come to embody the relationship between a company and its customers. From Virgin to Facebook, BMW to Gucci, and from Dove to IBM, every brand has a unique "equity" = a set of perceptions built up in people's hearts and minds based on all their experiences of that brand, both positive and negative.

People associate brands with a distinctive bundle of benefits, values and experiences that, along with factors such as availability and price, affect their propensity to choose that brand from competing offers. It is through the consistent delivery of superior brand benefits, values and experiences that organizations create *value* for their customers.

The concept of customer value

The concept of value is widely misunderstood to relate only to price. In fact, assessments of value are formed by customers by balancing the *perceived benefits* being offered by a product or service for the price charged, with those of competitors. Customers constantly assess perceptions of value relative to their changing needs, to affordability and to competing offers. Keeping one step ahead of this changing *value equation* is at the heart of great marketing.

As we explained earlier, to drive *demand-led growth*, organizations have to be able to consistently create better value for their customers by providing brands and innovative propositions that people find relevant, appealing and distinctive versus competitive offers. A central role of marketing is therefore to strengthen the value of an organization's brands by making them more salient, appealing and available to customers over time.

&& The key marketing task is to make a brand easy to buy; this requires building physical and mental availability. Mental availability/brand salience is the propensity for a brand to be noticed and/or thought of in buying situations. Physical availability means making a brand as easy to notice and buy as possible, for as many consumers as possible, across as wide a range of potential buying situations as possible.&&

The Role of Marketers

Professor Byron Sharp, *author of How Brands Grow[9] and Director of the Ehrenberg-Bass Institute for Marketing Science*

The effective creation and building of brands is at the heart of world-class marketing, but there are widely differing levels of understanding about the way this is best achieved and the implications for the role that the marketing function should play in practice.

In the research we conducted for this book with international business and marketing leaders, there were many examples quoted where marketing is seriously underrated and significantly underplaying its potential contribution as a *growth driver* for the business.

Pejorative references to the "colouring department" and the "pretty pictures department" are common, particularly in the service sector. Looking back on the time when he joined a major telecommunications business, one CMO observed that, *"The marketing department provided nothing more than a wrapper for the business, providing just the advertising for its products and services."*

At energy giant Shell, similar themes were once apparent. Mel Lane, General Manager, UK Retail, Shell UK Oil Products, explains, *"I think for a period of time we were very sales led, with marketing not necessarily leading and driving growth. That has definitely shifted in the last 18 months."*

While major progress is being made in some organizations, marketers in many others are experiencing a real crisis of confidence about the perceived value and scope of their role. Yet, as we aim to show, with greater clarity about this role and more support to build their capabilities to equip and enable them to operate more strategically, marketers can be a source of real competitive edge as key *growth drivers* within an organization.

The widespread misunderstandings about what marketers do arise from the fact that there are two dimensions to their role as *growth drivers*, dimensions which are often not adequately distinguished. One, the better understood dimension, is focused on driving growth through communicating and promoting the company's product and service offerings through advertising, promotion, PR, etc. However, the second more strategic dimension of a marketer's role is to ensure the organization is actively anticipating, creating and delivering products and services that consumers and customers need or want in the first place. Let's look in more detail at each of these dimensions in turn.

> *The marketing input used to be very much an 'end-of-funnel' support influence: so 'the product is finished, get me some users and deliver me some collateral to explain it to people'. Now, the focus is more on: 'the product idea is being formed – help us develop it, fine tune it – and also bring us the customers'.*
>
> Dan Cobley, *VP Marketing, Northern and Central Europe, Google*

Driving growth through communications and promotion

There is no doubt that driving growth through marketing communications and promotion is a vital function that marketers perform and one in which substantial corporate investment is made. Nielsen estimated that global spending on advertising in 2010 was an incredible $503 billion, up by over 10% year-on-year.[10]

Advertising and promotional budgets can account for as much as 30% of overall sales turnover; money which is invested because effective communications and promotional activities build awareness, salience, engagement, availability, consideration and loyalty for brands and therefore have a significant impact on customer demand.

There are many examples of outstanding multi-media brand campaigns that have had a dramatic influence on customers' perceptions and their purchase and usage decisions, driving commercial growth and business performance.

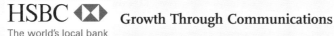

HSBC ◀X▶ Growth Through Communications
The world's local bank

Between 2002 and 2008, HSBC increased its operating income from $26.6 billion to $88.6 billion. A key driver in this success was "The World's Local Bank" campaign which was designed to create a stronger, more consistent, global HSBC brand. The communication idea was based on a belief that progress can best be achieved by embracing cultural diversity around the world, a powerful concept for a company trying to bring together a diverse range of local businesses. In its winning IPA Effectiveness Awards submission, HSBC estimated that a staggering $69.87 billion incremental growth could be attributed to the campaign between 2002 and 2008.[11]

Old Spice Growth Through Social Media

P&G's Old Spice campaign in the US revitalized the brand using social media channels to generate consumer engagement and sales growth. The campaign was based on a viral video featuring National Football

League star Isaiah Mustafa as "the man your man could smell like". In the first 24 hours, the campaign received 5.9 million views on YouTube. In the following six months, it achieved over 1.4 billion impressions. The results in sales terms were equally spectacular, with monthly volumes increasing by 107% year-on-year in the summer of 2010, cementing Old Spice as the leading body wash brand in the US.[12]

Driving growth through creating customer value

Although brand communications and promotional activity are extremely valuable to engage customers and stimulate demand, they only represent one dimension of a marketer's role in driving growth. The second, more strategic dimension, is to ensure the organization is creating and delivering the products and services that consumers and customers need or want in the first place.

If there is one factor that influences the effectiveness and efficiency of marketing communications more than anything else, it is the underlying quality and appeal of the product or service being promoted. Effective marketers understand this and are able to shape the creation and design of new product and service propositions, identifying opportunities to create value for customers by meeting their needs and wants in innovative and differentiated ways. Their task is then to combine strategic market insights with deep knowledge of the capabilities and commercial drivers within their business to unlock new opportunities for profitable growth.

&& People don't really understand what marketing is, and they marginalize it into this one box – communications – which is only one of the component parts. Focusing only on communications is like trying to ice a cake when you should be trying to bake a good cake in the first place, it is so fundamental. 99

Amanda Mackenzie,
Chief Marketing Officer, Aviva

British Gas 🌱 Customer-focused Transformation

British Gas, with its £12 billion revenue, recognizes this challenge well. It has recently undergone a major business transformation from its early roots as a nationalized industry, reorganizing its business, reshaping its operations and integrating its communications to place customers right at the centre. In so doing, it has successfully transformed perceptions of the British Gas brand, attracting 500,000 new customers in 2010, after losing as many as one million customers in one year in 2006.

As Phil Bentley, Managing Director of British Gas, says, *"There is often too much focus in other marketing departments on advertising and not enough on developing consumer-driven strategies. More time is spent worrying about who should direct a TV commercial than on being clear about the benefits of the product or service and how it fits with the strategic growth agenda. The overriding role of marketing is to own the growth agenda. I regard our marketing director as our chief growth officer."*

Driving growth through leadership

Once the expectations of marketing have been raised to a more strategic level, commercial success in driving growth will depend to a large extent on the quality and creativity of the strategies, insights and ideas that marketers generate on behalf of both the organization and its customers.

But that's not the only challenge. For an organization to become genuinely world class at driving growth through effective marketing, its marketers must be enabled and equipped to extend their influence to focus the entire business on a customer-driven agenda. Marketers cannot be left to operate independently within their own functional silo. They need the leadership skills to engage with their colleagues throughout the organization, and with multiple external agencies and specialists, to ensure their combined efforts are aligned in delivering customer value. We will return to this important subject in detail in the next chapter.

Key Marketing Challenges

The challenges facing marketers are considerable and don't end there. Let's be under no illusions, it's a demanding job! As markets mature, competition intensifies, and the pace of technological and social change accelerates, the relentless search for cut-through innovation and better value to maintain competitive edge is increasingly difficult to achieve.

"The development of the growth strategy of a company, particularly in a consumer facing company, lies at the heart of the strategic marketing agenda. If we look at a company like ICI Paints, then I believe the marketing function has a significant leadership role to play. They must build a fundamental understanding of consumers and translate the insights generated from this back into the processes of the whole business, from market strategies, to innovation and ultimately to value creation."

David Hamill,
former CEO ICI Paints/AkzoNobel (now Chairman Ideal Standard).

So let's look at what some of those challenges are and the most important aspects that need to be taken into account if marketers are to play their role as effective *growth drivers*.

Globalization pressures

The search for efficiencies and economies of scale to reduce cost has led many organizations to streamline their operations by moving towards global and regional brands. Whereas once a local market may have operated relatively autonomously, specialized centres of excellence for innovation strategy, research and development, manufacturing, sourcing and supply commonly now work across many countries simultaneously. This has led to harmonized formulations, packaging, design and communication campaigns – evident in the increasing uniformity of the global market place.

This rapid march of globalization means that marketers managing global brands in multinational companies have to achieve a very difficult balance between anticipating and addressing local customer needs, and achieving global scale and efficiency.

Marketers leading brands at a global level need to handle complex data and insights not just from one market, but from many, to determine the similarities across countries and provide platforms on which to build international competitive advantage.

Local marketers, meanwhile, may be equally stretched in covering multiple brands, sectors and markets. In many cases, they are no longer involved operationally in strategic brand development or communications activities, these being centralized into the global brand development teams and agencies. This creates enormous internal and external communications challenges, not least the need to clarify the roles of marketers operating at different stages in the value chain.

&& One of the biggest challenges we face is how senior leadership can embrace what is going on in the world today. When you entered marketing 15 to 20 years ago, there was a very modular, process orientated approach to marketing training. Everything was predicated on the old one agency partner model. Fast forward 20 years and my teenage children know more about iPods and Macs than I will ever learn. Their communication literacy is astounding. The environment we are in now is one that I don't think many experienced marketers have been tooled up for.&&

Simon Lowden, *CMO, Pepsi Beverages, North America*

Digital pressures

Perhaps the most far-reaching consideration for marketers in today's world, however, is the impact of digital technology on brands, businesses and the society around them. The emergence of the "networked society", in which social media is transforming the power and influence of word of mouth, is revolutionizing the world of marketing.

Increasingly, customers are more empowered, more informed, more sceptical and much harder to influence. They are also far less trusting about

Digital Transformation

- Facebook has 750 million active users of which 50% log on every day and 250 million access the site through their mobile devices. In total, people spend over 700 billion minutes per month on Facebook.[13]

- One quarter of the search results to the world's top 20 brands are linked to content generated by customers, not companies.

- Amazon now sells more e-books than printed books.

- Twitter users send over 140 million tweets per day, with over 400,000 new accounts being set up daily.

corporate and brand claims and have far higher expectations of the organizations that supply their goods and services.

Methods of listening to and engaging with customers are changing rapidly, as are the multiple channels and approaches to brand communication. The need to think beyond "paid-for" media and take into account the opportunities represented by "owned" and "earned" media is becoming essential. The availability of more data is enabling completely different approaches to the targeting and tailoring of customer messaging. Conventional marketing processes such as innovation and creative campaign development are being overhauled to involve customers as active participants along the way, often on a mass scale, rather than as recipients of the final output.

The digital world, with its 24/7 "always on" consumer communication, is forcing companies to open right up and integrate previously separate customer facing functions, as well as to become more transparent and demonstrably ethical in their activities.

The networked world has created the biggest shift in marketing seen for a generation. The change is not so much in *what* marketing involves in principle or *why* effective marketing is so critical to drive growth. The real impact is on *how* marketing needs to be carried out and the way marketers need to work in practice so that customer needs are recognized and systematically addressed across the whole organization.

Operational pressures

On top of these new challenges, the drive for cost effectiveness and efficiency has resulted in significant headcount reductions and an almost constant reorganization in marketing departments, creating unprecedented operational pressures for marketers. Time is a constant challenge, caused by multiple demands, ever tighter deadlines and massive internal complexity. A frequent complaint is that it's almost impossible "to see the wood for the trees".

At the same time as the external demands and complexities are accelerating, internal pressures to navigate complex and unwieldy internal structures are growing too. Unclear roles and responsibilities, uncertain boundaries and complex decision-making processes are causing the efficiencies of many marketing departments to suffer.

By contrast to a few years ago, there is much less time and far fewer opportunities to shadow more experienced managers on the job or to invest in core functional skill development. Even experienced marketers lack many of the capabilities needed to navigate the complexities and speed of markets today with the revolution taking place in digital and social media. So it is not surprising that marketers are struggling to cope and that marketing capabilities are increasingly considered to be off the pace.

Capability pressures

The growing marketing capability gap which we will address in the rest of The Growth Drivers is evident everywhere and is all the more serious given the wide range of activities that marketers perform. In some cases, their remit extends

" The skills set required of successful brand marketers going forward will necessarily have to be broader and deeper than it has been in the past. They need to have more in their 'toolkits' than what traditional brand marketers of 10 or 20 years ago required." [14]

Kevin Lane Keller, *Professor of Marketing, Tuck School of Business, Dartmouth College*

from high-level strategic analysis and portfolio planning, right through to operational, in-market brand activation and channel management.

Marketers must be as comfortable working with creative ideas as with financial and commercial data, balancing art and science, intuition and rigorous analysis. They must be able to engage and collaborate with consumers, customers and colleagues in other functions, as well as with the multiple external agencies and specialist suppliers that support them. In the words of one multinational company chairman we worked with, *"You have to be able to fly with the eagles and scratch with the turkeys!"*

The Role of Marketing Capabilities

Taken together, these challenges represent a paradox for marketing. In one respect, there has never been a more difficult era to be a marketer, but neither has there been a more exciting and important one. Times of great change often bring unprecedented opportunities. As we get used to the world transformed by social media, marketers need to be equipped to rise to the challenge and provide the customer-focused leadership their organizations need to deliver and sustain growth.

The big question is, therefore, not *whether* marketing as a discipline is important – if businesses want to thrive and grow in the future, it has to be. The real question organizations have to address is, how can they get *better* at marketing? Do they have the world-class capabilities needed to drive brand and business growth? And if not, how can these marketing capabilities be built in practice?

Beyond marketing training

In our view, the *growth drivers* – "marketing" as a discipline, "marketers" themselves and an organization's "marketing capabilities" – are more important than ever. And of the three, marketing capabilities need particular attention because without focus on these, the potential impact of the other two on commercial performance is unlikely to be realized.

The first task organizations usually think of when they identify the need to build their marketing capabilities is a "training programme" for marketers. And there is no doubt that skill development is an important driver of a marketer's ability to do their job successfully.

But, as we will demonstrate throughout *The Growth Drivers*, for organizations to drive sustainable, profitable, demand-led growth, they need to think and act well beyond the *individual* capabilities of marketers. The real challenge lies in building the *organizational* marketing capabilities needed to drive growth through effective marketing, by changing the way people and teams work in practice in the marketing function and integrating activities across all customer-facing and support functions.

The strategic imperative

The proposition at the heart of *The Growth Drivers* is that organizational leaders who want to drive demand-led growth need to take a *more strategic, holistic and integrated approach to the development of marketing capabilities.* By investing greater time, effort and resources in building the marketing capabilities of their people, teams and their organizations, they will be better equipped to improve commercial performance and drive growth.

Over the years, we have developed a proven, practical and user-oriented approach to planning and implementing marketing capability development strategies and programmes. This is based on working through three important stages which we describe as *The 3D Approach* (see Figure 1.2).

" For me it's a case of pay now or pay later. As a CMO, the sooner you establish the marketing capabilities you need to build your business and your brands, the better positioned you'll be to compete, the better positioned you'll be to win the war for talent, the better positioned you'll be to develop your people and the better positioned you'll be to succeed in your role. And given the data says that the shelf life of most CMOs is just 18–36 months, this is something we ignore at our peril. "

Barry Herstein, *CMO, HP Snapfish*

The 3D Approach

Figure 1.2: *The 3D Approach*
A practical approach to the key stages of marketing capability development

The 3D Approach is a powerful tool that can be used to guide business leaders through the process of marketing capability development:

- **Define strategy** – defining the key capability development issues facing the organization to create an inspiring marketing capability vision, strategy and plan

- **Develop solutions** – developing effective and efficient marketing processes, tools and ways of working and integrating these in a holistic way with blended skill development programmes, and with initiatives in the organization, people and culture drivers of capability

- **Drive embedding** – launching and embedding capability development programmes in an inspiring way that transforms the attitudes, skills and behaviours of people, teams and organizations and changes the way they work in practice.

Changing ways of working

The challenge of embedding changes in the way people work in practice is at the heart of successful marketing capability development. In that respect, it is very similar to the role of marketing itself, but the challenge is to drive improvements in business results by influencing the behaviour of *internal managers* as opposed to that of *external customers*. For this reason, as we shall demonstrate throughout *The Growth Drivers*, the disciplines and practices of marketing are also extremely useful in planning effective marketing capability development.

While marketing *skills* programmes are one important way to drive improved marketing capabilities and performance, we believe a more holistic approach is needed to make a significant impact on the way people, teams and organizations work to create better customer value. So, other factors we will explore in detail in this book are the role of marketing *processes*, the structure and clarity of the *organization*, the profile of talented *people* and the importance of a customer-centric *culture*.

But before we turn to these issues, we need to first define more precisely the marketing activities that contribute to driving growth, and those responsible for them, to help set the agenda for marketing capability development and this will be our focus in the next chapter.

CHAPTER 1 – AT A GLANCE

- The business world faces a substantial challenge – how to deliver sustainable, profitable growth. Costs can only be cut so far and organizations need to create shareholder value by actively driving growth in a more proactive and sustainable way.

- The benefits of sustainable growth are far-reaching, not just for shareholders, but for all the stakeholders connected to an organization – its consumers and other customers, employees, business partners and society as a whole.

- Organic business growth is best driven by increasing customer demand, which means more people choosing to buy products and services, buying them more frequently, buying greater quantities of them or being prepared to pay more for them.

- To drive *demand-led growth*, organizations have to be able to consistently create better value for their customers. The unique role of the marketers in the marketing function is to create better customer value, by building salient brands and innovative propositions that consumers and customers find relevant, appealing and distinctive, to drive sustainable, profitable, demand-led growth.

- Marketing is a widely misunderstood and undervalued business discipline. Brand communications and promotional activity represent just one dimension of a marketer's role in driving growth. The second, more strategic dimension, is to ensure the organization is creating and delivering the products and services that consumers and customers need or want in the first place.

- The three interrelated *growth drivers* in terms of creating customer value are the discipline and practices of *marketing*, the *marketers* responsible for managing functional marketing activities, and the *marketing capabilities* of people, teams and organizations as a whole.

- Effective marketing is extremely challenging, particularly in the context of pressures arising from globalization, digital technologies, internal operational demands and capability challenges.

- Building marketing capabilities is a key strategic priority for any business wanting to drive sustainable, profitable, demand-led growth.

Notes

1   http://www.macstories.net
2   *Value-based Marketing* by Peter Doyle, Wiley 2000, page 54.
3   Business Week column, 2009.
4   Written testimony to the US House Oversight Committee.
5   www.unilever.com/pressreleases 2010.
6   www.plana.marksandspencer.com, 8th May 2011.
7   "Can CSR make money?" by Michael Barnett, *Marketing Week*, 14th April 2011.
8   Marks and Spencer Annual Report 2010.
9   *How Brands Grow* by Byron Sharp, Oxford University Press 2010
10 www.nielsen.com, 4th April 2011.

11 "HSBC – how a brand idea helped create the world's strongest financial brand" by Ian MacDonald and Orlando Hooper-Greenhill. Institute of Practitioners in Advertising Effectiveness Awards 2010.

12 Old Spice Case Study Video, Wieden & Kennedy, www.wearesocial.net

13 www.facebook.com/press/info, 8th May 2011.

14 "The new branding imperatives" by Kevin Lane Keller, fastforward BRANDING, Marketing Science Institute

Chapter 2

In Chapter 1, we emphasized that marketing is all about creating better value for customers to help drive business growth. Yet this clearly isn't something that people in the marketing department do alone; it is the remit of the *entire organization*. From the technicians in the R&D labs to the salespeople in the field, from the shop floor workers to the call centre operatives; every part of an organization needs to play its part in creating better value for customers at each customer "touch point".

But if marketing is the task of the entire organization, what unique role should the function of 'marketing' play to drive profitable, demand-led growth? What are marketers uniquely accountable for? And what key capabilities do marketers need? These are the key questions we aim to answer in this chapter, before we move on to explore how to build the marketing capabilities needed to drive demand-led growth.

Marketing – small 'm' versus big 'M'

Each year, the "Marketing Leaders Programme" is run by The Marketing Society in association with Brand Learning. Top business and marketing leaders gather in London to share their personal leadership stories and inspire a group of aspiring and new marketing leaders. At one of these sessions, Mike Moran, the Marketing Director of Toyota (GB) at that time, described two uses of the word marketing; one with a small "m" and one with a big "M". He used this distinction to separate what the whole company needs to do in terms of marketing (small "m"), from the functional role of the Marketing department (big "M")[1] – a naming convention we will use from now on.

So let's first look at the Marketing function in more detail and at what Marketers should be doing in practice to drive growth. And, for those less familiar with marketing, or keen to challenge their own thinking as to what marketing really involves, let's briefly open the black box and take away some of the mystery.

Our recommendation is that all readers, even Marketing specialists, make the time to read this chapter, not least because it contains *The Growth Propeller*, a useful practical framework that helps explain the unique role that Marketers play and identifies the core marketing capabilities needed to drive sustainable, profitable, demand-led growth.

The black box of marketing

In our experience, for many executives outside Marketing (and a good many inside it!) the definition, role and expectations of the Marketing function and the "nuts and bolts" of brands and brand management are not well understood.

A senior Marketer in one of the top FTSE 100 companies revealed to us, "*Our chief executive took a lot of face time to understand what we mean by the term brand, what we mean when we say we're going to do a brand launch and how the brand can be so important that it needs a standalone function.*"

One reason for the widespread confusion surrounding marketing is that the language

" If you take Marketing out of this organization you don't have the kind of products the consumer wants, you don't have the right spec, you don't have any stock and you've got no way of getting people through the showroom door. But Marketing is losing traction because we're not able to demonstrate all of this. "

Ian Armstrong, *European Communications Director, Honda Motor Europe*

and definition of "customers" is fraught with complexity. In some organizations "customer" means just that; in others the customer can be a retailer or a channel partner, a physician or a buyer, while the end-user or "customer" may be known as the "shopper", "buyer", "patient", "drinker" or "consumer".

It is therefore extremely difficult to define where Marketing as a function begins and ends, because its customer-focused role links so closely with the work of other organizational functions – such as Insight, Sales, R&D, Channel Marketing, Finance, IT, Corporate Brand and HR, as well as with a host of external third party specialists, agencies and consultants.

> *The role of Marketing in driving growth is not well understood in other functions or sometimes by those general managers who are not Marketers by background. As a result we either get boxed into a more limited role – creative, communications, promotions, sponsorship. Or at the other extreme, any issues relating to KPIs on price, revenue management streams, distribution, availability, manufacturing strategies . . . all these questions are laid at the door of Marketing.*
>
> Simon Lowden, *CMO*,
> **Pepsi Beverages, North America**

The "black box" confusion surrounding Marketing is compounded by different industry business models (e.g. consumer packaged goods, retail, financial services, technology), each with differing expectations of their Marketing functions. The different organizational models within businesses don't help (e.g. multi-brand, mono-brand and global versus local brand structures) and neither do the multiple job titles (e.g. marketing, brand, customer, commercial).

The trend in many consumer packaged goods companies towards a more hybrid Sales/Marketing commercial role is yet another challenge where the benefits of a more integrated commercial function, if not managed carefully, can diminish or undermine the specialist *Marketing* capabilities needed to drive growth.

One senior Marketing leader in a new global financial services role candidly admitted that they did not know who in the organization had a "marketing" remit, that many with "marketing" in their job title had few marketing credentials and little expertise, and that others who did have expertise were in roles without a clear marketing remit!

The disciplines of marketing

So, what are the core disciplines of effective marketing? Is there any common agreement, beyond a superficial appreciation of the 4Ps (Product, Price, Place and Promotion), as to what marketing is, what it involves and what the Marketing function can contribute to a business in practice? And is there an explanation that works across industries, applies in both B2B (Business to Business) as well as B2C (Business to Consumer) organizations and is relevant to global Marketing as well as to local Marketing roles?

There is no doubt that organizations in different sectors and categories need different marketing approaches to succeed. The nature of the customer base, the competitive context and the heritage of different companies and brands, will all influence the effectiveness of marketing strategies in driving growth.

However, looking beyond these differences, across the many multinational clients we've worked with, we believe that there are some *core marketing activities* that underpin *any* organization's ability to consistently drive growth. We have captured our thinking in *The Growth Propeller* – a practical tool that captures what we believe are the central elements of "world-class" marketing and how it drives brand and business growth.

The Growth Propeller

The Growth Propeller (see Figure 2.1) provides a framework that outlines the key drivers of marketing effectiveness and therefore helps define the role of Marketers *in practice*. In so doing, it identifies the core capabilities that Marketers need to drive sustainable, profitable, demand-led growth.

This does not mean that every *individual* Marketer needs to excel at all these areas, but that any *organization* aspiring to be world class at marketing needs to consider how well it performs, as a whole, against *The Growth Propeller* dimensions.

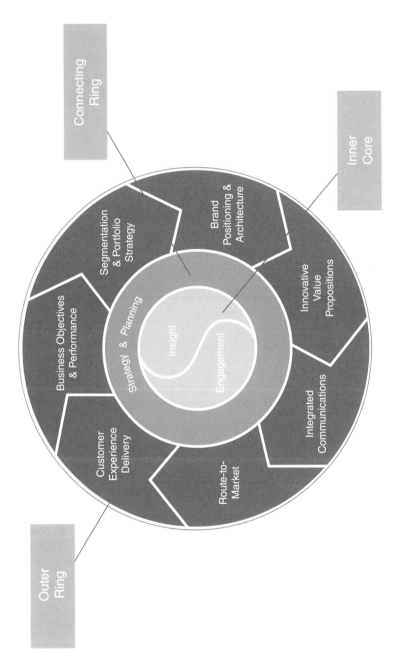

Figure 2.1: *The Growth Propeller*
The core marketing capabilities needed to drive growth

The Growth Propeller – Overview

- **The Outer Ring**: outlines 7 core marketing capabilities from the definition of Business Objectives and Performance, Segmentation and Portfolio Strategy, through the development of Brand Positioning and Architecture, Innovative Value Propositions, Integrated Communications, Route-to-Market and into Customer Experience Delivery.

- **The Connecting Ring**: captures the Strategy and Planning capabilities needed to connect marketing activities, integrate them with other functions and allocate the business resources to effectively implement marketing activities to drive growth.

- **The Inner Core**: drills down to the twin core capabilities of continuous Insight and Engagement that we believe provide the fuel for world-class marketing to operate as an effective growth driver.

The Growth Propeller – Outer Ring

The Outer Ring of *The Growth Propeller* covers the core marketing capabilities needed for the main ongoing processes of strategic marketing, from clarifying strategic objectives and direction right through to the delivery of the customer experience and measurement of its impact on business performance.

1. Business Objectives and Performance

Marketing's role should begin with, and be defined by, the strategic goals and objectives of the organization. The extent to which *business objectives* are met is the ultimate basis on which Marketing's performance as a function should be assessed.

However, this does not mean that business objectives should be defined in purely commercial or financial terms. One of the primary tasks of senior Marketers is to ensure that customer interests are built in to the strategic objectives of the company and can, where needed, shape business goals.

In too many organizations, strategic and commercial goals are based on objectives which are disconnected from customer needs, wants and motivations and this is a fundamental barrier for any business wanting to drive demand-led growth. It is also counter-productive as there is strong evidence to suggest that the organizations that excel in terms of customer satisfaction also tend to generate higher shareholder returns in the longer term.[2]

At the highest level, the organization's purpose or mission should be customer focused and inspire everyone in the business with the role they can play in delivering superior value to customers. The customer comes first and the business results and broader organizational benefits follow.

> *"I think organizations lose sight very quickly of consumer conversations and get into conversations that are much more about the financial targets and numbers they need to hit. The focus tends to be more on 'what do we need to deliver to our shareholders?' than on 'what is it that our customers want?'"*
>
> Jon Harding, *Head of Organization Development, Barclaycard*

P&G Mission – the Power of Purpose

"We will provide branded products and services of superior quality and value that improve the lives of the world's consumers, now and for generations to come. As a result, consumers will reward us with leadership sales, profit, and value creation, allowing our people, our shareholders, and the communities in which we live and work to prosper."[3]

It stands to reason that if an organization is seeking to drive customer-led growth, then customer-focused objectives should be established alongside financial objectives as key measures of business performance. The underlying rationale being that customer metrics precede and drive the financial metrics in the longer term, so they are critical *drivers*, not just indicators, of future business performance.

Sainsbury's   Customer-focused Metrics

In the mid-2000s, Sainsbury's had slipped back to number 3 behind Tesco and Asda in the UK grocery retail sector and sales were in decline. CEO Justin King launched a recovery plan entitled 'Making Sainsbury's Great Again' and set a target revenue increase of £2.5 billion within a three-year period. In working through how they could contribute to this goal, the Sainsbury's Marketing team made the simple calculation that if its 14 million customers spent just £1.14 extra every week over the three years, the £2.5 million revenue objective would be delivered.

This internal business insight was combined with an external customer insight: "We are all 'sleep-shopping', buying the same products week in week out, eating the same old meals for lack of inspiration".

The result was a new marketing strategy based on the brand idea "Try Something New Today". The entire organization was engaged in inspiring customers to experiment with simple new food ideas and add a little extra to their shopping basket each week. The strategy delivered results – three years later the actual sales revenue increase achieved by Sainsbury's was £2.7 billion.[4]

This Sainsbury's case highlights one of the main principles of marketing – that increasing sales revenue on a sustainable basis requires tangible changes in the attitudes and purchasing behaviour of customers. For an organization to drive sustainable, profitable, demand-led growth, its customers have to choose its brands, products or services more often than competitive offerings.

As such, a critical capability needed by Marketers in their role as *growth drivers* is to make sure they fully understand the connections and correlations between customer attitudes, behaviours and business outcomes so they can help shape business strategy and set the customer-focused marketing goals needed to deliver against business objectives and performance targets.

"We used to talk about 'putting consumers' at the heart of everything we do. Now we talk about customers and consumers 'being' at the heart of everything we do. Either way it's about driving top line growth and therefore having the Marketing group understand what it is about our brands that makes consumers want to choose them and ultimately, choose them more often, over other brands in their repertoire."

Nick Rose, *former Chief Financial Officer, Diageo*

2. Segmentation and Portfolio Strategy

Once business objectives are clear and articulated in customer terms, the next step in driving demand-led growth is to define the markets in which the organization will compete and to segment them on the basis of customer needs, wants or motivations.

In its article "The Granularity of Growth", McKinsey & Company reported on research undertaken using a database of over 200 companies that

had outperformed their rivals on both top-line growth and shareholder value. They found that, whatever the industry sector, the single most important factor explaining their success was the fact they were competing in markets or segments that were faster growing than their peers. The article's authors concluded that, "*Executives should identify and allocate resources to the fastest growing segments in which the company has the capabilities and resources to compete successfully.*"[5]

The ability to define markets and segments in customer-oriented ways is one of the core capabilities needed by effective Marketers. They must be able to assess and determine which market segments offer the greatest profitable growth opportunities for the organization based on the business capabilities it has, or can acquire, relative to its competitors.

Segmentation and Portfolio Planning is an important cross-functional activity which should involve all relevant functions, for example Insight, Strategic Planning, Sales, R&D and Finance specialists. Marketing's key contribution is to make sure these market opportunities are defined, understood and prioritized from a *customer-focused* perspective.

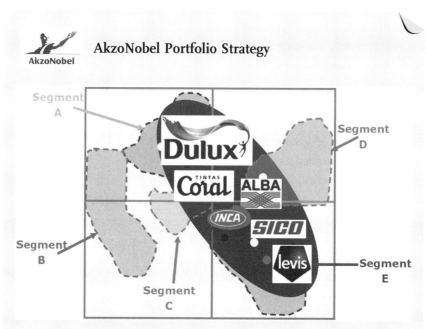

AkzoNobel Portfolio Strategy

It was ICI's capability development in segmentation and portfolio planning in particular, that transformed the business and revolutionized the role of Marketing within the organization. According to Kerris Bright, former CMO of ICI and later AkzoNobel, *"Historically, we had used an attitudinal approach to segmentation, and the business was finding this hard to action. So we took a step back and decided to invest in a new approach to market segmentation based on need states, as we thought these were driving customer choice. This created some real insights. We knew where Dulux was strong, but we suddenly could see one or two really big segments where we were weak and where the growth opportunities were. And because we'd used a needs-based segmentation, that also helped us to see where the innovation opportunities could be."*

Bright's team went on to use segmentation to rationalize the number of brands in the ICI paints portfolio and to plan the architecture and development of Dulux as a master brand.

❝*The creation and execution of an optimized global brand portfolio model provided us with an opportunity to drive the direction and performance of the business like never before.* **❞**

Kerris Bright, *former CMO, ICI Paints/AkzoNobel (now CMO Ideal Standard)*

There are two key segmentation questions all Marketers should be able to answer. First, which markets, categories, segments and channels are we aiming to grow *in*? And, second, what are we going to grow *with* in terms of our brand and product portfolio?

Assessing the opportunities in each category and clarifying the role of each brand in the portfolio is a critical contribution that Marketers can make to corporate strategy. This is both in terms of the different role each brand or proposition plays in creating better value for customers, and how each contributes to driving the commercial growth agenda.

 Brand Portfolio Rationalization

In the automotive sector, Ford has undertaken significant brand and model rationalization since the arrival of Alan Mulally as President and CEO in 2006. Since then, the Aston Martin, Jaguar, Land Rover and Volvo brands have all been sold, enabling Ford to dismantle its sprawling "house of brands" and focus on its core business.

"We have eliminated a number of brands from our portfolio in order to devote fully our financial, product development, production and marketing, sales and service resources toward further growing our core Ford brand and enhancing Lincoln."

In reducing the number of models in its range by 50%, Ford has delivered a rapid improvement in performance. In 2010, Ford achieved its first back-to-back market share increase in the US since 1993 and impressive growth rates were achieved in other markets, notably India and China. Revenues rose by 14% to over $120 billion and profits increased from $2.8 billion the previous year to $6.6 billion, its best performance for ten years.[6]

3. Brand Positioning and Architecture

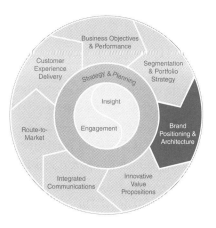

Once priority categories and brand portfolios have been defined, the next step in driving demand-led growth is for Marketers to ensure that each brand within the portfolio has a clear, distinctive brand positioning. Importantly, this should be expressed in customer language so it can be clearly understood and leveraged across all customer touch-points.

While segmentation and portfolio planning work out *where* the organization is going to grow and *what* it is going to grow with, brand positioning and architecture define *how* it is going to grow, by clarifying the brand benefits most likely to attract and retain customers.

Strong and enduring brands appeal to customers and create competitive advantage because they are associated with a coherent set of distinctive benefits and engaging experiences that connect with people's heads, hearts and spirit.

Brand Positioning encapsulates what a brand's associations are (or, in the case of a positioning vision, what a business wants them to be) among its target customer segment. So Marketers need the capabilities to define positioning accurately, based on customer insight, and to distinguish the key functional and emotional benefits each brand provides relative to its competitors. Key questions to ask here include: What is the reason for this brand? Why should our customers choose us? What perceptions does our brand evoke in people's hearts and minds?

"Companies should create 'purpose-driven' marketing strategies. We are at an inflection point. If we continue with the old marketing techniques, we might only survive until the next economic downturn. However, if we focus on serving, touching and moving people, we will thrive." [7]

Marc Pritchard, *Global Marketing and Brand Building Officer, P&G*

Zappos — Delivering Happiness

Zappos, the US online footwear and clothing retailer, illustrates the growing trend towards brands basing their positioning on a mission or purpose that appeals to people's spirit. Back in 1999, the Zappos brand promise was very functional, focusing on providing the largest selection of shoes. As it established itself, customer service and the culture required in the business to deliver it successfully, became ever more important.

Since 2009, the Zappos positioning has moved to one of "Delivering Happiness". As CEO Tony Hsieh explains in his book of the same name, *"We've always had customers tell us they think of the experience of opening up a Zappos shipment as 'Happiness in a Box'. Whether it's happiness customers feel when they receive the perfect pair of shoes . . . , or the happiness that customers feel from our surprise upgrades to overnight shipping . . . , or the happiness employees feel from being part of a culture whose values match their own personal values – the thing that ties this all together is happiness."* [8] The sales turnover of Zappos now exceeds $1 billion per annum.

The other central task is to distil the strategic thinking into big, inspiring, practical ideas that provide differentiation, direction and engagement for everyone across the organization.

Having developed a brand positioning based on a clear segmentation and portfolio strategy, a critical next step for Marketers, before they embark on any innovation or communication development, is to clarify the strategic structure of each brand's portfolio by developing a clear *Brand Architecture* description.

A brand's architecture provides answers to a number of important questions. What are the key range and sub-brand platforms? How do naming conventions work and how is any sub-branding organized? What is the relationship between products and pricing tiers? And, as an important springboard to the next step in *The Growth Propeller*, where should innovation and communications be focused to secure competitive advantage?

4. Innovative Value Propositions

Brand positioning comes alive when Marketers translate it into tangible, *Innovative Value Propositions* that are appealing to customers. There is a real art to crafting propositions – whether these lie in the brand's core category or in adjacent categories – and it is a key marketing capability required to drive demand-led growth.

An innovative value proposition creates a new targeted product or service offer for a specific customer segment (either to retain current customers with a

"We tend to be an innovative company. We're looking for new things to do. And we tend not to go into the exact space that a competitor is in, because it's easier to go into a space where no one is doing a good job. If you're a little imaginative about these things, you see many, many areas needing attention."

Larry Page, *CEO and co-founder, Google*[9]

higher value offer or to attract new customers). It provides a relevant and differentiated set of benefits that address customer needs, wants and motivations for an accessible price.

Mountain Dew

PepsiCo's soft drink Mountain Dew involved 50 brand "fanatics" in

generating new soda flavours as part its highly successful "DEWmocracy" campaign. Four different flavours were provided online and consumers then decided which one they preferred. Fan communities sprang up behind each option called "flavor nations" and over a million people participated in the product and communication development process. Each nation had its own Facebook page and Twitter account to enable communication, sharing of ideas and voting.[10]

❝By giving consumers the selection and design of the flavor they wanted – it gave them a playing field, but within controlled parameters. We retained some semblance of control, so it was a lovely marriage. Commercially it was extremely successful too – Mountain Dew is PepsiCo's fastest growing brand, domestically and internationally. It has flourished because it has stuck hard and fast to its proposition for the past decade. It stands for 'exhilaration' and it has been brave in terms of how it has given consumers a chance to get involved with the brand.❞

Simon Lowden, CMO, Pepsi Beverages, North America

In addition to the strategic analysis of innovation opportunities we have described so far, successful proposition development depends on a highly creative idea generation phase. Here, Marketers work closely with cross-functional teams and other specialists, internally and externally, to generate new customer insights and develop compelling concepts to address the greatest opportunities to drive growth.

It is particularly important for Marketers to connect and network with the outside world, seeking stimulus, expertise and ideas from consumers, customers, competitors, external specialists, strategic partners, agencies and other thought leaders. Increasingly ideas are co-created with consumers, real time, using virtual customer panels and online collaboration.

---

essential Waitrose **Democratizing Food Quality**

The launch in the UK of the Essentials range by the retailer Waitrose provides an excellent example of a successful innovative value proposition. The case won the Grand Prix in the Marketing Society's annual Awards for Excellence in 2010.[11]

Well-established as a premium food retailer, with a reputation for ethical sourcing, the company set out in 2008 to double the size of its business within 10 years. In March 2009, during the global recession, Waitrose skilfully launched the Essentials range. Its ambition was to *"democratize food quality"* and broaden the base of its business using the proposition: "Quality you would expect at prices you wouldn't".

Within six months, and in direct contrast to the decline in much of the sector, total Waitrose sales were up 17%, with the Essentials range accounting for 16% of total turnover. Waitrose managing director Mark Price described the launch as a "calculated gamble", revealing that, "It cost us £25 million to reduce the prices, but we thought if we got 5% volume uplift it would net out. In the end, sales went up 17%."[12]

Getting pricing right is critical in the development of value propositions. Customer value is a function of both perceived benefits and price relative to competitors. In world-class marketing, pricing is actively managed as an important strategic input to customer value perceptions. In many organizations, however, Marketers are not given any input into pricing decisions and do not understand the pricing lever. They focus predominantly on promotional price offers to the detriment of real added value. They also forget that where additional benefits are offered, price increases may be justified and can sometimes positively contribute to customer brand perceptions.

When leveraged effectively, pricing is an important driver of profitable growth, but it needs to be planned strategically. If not, the outcome may be an excessive reliance on unprofitable "volume-chasing" promotional activities which end up undermining the perceived value and the profitability of brands.

5. Integrated Communications

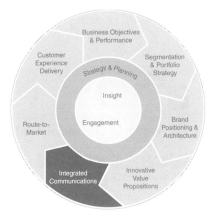

Integrated Communications are a core driver of brand and business growth. At the heart of successful brand communication is its powerful ability to influence the choices people make by building a compelling, distinctive brand identity that connects with current and potential customers and builds rational and emotional engagement.

Historically, the focus for effective integrated brand communications was on two key building blocks:

- The search for excellent creative ideas to bring brand positioning to life and connect marketing activities across different multi-media executions.

- Cost-effective media channel plans, to leverage the right range of customer touch-points, the goal being to "deliver" the right messages to the right customers at the right time.

While big ideas and effective selection of media channels remain essential, the explosion of digital technology and social media has added a critical new dimension to the marketing challenge. Customers now take ownership for, and independently engage in, communication with brand owners and among themselves as a channel in their own right. This has created the discipline of "social media" or "network" marketing.

"Word of mouth" has always been a powerful channel for marketing communications, typically handled under the banner of public relations (PR), corporate relations (CR) or corporate social responsibility (CSR). Now social networks like Facebook, MSN and Mumsnet have transformed the pace, reach and power of customer conversations and the business world is racing to catch up.

> *"If I had $10 for every time I heard someone say 'do we have a social media strategy?' I'd be a rich man. To me that misses the point. The question should be, 'do we have a communication and customer engagement strategy and what is the role of social media in that context'?"*
>
> Barry Herstein, *CMO, HP Snapfish*

The Explosion of Social Media

At the time of writing, Twitter has nearly 200 million registered users, with well over 100 million tweets being posted daily. The fastest growing group on Facebook is the over 50s, anxious to "join the party" and avoid missing out on the lives and worlds of their children and grandchildren. And while Facebook is still the dominant service globally, RenRen China now has over 160 million users and Google's Orkut is also strong, particularly in Brazil.

In a relatively short space of time, the communication landscape has been transformed by these and other social media platforms. Increasingly, people are starting their online journeys from their social media site rather than through their ISP or Google.

The implications are profound, as demonstrated by the influence of social media in recent political upheavals. For organizations and brands, the changes bring risks and opportunities in equal measure. Companies like Starbucks and Dell have been famously successful in harnessing the involvement and ideas of their customers. Others, such as Eurostar, Gap and Nestlé, have been on the painful receiving end of consumer discontent.

For most, though, the agenda to date has been one of experimentation, a search to learn and build up experience about what does and doesn't work. The new technologies, and the social activities that go with them, will no doubt continue to evolve rapidly. Marketers must do the same.

A radical shift is taking place from one-way communication to a world where Marketers and their agencies need to manage an extremely complex, constantly evolving dialogue with customers, suppliers, employees, shareholders, industry regulators, competitors and many other stakeholders.

As a result, Marketers have to get to grips with a whole new range of issues, concepts and capabilities in the area of communications development – from customer data capture and analysis, to search engine optimization, the crowd sourcing of campaign ideas and the evaluation of new channel effectiveness. The landscape for effective marketing is changing radically and the key imperative for Marketers is to learn and adapt as fast as possible to the networked society in which we all now live.

" This is not just about things 'going digital'. It is more fundamental as there is a complete sea change in how consumers are operating. You could argue that consumers always wanted to be in control, but now they have the resources and the tools to really exert that control in their dialogue and purchasing decisions. To compete in this incredibly complex world, Marketers simply have to build their capability to understand not just how each channel works, but also how they interact and how best to use which one, at what time, against which segment. "

Barry Herstein, *CMO, HP Snapfish*

6. Route-to-Market

Major changes are also taking place in the way brands plan and execute their *Route-to-Market* through distribution channels and retail

customers. Important new opportunities for growth are opening up, particularly through the explosion in
e-commerce, which is leading to a
greater need for collaboration and
"joined-up thinking" between Marketers and their Sales, Channel and Trade
Marketing colleagues.

The main focus for Marketers, in
partnership with their colleagues elsewhere in the business, is to ask – are we
exploiting all possible channel opportunities to the full? Do we provide retail
customers and channel partners with superior value propositions? What incentives do we provide to encourage channel partners to stock and display our
brands in the best way, to attract shopper or end-customer attention and purchasing power? Are our channel marketing initiatives fully integrated with all the
other aspects of our marketing plan?

 ## Growth through Integration

SABMiller, with global brands Grolsch, Peroni, Pilsner Urquell and
Miller Genuine Draft, is one company seeking to drive growth by
creating much closer integration between the functions of Marketing,
Sales and Trade Marketing.

"You've got to make the whole machine work", explains Nick Fell,
SABMiller's Group Marketing Director. *"We're effectively redefining
Marketing from having a traditional Marketing function to joining up
Marketing, Trade Marketing and Sales. We believe these three have
to work in concert to win in the marketplace."*

*"The great tragedy is the Marketing guys have become specialists,
the Trade Marketing guys and Sales guys too"*, Fell continues. *"The
language, process and segmentation systems necessary, so they can
all see the customer's world the same way, don't exist. And we're now*

into our first generation of people that have only ever known the specialist model."

One of the key learnings at SABMiller is that integrating the work of the functions isn't just about integrating plans for brands, channels and customers at an executional level. Nick Fell acknowledges the challenge involved in doing this more strategically, emphasizing that, *"Getting a clear line from the 'where to play' decisions all the way through to the 'how to win' decisions is the single biggest struggle."*

Coca-Cola famously drove its distribution strategies for many years using the mantra, "Within arm's reach of desire". Many other companies are now equally savvy about leveraging multiple channels to drive their availability, and the digital revolution is creating many new opportunities.

The shift in commercial activity online has transformed the shape of many industries, with a host of new players emerging and established players looking to capitalize as best they can. An interesting new development looks set to be the evolution of social media sites such as Facebook into e-commerce channels. For example, the "Friends Store" on *Levis.com* showcases products recommended by Facebook friends to "like", "review", "comment" and "share" a purchasing intention, and allows you to invite friends to co-browse the store.

New Routes to Market

With the launch of the "Boots Laboratories" skincare brand into France, Boots reached 5,000 pharmacies through a highly price-competitive wholesale channel. The ability to use unconventional, lower cost, brand-building communication to drive customer awareness and consideration through digital channels, created the opportunity for a new business model opening up new routes-to-market.

"Wholesaling is a really small margin, but big scale business in France. It is a very different business to the one which we are used to in consumer goods marketing. Ten years ago, we would not have contemplated launching this product because we couldn't imagine doing it without classic brand-building investment. But by seeding it through PR, virals, blogging and guerilla marketing, which all costs very, very little, we managed to achieve market leadership in the French market within two months – and there are 500 anti-ageing brands in France!"

Torvald de Coverly Veale, *International Brand Development Director, Alliance Boots*

7. Customer Experience Delivery

The final capability in the Outer Ring of *The Growth Propeller*, and critical to driving demand-led growth, is the delivery of the *Customer Experience*. This is where promises are delivered and customer value is created in practice. At this stage, the drive for growth shifts from strategic planning and development to outstanding operational excellence.

In many centralized organizations and service businesses, this is where responsibility for brand activities moves from central innovation, proposition or brand teams to local or dispersed operating units, teams and outlets. But as more teams get involved and ownership disperses, the risk is that the understanding and respect for the value proposition can get diluted, thereby undermining customer value assessment, purchase choice and loyalty.

 Challenging Category Norms

Virgin has recently entered the Australian market with its Virgin Active health clubs and wants to break away from the traditional category approach of locking people into contracts.

❝Our utter focus is on engaging with consumers, not just when we sign them up, but through the lifetime of their membership. This is core to the brand proposition. Your health club contract is often more difficult to get out of than your marriage! We're going to change that, by having systems and processes in place which constantly ask consumers how they're getting on, providing them with the information they need and giving them the service they want in the right way.❞

Mark Gilmour, *Brand Director for South East Asia, Virgin*

At this stage in *The Growth Propeller*, having well-articulated and embedded customer-centric values, processes, role clarity and communication *across* functions now becomes business-critical. Only then will the brand proposition be respected and consistently brought to life through every customer touch-point.

In the consumer packaged goods sector, P&G talks about the delivery of the customer experience coming down to two key moments of truth – the point when the consumer chooses the product they will buy on-shelf and the point when the product is actually used.

To build its understanding of the first of these moments, P&G launched a drive to improve performance in areas such as in-store availability, promotion planning and merchandising in its US drug channel, an initiative which it estimated delivered a 5% incremental sales uplift.[13]

Over the years, in most companies, the first of P&G's "moments of truth" has probably received less attention from Marketers than the second, in part because of the silos between the Marketing and Sales functions referred to earlier.

As a result, significant work is currently underway among consumer packaged goods companies and retailers to generate deeper insight into the behaviour of *shoppers*. The growth drivers at this level can be highly detailed and operational, ranging from supply chain reliability through to store layouts, range and shopper response to display optimization, pack design and promotional mechanics. P&G itself uses a research facility called "The Cave" to test consumer reactions to store layouts, shelving and product and packaging design, all in shop environments created using computer-generated imagery.[14]

The Growth Propeller – Connecting Ring

Having covered the "Outer Ring" capabilities in some detail, we will now move one level inside *The Growth Propeller* (see Figure 2.2) to address the *Strategy & Planning* capabilities needed to join up marketing activities, integrate them with those of other functions and allocate the business resources to execute activities in the market.

Without this, marketing efforts can become so fragmented, disjointed and overstretched by competing activities and operational complexity that Marketers are unable to focus resources on driving sustained, effective growth.

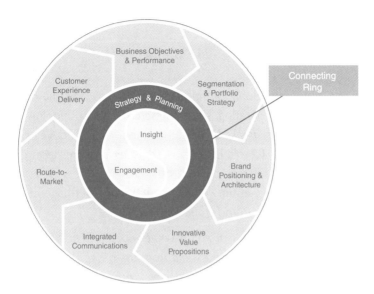

Figure 2.2: *The Growth Propeller – Connecting Ring*

8. Strategy & Planning

Marketing *Strategy & Planning* has a unique role to play in marketing capability development. It connects the marketing activities in the 'Outer Ring' with the 'Inner Core' capabilities of *Insight* and *Engagement* that we believe are so important to creating superior customer value to drive business growth.

Effective strategy and planning is essential for Marketers to make informed choices, both long-term and short-term, about competing ideas on what to offer customers and when, where and how to invest behind those offers. It also provides the focus and direction Marketers need to guide brand-building activities and integrate them with broader organizational activity plans.

Strategy & Planning are important for any organization, but where the marketing activities around *The Growth Propeller* are managed by separate people, teams or business units they become even more significant. Capability gaps in this area can be particularly damaging where strategic brand development is structurally separated from operational brand activation, for example when brands and businesses are managed on a global basis and in mono-brand organizations.

Integrated Strategy and Planning

Unilever

Unilever's integrated global brand planning process uses the concept of "BrandZip", incorporating key commercial and positioning goals and strategic plans in areas such as innovation, channel development and communication. Its role is to "zip" together the long-term global brand visions and strategies created by Unilever's *Brand Developers* on a three- to five-year time horizon, with the shorter-term, local operational plans of its *Brand Builders*.

❝ You have to have realism about what you can plan globally and locally and what each side can expect from the other. It's always easy for the local guys to beat the global guys with a stick because they haven't got the same level of local granular analysis. But how could they have? In fact, why should they have? If we're not careful, everyone ends up trying to do the same job, like kids playing football – everyone runs to the same side of the field. The global strategies really must keep a long-term global perspective otherwise there is a risk that brand teams will never start anything substantial. ❞

Helen Lewis, *Consumer Insight & Marketing Strategy Director, Unilever Marketing Academy*

At its most effective, Marketing *Strategy & Planning* is far more than an analytical, financial budgeting process. It provides a way to ensure that the business has a clear roadmap to know how to drive growth by relentless focus on addressing significant customer insights. It also adds clarity to the interpersonal dynamics that need to be managed between those working in different business units or departments.

The Growth Propeller – Inner core

Let us now move right into the core of *The Growth Propeller* to look at the twin capabilities of *Insight* and *Engagement* that we believe provide the fuel for world-class marketing (see Figure 2.3).

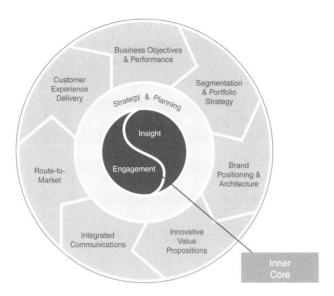

Figure 2.3: *The Growth Propeller* – **Inner Core**

While the Outer and Connecting Ring capabilities are important and challenging in themselves, it is the *Inner Core* capabilities that make the most difference in enabling Marketers and their organizations to successfully create and deliver the superior customer value at the heart of growth.

9. Engagement

We have already stressed the importance we place on the ability of Marketers to *engage* other customer-influencing functions in everything they do, from the creation of high level business goals, through to portfolio planning and all aspects of brand development and delivery. No matter how good a Marketing department is at the functional tasks of

marketing, its ability to engage the rest of the business to create superior value for customers is vital for a truly *world-class* approach.

Engagement, however, is not a simple task and does not take place in isolation. Unless a customer-centric culture has been established from the very top (see Chapter 6), other functions may be pursuing their own agendas, making the task of Marketing to get the *customer* agenda heard, feel like "pushing water uphill".

To fulfil their potential as *growth drivers*, Marketers need to build the capabilities and experience to operate not just as functional experts but as business leaders. They need to create an exciting vision of market and commercial opportunities and inspire people to share their passion for the brand's purpose and values. And, ultimately, they must take responsibility for leading the delivery of results consistent with the agreed business objectives, marketing strategy and brand vision.

Being an effective Marketing leader does not, however, mean egotistically insisting that every other function is "Marketing led". It means focusing the whole organization on the *shared* task of creating superior value for customers.

Engagement is not just an internal driver of growth. The continuous engagement of customers and other relevant stakeholders like shareholders, government and regulatory bodies, agencies and suppliers is a central driver of corporate success. This is becoming increasingly important in today's networked society, where the boundaries between the "internal" corporate world and the "external" have been blurred beyond recognition.

Effective engagement is an essential marketing capability and a powerful driver of growth. In addition, by its very nature of involvement and two-way communication, it is also an extremely powerful and ongoing source of customer insight.

> *Engagement is unbelievably important. You simply have to engage the people who know how to make the system work. And if you engage them, somehow they make the things you're doing better. If they feel ownership for things themselves, then they happen far better, faster, cheaper than they otherwise would have.*
>
> Amanda Mackenzie, *CMO, Aviva*

Co-creation Labs

BMW has been an early pioneer of co-creation programmes with its customers. As far back as 2001, BMW had set up a Virtual Innovation Agency to enable creative consumers and other external stakeholders to submit ideas to the company. Since then, co-creation initiatives have been launched in areas as diverse as sustainable energies, driver assistance and future mobility services.[15]

In 2010, BMW integrated all its various activities into the BMW Group Co-Creation Lab.

In a recent contest, BMW sought ideas for individualization of car interiors. In total, over 1,100 members submitted 750 ideas and provided 28,000 evaluations and 13,500 comments.

❝The BMW Group Co-Creation Lab is a virtual meeting place for individuals interested in cars and all related topics, who want to share their ideas and opinions on tomorrow's automotive world with one of the leading car manufacturers. It invites people from all over the world to contribute their suggestions for specific topics and to connect with like-minded others. Participants not only evaluate concepts which are developed by the BMW Group but they also actively contribute their ideas and suggestions – they become active 'co-creators' of innovative products and services. ❞

www.bmwgroup-cocreationlab.com[16]

10. Insight

Finally in this chapter, we come to the role of *Insight*, potentially the most important capability needed for world-class marketing. Many varied definitions of customer insight exist and insight is a crucial, expanding and much debated area. Here we'll refer to it simply as *"a discovery of underlying customer needs, wants or motivations that releases an opportunity to create value for both customers and the business"*.

⠿ BlackBerry™ Insight in Action

In 1997, Mike Lazaridis, CEO at Research In Motion (RIM), had an insight that changed the future of his business. He asked, "When is a tiny keyboard more efficient than a large one?" The answer: "When you use your thumbs." A year later the BlackBerry was born. It now has over 50 million users.[17]

Insights arise from a combination of rigorous analysis of data and creative and imaginative thinking. Through insight generation, Marketers reveal important new opportunities to meet customer needs, wants or motivations in competitively superior and commercially profitable ways.

For this reason, the capabilities required to enable the systematic generation and application of insights lie at the very heart of Marketing's ability to act as the growth driver of an organization. And, just like engagement, insight has both an external and an internal dimension, as it requires a deep understanding of what makes both customers and the business work.

Insight capabilities are essential to feed and inspire all aspects of marketing, from the basis for strategic segmentation and the foundation for a brand's positioning, through to the detailed development of the brand's product, packaging, communicaion and distribution mix.

Insight is a vital capability in which the art and science of marketing come into sharp relief. On the one hand, insights can sound intangible, being generated partly through intuition, empathy, curiosity and creative ways of thinking. On the other, and of increasing importance in this digital era, is the power and influence of real time, measurable data and systematic ways to mine data, information, experiences and observations to uncover new perspectives.

To add to the challenges, there are constantly new sources of customer information becoming available to Marketers. For example, the quantitative analysis by marketing scientists such as those at the Ehrenberg-Bass Institute is building up powerful evidence about how consumers behave in practice, data that is adding to the debate and challenging thinking about how brands grow.

There is also breakthrough science in psychology, social science, heuristics and behavioural economics offering new techniques to increase our understanding and prediction of human behaviour. Similarly, advances in neuroscience mean there is an ever-increasing understanding of how the brain works. Consensus seems to be emerging that instead of people making decisions in the sequence of *feel – think – do*, actual behaviour seems to be based more on a model of *feel – do – post rationalize*. This clearly has big implications for the way Marketers seek to understand and communicate with their customers.

New methods of market research are being developed as a result, ranging from the scanning and measurement of the brain's activity, through to the tracking of eye movement and galvanic skin response. These new techniques provide exciting new ways to understand how customers

"Our ambition is to constantly create the experiences customers never dreamt of. It's an aspiration you never quite reach. And that's what inspires you to keep driving. Those experiences start with a personal and evolving understanding of customers that goes well beyond traditional segmentation boxes. This insight must go beyond what customers say they want, to what they mean they want."

Ronan Dunne, *Chief Executive Officer, O2*[18]

"The one thing Marketers should be able to do better than anyone else is bring the outside in. We must be able to look at what is happening with consumers, the competition, general market dynamics and have a better feel for these things than anybody else. The insights Marketers generate ought to be as quantified as possible. The ability to collect the right data, analyse the data in the right way, report it in the way that generates the right actions is very hard. But it's vital."

Martin George, *Managing Director for Group Development, Bupa*

behave and make decisions and the best Marketers are already experimenting to see what they can learn from them.

Becoming World Class at Marketing

In conclusion, Marketing is a complex and challenging, yet vital function. The ongoing process of creating better value for customers to help drive growth clearly isn't something that Marketers can be expected to do alone; it is the remit of the entire organization to deliver value to customers at each and every customer touch-point.

" We now know the brain takes an emotional response first before rational evaluation, and we're uncovering lots of learnings within the car buying process from that. We are also measuring the physiology of the body as opposed to just understanding what the outputs are – getting the principles of neuroscience, science and biology to test our hypotheses. "

Ian Armstrong,
European Communications Director,
Honda Motor Europe

Yet, *The Growth Propeller* helps explain the unique role that Marketers have to play. It clarifies the role of Marketing and the key drivers of effectiveness, helps define the role of Marketers in practice and identifies the core marketing capabilities needed to drive sustainable, profitable, demand-led growth.

As we have demonstrated, marketing is a tough and demanding discipline facing unprecedented internal and external pressures. *World-class* marketing requires a complex, ever-evolving blend of capabilities and leadership characteristics. In the next chapter we will move on to the challenge of building these capabilities and what that involves in practice.

CHAPTER 2 – AT A GLANCE

- Effective marketing is not something that Marketers can deliver alone – it is the remit of the entire organization.

- The definition, role and expectations of the Marketing function and its potential as a growth driver are widely misunderstood.

- *The Growth Propeller* explains the core marketing activities that underpin any organization's ability to drive sustainable, demand-led growth. It outlines how world-class marketing should work *in practice* and identifies the core capabilities Marketers need to drive growth.

- Not every individual Marketer needs to excel at all the activities identified, but any organization aspiring to be *world class* at marketing needs to consider how well it performs, as a whole, against *The Growth Propeller* dimensions.

- The Growth Propeller's Outer Ring outlines seven core marketing capabilities from the definition of *Business Objectives and Performance*, *Segmentation and Portfolio Strategy*, through to the development of *Brand Positioning and Architecture*, *Innovative Value Propositions*, *Integrated Communications*, *Route-to-Market* and *Customer Experience Delivery*.

- The Growth Propeller's Connecting Ring captures the Marketing *Strategy & Planning* capabilities needed to connect marketing activities, integrate them with other functions and allocate the business resources to make them happen.

- The Growth Propeller's Inner Core drills down to the twin capabilities of continuous *Insight* and *Engagement* that we believe provide the fuel for world-class marketing to operate as an effective growth driver.

- *World-class marketing* requires a complex, ever-evolving blend of capabilities and leadership characteristics that enable people, teams and organizations to create the value for customers that drives brand and business growth.

Notes

1 "Creating alignment: marketing with a small m" by Mike Moran, *Market Leader*, Summer 2004

2 "The long term stock market evaluation of Customer Satisfaction", American Marketing Association, Aksoy, Cooil et al., 2008

3 "The power of purpose", www.pg.com, May 2011

4 "Sainsbury's – how an idea helped make Sainsbury's great again", by Tom Roach, Craig Mawdsley and Jane Dorsett, Institute of Practitioners in Advertising Effectiveness Awards 2008

5 "The granularity of growth", Baghai, Smit & Viguerie – *McKinsey Quarterly*, July 2007

6 Ford Annual Report 2010

7 "P&G urges brands to move people" by Stephen Jakes, marketingmagazine.co.uk, 29th June 2010

8 "Delivering happiness" by Tony Hsieh

9 www.google.com/press/podium/brin, 22nd January 2011

10 Social media marketing case, socialemailmarketing.eu, 4th May 2010

11 Essential Waitrose, Marketing Society Award submission 2010

12 *Sunday Times* article (September 2010)

13 "Leadership in action" by Allison Ackermann & Alarice Padilla, consumergoods.com, April 2009

14 "P&G takes shoppers to another world in war of the brands" by Alan Mitchell, *Financial Times*, 17th October 2006

15 "The BMW Co-creation Lab" by Jawecki, Bilgram and Wiegandt, ESOMAR Innovate 2010

16 www.bmwgroup-cocreationlab.com, 30th April 2011

17 www.economist.com, 22.02.2011

18 *The Future of Marketing* by the Marketing Society 2009

Chapter 3

"*M*arketers are not like mushrooms – if you keep them in the dark, they won't grow!" So exclaimed Aviva's CMO, Amanda Mackenzie, in a discussion about investing in a marketing capability development programme to transform the effectiveness of her global Marketing team. "*I had to fight for that money*", she elaborates. "*We manage £380 billion worth of assets, our turnover is £40 billion and there I was killing myself to get £2 million to invest in building marketing capabilities.*"

But Mackenzie was not trying to introduce a marketing *training* programme – that would have been far less controversial. Instead, she was making the case for a fundamental change in the ways of working across Aviva to *build marketing capabilities*. Her goal was to change the hard and soft wiring of Aviva's organization, and its Marketing department in particular, to make the business more customer-centric. Marketing capability development became a transformational catalyst for broader organizational change.

We will now move on to focus on the challenges inherent in transforming marketing capabilities. But first, what does that term really mean? And what does it involve? Is it just another name for "marketing training"? And what are the most important aspects of capability development for organizations wanting to build marketing excellence?

In this chapter of *The Growth Drivers*, we will answer all these questions and overturn the common misconception that "capability building" is just about addressing skill gaps or training needs. We will also introduce another useful tool, *The Brand Learning Wheel*, which defines the key drivers of marketing capability and helps organizations think differently about the scale of their ambitions.

 Aviva's Transformation

Aviva's strategy defines an ambitious role for capability development. Its website confirms, *"We will succeed by building on four core capabilities: marketing and distribution expertise, financial discipline, technical excellence, and operational effectiveness. By focusing our efforts and resources, we aim to excel at each of them, and enhance Aviva's position as a leading insurer and asset manager."*

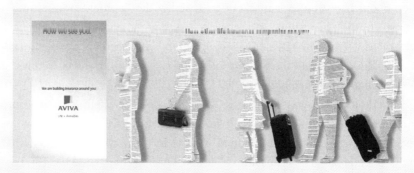

Aviva's performance is certainly on track to achieve this goal, as Group Chief Executive Andrew Moss confirmed in his annual review for 2010. *"Despite the tough economic environment, we have grown the business and the benefits of Aviva's transformation over recent years have started to come through. We have seen strong growth during the year: IFRS profits were up 26% to £2.55 billion and total sales were up 4% to £47.1 billion. We are selling more and improving profitability."*[1]

In changing Aviva's perspective on the potential for marketing to help drive growth, CMO Amanda Mackenzie initially faced some key challenges from those who did not fully understand the Marketing

CHAPTER 3 - TRANSFORMING MARKETING CAPABILITIES | 73

department's role: *"There was a definite sense among many people that we were trying to introduce something new and that surely we could live without it. They just couldn't see the point – it was like we were spending £2 million on doughnuts!"*

First, she needed to change perceptions around the strategic role that Marketing could be playing. And second, she had to explain that this initiative was serious and significant in both ambition and scale – seeking to change the way the business operated in practice and to better equip Aviva's Marketers to drive its business results.

The Aviva Way

Aviva's Global Marketing & Communications Leadership team defined a global marketing strategy focused on three core themes: to strengthen brand health ("Build the Brand"), enhance customer satisfaction ("Win the Crowd") and improve the effectiveness and efficiency of marketing investment ("Deliver More").

As part of this strategy a marketing capability programme was launched to build skills, confidence and consistency across the Marketing organization, rallying people behind the strategy and equipping them for the journey. Common tools and language were introduced in "The Aviva Way" and learning support initiatives rolled out globally in the form of workshops, virtual classrooms and e-tutorials.

To help look after your baby's future we'll give both you and mum £10,000 of free life cover until baby's first birthday.

Call 0800 046 6446
or speak to your financial adviser

aviva.co.uk

AVIVA

As Jan Gooding, Aviva's Global Marketing Director, explains, *"For me, the greatest evidence for why we've been successful is the fact that the gigantic name change and unification behind the Aviva brand has been executed so well. At the end of last year, for the first time ever, an independent strategic assessment formally recognized our marketing as being a core strength of Aviva."*

Aviva's commercial results support this claim. Centralizing media buying has saved over 10% of the global media budget. Other highlights include programmes in the US to improve the customer experience which have increased loyalty by 30% and saved specific parts of the business over $44 million. In the UK direct insurance business, sales have increased by 12% in 2010 and 160,000 new customers have been added since the previous year.[2]

The Training Trap

One of the biggest obstacles to effective marketing capability development comes from a deep and widespread misunderstanding about the level at which capability development needs to operate. So we want to take this opportunity to address the widespread confusion between *training* and *capability development* and to clarify the very substantial differences between them.

The word "capability" can be used at three different levels: the ability of an *individual* Marketer to do their marketing job (often called "competency"); the capability of the *Marketing function* as a whole; or the ability of the *entire organization* to work more effectively to deliver better value to its customers – marketing with a small 'm'.

The problem with "training" is that it largely focuses on the first of these levels – on individual skill development – and therefore fails to take into account the crucial "organizational wiring" needed to change the ways of working in the Marketing function, and across the organization as a whole, that is so vital for effective change management. We call this the *training trap* because, like stepping on the accelerator in a car that is not in gear, investing in skills training without connecting it with the other drivers of organizational capability will have little impact on the organization's ability to drive growth.

In our view, the lack of integration between the three levels of capability has been driven in part by the silos that exist between the Human Resources and Marketing functions. Marketing "training", designed to build individual competencies, has been typically managed by HR, whereas the way Marketers work in practice – the day job – is the primary responsibility of Marketing leaders.

Exploring the training trap

The conventional approach for an organization concerned about its marketing effectiveness (see Figure 3.1) has been to brief HR to identify the skill gaps of Marketers. Once these have been defined, usually by some sort of skills audit or benchmarking, HR is tasked with providing a suite of training solutions to address the priority needs.

Training, managed like this, is often sourced from a range of different suppliers – academics, consultancies, agencies and training companies – who all bring their own content and approaches to learning. These suppliers introduce valuable new concepts, but with language and terminology that has been developed independently. As a result, training inputs tend to be fragmented and poorly integrated across different marketing skill areas.

"Training is short term, it is a quick hit. You get some content and then hopefully you use it. 'Hopefully' being the key word. Training is something that happens in the classroom and it's of the old world. If you want to change an old habit you have to do it for 30 days. Show me a training course that lasts 30 days!"

Richard Davies, *Global Marketing Manager, Shell Bitumen*

Of more concern is the way that such training inputs tend not to be connected to the way Marketers work *in practice* – to the processes, tools and techniques they use every day. Too much of this training activity has traditionally been limited to classrooms and it is not sufficiently linked to the real issues, challenges and tasks that Marketers need to address on the job.

Organizations stuck with a conventional training approach can find themselves in an impossible situation. They are often left with an unwieldy set of disparate learning solutions that are complex to manage, costly to run, difficult to integrate, and very challenging to embed in terms of ongoing knowledge management. As a result they strive to cut costs, try ever shorter, "bite-sized" interventions and find cheaper suppliers – they are caught in the *training trap*.

"Training in a traditional sense wouldn't apply in our business because it's a whole change programme we need to go through – changing processes, changing attitudes, changing behaviours, a whole raft of things. It is not something that happens just over one workshop or attendance at one programme, but it happens in people's day-to-day tasks and that needs to be embedded over a period of time. It takes many months, even years to achieve that, but when you get there it will make a significant impact on the business."

Navjot Singh, *Global Marketing Manager, Recruitment & Global HR Communications, Shell*

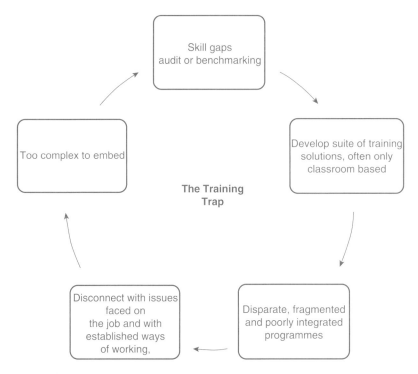

Figure 3.1: *The Training Trap*

In our experience, marketing capability development needs to be approached far more strategically, in a way that is focused on supporting the marketing capability needs and strategy of operating teams, business units and the whole *organization* – not just of the *individuals* within it.

Strategic capability building

Marketing training programmes of the type we have just described have a fundamental problem in that their development starts

" It's very clear when I look at what has got traction in the company, they have been the things which were really delivering against the main change agenda of the business. Where we've been less effective is when we've tried to complete the curriculum for its own sake or tidy things up to provide people with a full service. At any one stage, the business has got a few critical things it has to do and that's where we must focus our capability building efforts. "

Helen Lewis, *Consumer Insight and Marketing Strategy Director, Unilever Marketing Academy*

from the wrong place. They are constructed with a "bottom up" perspective, analysing and grouping *individual* skill gaps and then aggregating them back up in an attempt to create a manageable whole.

Just to be clear, we are not arguing that skills audits, gap assessments and focused learning programmes do not have a value; they certainly do, as we will demonstrate later. But to build *world-class marketing capabilities* we believe that a far more holistic and strategic approach is essential.

In our experience, marketing capability development should always be planned and executed starting from a strategic and "top down" perspective, focusing first on the business strategy and marketing capability needs of the organization, and then moving on to define individual development needs in that context. It's a crucial distinction.

The Drivers of Marketing Capability

In the first two chapters, we defined what marketing is all about and the role it plays in driving growth. We also explained the key elements of *The Growth Propeller* – the core marketing capabilities required for Marketers to drive profitable, sustainable, demand-led growth in practice.

It stands to reason therefore, that if an organization is to succeed in driving the growth of its products, propositions or services, it must ensure it builds world-class marketing capabilities both within its Marketing function and across the organization as a whole. But how should an organization focus its marketing capability development resources? How should it decide how best to equip and enable its Marketing executives to drive brand and business growth?

Early on in our work with multinational companies, we realized an outdated concept of "training", as opposed to *capability development,* was so deeply entrenched in some quarters, that we needed a simple way to challenge that thinking and to explain the power of a more holistic approach. This would move beyond the focus on individual skill development and training, to embrace the impact of a range of other important drivers of capability that influence the way Marketers work in practice.

We explained this new approach by creating *The Brand Learning Wheel* (see Figure 3.2). This simple model has been proven to help organizations appreciate

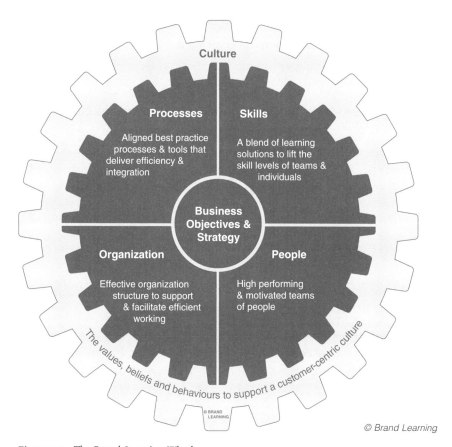

Figure 3.2: *The Brand Learning Wheel*
The core drivers of marketing capability

what building marketing excellence requires in practice and enables them to assess and prioritize each of the core drivers of their own organizational marketing capability.

The Brand Learning Wheel is a robust and highly effective strategic framework and many multinational companies now routinely use it to help structure and plan their marketing capability development strategy and initiatives.

Just as Business Objectives form the start of *The Growth Propeller*, we have put *Business Objectives & Strategy* at the heart of *The Brand Learning Wheel*.

These define what an organization is trying to achieve and provide the strategic direction for the Marketing function's goals and activities.

The Brand Learning Wheel – Core drivers of marketing capability

- **Processes:** the best practice ways of working, systems and tools that Marketers use in their work (both within the Marketing function and with others in the organization).

- **Skills:** the blend of integrated learning solutions that equip people and teams with the attitudes, knowledge, skills and behaviours needed to perform effectively.

- **Organization:** the effective structure of clear marketing roles and responsibilities defined within and across each department, each business unit and for specific job roles.

- **People:** the attraction, development, motivation and retention of the right calibre of Marketer for each job role and of people capable of delivering a consistent brand experience to customers.

- **Culture:** the values, beliefs and behaviours that drive the way things get done and decisions get made within the organization.

But which capability driver is the most important? What roles do they all play? And how do they all work together to help business leaders drive growth? We will answer these questions as we work through *The Brand Learning Wheel* in detail in Part 2 (Chapters 4–7) of *The Growth Drivers*, but first let's give a brief overview of each of the core capability drivers.

1. Business Objectives & Strategy

At the centre of *The Brand Learning Wheel* are the *Business Objectives and Strategy* (see Figure 3.2a). In addition to identifying clear, focused objectives,

Figure 3.2a: *The Brand Learning Wheel – Business Objectives & Strategy*

the business strategy provides essential direction to the role the Marketing function needs to adopt within the organization, and how different departments or business units need to collaborate in delivering superior customer value.

By providing the focus for both 'what' Marketers need to do (*The Growth Propeller*) with 'how' marketing capabilities should be developed to support them (*The Brand Learning Wheel*), a far more integrated and focused approach to building marketing excellence can be delivered.

"Any marketing capability development initiative has to deliver results to justify the investments made. So, by ensuring the business goals and objectives are integral to the initiative right from the start, a positive outcome is far more likely."

Nilgun Langenberg, *former VP Talent Development & Learning, Sara Lee*

The direct link between business objectives and capability development programmes is critical if marketing capability initiatives are to deliver the improvements needed to deliver better customer value and to drive growth. By ensuring capability development is focused on supporting the business objectives, and that initiatives are integrated across all the key drivers of marketing capability, the effectiveness and efficiency of capability investments can be significantly enhanced.

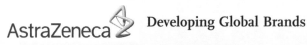

AstraZeneca — Developing Global Brands

In global pharmaceuticals business AstraZeneca, a key strategic thrust has been to enhance its business performance by improving the differentiation of its global brands. These include drugs in therapy areas such as oncology, neuroscience and cardiovascular. As a result, significant effort was made to clarify the brand development process "roadmap" between global and local Marketing teams and a new organizational model has been defined for Global Marketing.

Tim Bailey, Head of AstraZeneca's Marketing Academy, explains, "We have a new remit for Global Marketing teams. They now focus more on activities like strategic positioning and less on the tactical activities, where they were tripping over the local marketing companies. They also provide commercial input earlier to R&D. We have set out to be 'world class' in Marketing, not just 'best in class'. But we now have half the number of people and many have been here years. As a result, the big question is, given the new remit and the new vision, how will they be able to deliver?"

To support these significant organizational and process changes, a marketing capability development programme was developed and implemented. This focused on inspiring a change in the mindset of Marketing teams and actively supporting them on the job with "live action learning" – learning designed specifically for operational teams to build their capabilities while simultaneously addressing current marketing issues. Leadership initiatives have also been launched to increase the customer orientation and collaboration culture within the business.

❝There is now a 'red thread' running through from the business vision to the remit and capability needs of the teams. The capability programme has been put in place to address the capability gaps – it all fits together and it makes sense to people.**❞**

Tim Bailey, *Head of Marketing Academy, AstraZeneca*

2. The Process Driver

The *Process Driver* is a critical driver of marketing capabilities (see Figure 3.2b) which involves building aligned best practice processes and practical tools that enhance the efficiency and effectiveness of marketing activities.

As we explained earlier using *The Growth Propeller*, world-class marketing involves a series of different marketing activities in order to deliver against business objectives, such as insight, market segmentation and brand positioning. So understanding which core marketing processes and tools are most needed, and how they fit together, is a fundamental aspect of effective marketing capability development.

Important questions to ask here include: is there an "end-to-end" marketing process that clarifies the role of Marketing in the organization? If so, does it explain how the various marketing processes fit with the related processes in other functions such as Category Management, Sales, Manufacturing and Research and Development? Which individual processes are priorities for review? Are there pockets of best practice in some parts of the organization which can be leveraged elsewhere? And which practical tools are most needed to support Marketers in the work they do, for example a clear agency briefing template or tools to help determine how to build a marketing strategy and plan?

Figure 3.2b: *The Brand Learning Wheel – Process Driver*

DIAGEO The Diageo Way of Brand Building

Investing time and effort to develop effective and aligned processes is essential to building marketing excellence. When the ambition is global change in line with a major merger or organizational change, such as with the creation of Diageo plc (from Guinness plc and Grand Metropolitan plc), the commitment to changing the way Marketers work needs to come from the very top.

Paul Walsh, CEO of Diageo, wrote to all employees when they embarked on the global "Diageo Way of Brand Building" (DWBB) programme stressing the value of this initiative, "*We need outstanding execution and consistency in a few critical areas.*"

Diageo approached this challenge in two phases with between five and eight processes tackled each time. The first group included Insight, Innovation, Consumer Driven Strategy, Brand Essence & Positioning and Game Planning, then a series of more specific marketing disciplines such as Relationship Marketing, Pricing and Packaging were handled in a second phase.

High levels of dedicated internal leadership were committed to the task, with both internal and external support resources playing key roles. The development time for each group of marketing processes was 6 to 12 months tackled simultaneously, moving from the project "kick-off meeting", through best practice capture, to the creation of processes and tools. These were bought to life and explained in a series of 15 user-friendly manual and online "learning guides". A series of facilitated learning events was cascaded globally, led by Diageo executives, and participation was extensive from board level right down to new marketing hires.

Nick Fell, now Group Marketing Director at SABMiller, was an executive who played a leadership role in the development of the DWBB programme during his time at Guinness and Diageo. He engaged Mhairi McEwan to help develop the content materials across all 15 processes, working alongside Diageo internal marketing and subject matter experts, HR and learning experts. He reflects on the challenges Diageo experienced before the DWBB initiative: *"There were Procter guys, Pepsi guys, Unilever guys, Kraft guys, Kellogg guys – I mean everybody from everywhere was there! One of the internal battle cries of Marketing was that this is the Tower of Babel. Senior people would say that every time I've got a market right and I've got my relationships right and the guys are doing the right thing, the local General Manager changes and they bring in someone who used to work for Pepsi and I have to start all over again! We were wasting time on competing thought systems."*

A key benefit of Diageo's DWBB programme was that, whatever their background, Marketers could all unite their efforts behind a shared appreciation of the consumer issues and of the required tasks. People became able to focus on the outputs, not the inputs, of great marketing thinking.

Marketing is inherently a dynamic and creative activity. While process development undoubtedly aids efficiency and effectiveness, especially in complex or global organizations, there is a delicate balance to avoid processes becoming too mechanistic. We recommend organizations stay clear of complex over-engineered process task menus which can increase operating costs and lead to the process becoming an end in itself.

We advocate instead the value of keeping to simple frameworks that collate the main stages in each marketing process, clarify the key inputs and outputs at each stage, and focus on providing a few practical tools to help Marketers do their jobs better or more

❝Personally I would always go for a light touch as I think Marketers have to be liberated to break the market rules. If you give them boxes – this is how you do a, b, c – you end up with formulae, and we all know that brilliant stuff often has no rhyme nor reason.❞

Torvald de Coverly Veale,
International Brands Development Director, Alliance Boots

easily. Processes should be useful guides to enable better ways of working, never a straitjacket that cramps creativity. We will explore this driver in more detail in Chapter 5.

Key Principles – *The Process Driver*

- First develop an *end-to-end* map of marketing processes – don't address specific processes in isolation without a clear sense of the high-level "big picture".

- Work out where and how marketing processes connect with other business functions and prioritize processes for development in line with business needs and competitive context.

- Involve key stakeholders at all stages in the development of processes, tools and new ways of working.

- Capture marketing best practice from inside and outside the organization and keep processes and tools simple, practical and "fit for purpose". Avoid over-processing to the point where a tick box mentality takes hold.

- Be end-user focused in the way processes are brought to life, communicated and cascaded throughout the business.

- Adapt processes over time to ensure the business is learning and evolving.

3. The Skills Driver

The next core driver of marketing capability around *The Brand Learning Wheel* is the *Skills Driver* (see Figure 3.2c). This covers the blend of integrated learning solutions that an organization needs to develop to equip its Marketers with the knowledge, skills and expertise needed to undertake all the marketing activities identified in *The Growth Propeller*.

Issues to address in this driver include: do the Marketers in the organization have the skills they need to compete and to implement effective

Figure 3.2c: *The Brand Learning Wheel – Skills Driver*

marketing activities? Where are the gaps? Are the skills of Marketers able to cope with the heavy demands caused by advances in digital technologies and social media? How do formal learning programmes link with a strategy to promote continuous learning on the job?

An important benefit of skill development is that it can be extremely motivating to the Marketing community. Most Marketers are keen to actively learn and enhance their skills over time, enabling them to enjoy stimulating roles, secure professional development and achieve career advancement. We will explore this driver in more detail in Chapter 5.

NOVARTIS Skill Development Programme

The Novartis Pharmaceuticals business has taken active steps to build the skills of its Marketing communities in recent years. In the General Medicines division, a Marketing College provides a suite of learning programmes focused on five key "competency" areas (e.g. Customer Insight and Analytics, Marketing Mix and Execution, etc.).

Cathy Strizzi, Director – Learning and Capability Development, explains, *"We have a mix of e-learning and classroom interventions for each competency and are looking to increase the blended learning possibilities to provide our learners with various methods to best suit their learning needs. The programmes are designed to grow current functional capabilities and skills that can take them into their next role."*

The Oncology Division in Novartis has had a less mature marketing skills programme, and work is under way with General Medicines to develop a more comprehensive capabilities curriculum. Huw Jones, Senior Director – Global Commercial Excellence, observes that marketing as a discipline has become more important in Oncology in recent years: *"The market has become a lot more competitive and we can rely less heavily on unique blockbuster drugs. So it's no longer the case that 'we've got the answer so now let me help you find the patients'. The situation is 'we've got an answer – let us help by differentiating our answer from somebody else's answer to show you why our solution is right for the patient'."*

A live-action learning programme called "Customer Solutions Initiative" (CSI) has been rolled out internationally to coach brand teams how to address important business issues from a customer perspective, rather than a purely medical or clinical perspective. Huw Jones explains *"CSI has played an important role in encouraging people to think in a way that they've never thought before, to work in ways collaboratively and cross-functionally that they've never done before, and to ask themselves questions and look at situations from a customer's point of view that they've never done before."*

Key Principles – *The Skills Driver*

- Create a marketing capability framework that specifies the key capabilities needed within the organization and the Marketing function.

- Assess marketing skills against both the organization's commercial goals and strategy and against competitive benchmarks.

- Integrate "top down" strategic capability initiatives with "bottom up" programmes focused on the skill development needs of individuals.

- Connect skill development with the marketing processes and ways of working in the business.

- Link individual skill development with the personal performance and development planning process.

- Skill development support is proven to be important in attracting, motivating and retaining Marketers.

- Adopt a blend of both formal and informal learning delivery methods to embed new skills.

4. The Organization Driver

The *Organization Driver* of *The Brand Learning Wheel* (see Figure 3.2d) involves building an effective organization structure to facilitate more efficient decision making, knowledge sharing and ways of working. At the heart of this driver is the way in which the company is organized, and

❝In Pepsi, the brand manager or marketing manager was the fulcrum around which the business turned; in Google, it's the product manager who plays that role. Product management is much more technical, very close to engineering, and Marketing plays more of a support role in that equation.❞

Dan Cobley, *VP Marketing,*
Northern and Central Europe, Google
(formerly at PepsiCo)

Figure 3.2d: *The Brand Learning Wheel – Organization Driver*

specific marketing roles and responsibilities defined, to facilitate more customer-oriented ways of working.

 Shift to Customer Focus

Best Buy, the US consumer electronics retailer, is a business that has
achieved impressive results from reorienting its business around its
customers. In the early 2000s, faced with a formidable emerging band
of competitors including Wal-Mart, Amazon, Dell and Costco, Best
Buy was in a "growth trap". On the one hand, if it drove for improved
top line sales, it risked undermining its margins. Yet if it sought to
enhance its profitability, it risked a fall in volume.

In 2004, CEO Brad Anderson announced the launch of a new
operating model designed to create differentiation for Best Buy through
its overall customer experience. At the heart of its reorganization
was a shift in orientation from product categories to customer segments. Initially, five permanent cross-functional segment teams were
established to develop and implement segment-specific strategies in
its stores. Once these had been piloted and sales had been seen to
increase by an average of 9%, the approach was rolled out to all stores
by 2009.

Brad Anderson summarized the change in approach, *"We saw
ourselves . . . as being the leading agent that helped bring the product
from manufacturers like Sony and Panasonic . . . to the customer's
home. We've now begun a change to seeing ourselves as a customer-
centric company, one whose focus is on customers' needs in the
lifetime application of the product that we sell, as opposed to an
agent that efficiently distributes the product. And that's a very profound change indeed."*[3]

Key questions for this driver include: Is the difference between Marketing with a big "M" (functional level) and a small "m" (company level) well understood? Is the organization as a whole focused "externally" around its key customers and segments, rather than internally around its own products or services? What is the structural relationship of Marketing with other functions in the business? And how strong are the links between business unit Marketers and specialist teams such as Insight, Innovation, Pricing and Digital?

There are major changes underway in how Marketing departments themselves are being organized. An extension in their remit to take in a broader range of customer-facing functions is common. There are also big debates about the impact of digital technology and the best way to organize responsibilities and the required ways of working to address the implications of social media. We will explore this driver in more detail in Chapter 6.

Key Principles – *The Organization Driver*

- Recognize that organizations need to change radically to embrace the opportunities and challenges of digital technologies and social media.

- Ensure the organization as a whole is genuinely designed around meeting the needs of customers.

- Establish a clear vision and remit for the Marketing function that extends beyond brand communication into a more strategic growth-driving role.

- Consider how Marketing's role will interface with other functions to make it more effective.

- Clarify the responsibilities within the Marketing department of specialist teams and between global, regional and local managers.

- Create job profiles for key Marketing roles with clear roles and responsibilities.

5. The People Driver

The next core driver of marketing capability in *The Brand Learning Wheel* is the *People Driver* (see Figure 3.2e), which involves attracting, recruiting, developing and motivating talented people to fill the Marketing roles within the organization. At a higher level, there is also a requirement to make sure the organization as a whole is recruiting people of the right profile to build the culture needed to deliver a brand experience that is true to the company's brand promise to customers.

The connection between brand values and company values, the strategic planning of recruitment and talent management, and the learning and development needed to build and sustain a world-class Marketing community, all require an integrated approach across HR and Marketing.

Key questions here include: what is our Marketing talent management strategy? Is it better to recruit in talent or grow our own? How easy is it to find and retain great people with the right skills and experience to fill Marketing roles? How good are our HR processes, and our on-boarding and induction for Marketers? And how can we ensure the people we recruit into the business outside Marketing support the customer-focused culture we want to create?

Strong leadership capabilities are critical if Marketers are to succeed in the engagement of the rest of the organization which, as we explained in

Figure 3.2e: *The Brand Learning Wheel – People Driver*

Two key dimensions of a world-class marketer

In benchmarking work we have done with several leading multinational companies, two key dimensions that go towards making up a "world-class" Marketer have emerged.

- The *technical* ability to carry out the functional tasks of Marketing, i.e., skills in the diverse range of activities outlined in *The Growth Propeller*, from insight generation and brand development through to operational marketing activation.

- The *behavioural* characteristics that determine the effectiveness of Marketers. Traits for effective Marketing leaders include passion, future orientation, empathy, curiosity, creativity, entrepreneurial drive, organizational awareness, attention to detail, resilience and commerciality.

Through this benchmarking, it became clear that "who" Marketers are being as people (i.e. their behaviour) is just as important to their impact as 'what' they are doing technically (i.e. their skills).

Chapter 2, is at the heart of *The Growth Propeller*.

Finding this kind of talent, "off-the-shelf", with the technical, commercial and leadership capabilities required is extremely tough. Given this challenge, some forward-thinking HR departments are now investing in building their *own* marketing capabilities to help them better target, attract, recruit and retain the best people. In this case, their *customers* are potential candidates and current employees, rather than consumers.

“Employer branding is something a lot of organizations are looking to do a lot more of, purely and simply because it's more difficult to find really good talented people to bring in to your business. People want to be attracted to a brand. You need to offer something more – a company's reputation, an offering that goes beyond just pay and benefits. I think leadership development and the development of people's skills, their progression, is an important area to highlight.”

Steven Dyke, *Head of Global Early Career & UK Recruitment, Rolls-Royce*

Marketing Techniques Applied to HR

Shell has been a much applauded pioneer in the use of marketing techniques by HR to develop a compelling "employer brand", "employee value proposition" and recruitment communication campaigns to attract high calibre talent across its entire business.

❝There is now a clear set of global marketing planning principles for recruitment which we use in all markets. This was never the case before – every country was doing their own thing. Secondly, all the information that has been captured – the channels we go to, the penetration we have, what's working and not working – all of this can be shared from one market to the next. And thirdly, if you look at it from a cost perspective, we have managed to reduce our recruitment cost by over 80% ❞

Navjot Singh, Global Marketing Manager, Recruitment & Global HR Communications, Shell

Key Principles – *The People Driver*

● Ensure Marketing and HR work together closely to develop a winning talent management strategy.

● Define the specification for Marketing talent in both technical and behavioural terms.

● Strike a balance between recruiting new talent and growing your own.

● Invest in effective on-boarding and induction to equip and retain Marketers.

● Create "employee value propositions" and leverage other marketing planning techniques to better attract and retain talent.

● Encourage Marketing to collaborate closely with HR to make sure brand values are integrated with the cultural development of the organization as a whole.

We will return to this driver in Chapter 6 and explain in more detail how Shell has used marketing disciplines to transform its Attraction and Recruitment process globally.

6. The Culture Driver

The final driver of marketing capability in *The Brand Learning Wheel* is the *Culture Driver* (see Figure 3.2f). This is the least tangible driver but potentially the most powerful of all. By culture we mean the prevailing attitudes, values and behavioural norms that condition and shape the way things get done in any organization. Often, while a statement of values may be posted in reception, the real essence of the culture is not written down and has to be learnt

Figure 3.2f: *The Brand Learning Wheel – Culture Driver*

or acquired by experience, sometimes painfully, in the early months of a new job.

Key questions here include: can we articulate our culture? Is our culture customer-centric or focused internally? Is the culture enhanced or diminished by the behaviour of senior management? Is the culture vibrant and alive in pockets or across the whole company? Do we have a lot of attrition with new hires unable to adapt to our culture?

In start-up companies, the culture usually springs directly from the beliefs and behaviours of the founders and is kept alive by their personalities and by the leaders that follow them who ensure the consistent application of shared values to every decision and business intervention. But in larger organizations, many different and sometimes competing cultures influence the way that "things get done around here", and just as often "who gets on around here!"

The most important characteristic of a marketing culture is a *passion for customers*, an obsession which moves off the mission statement and into the reality of every business decision and choice made. We will return to cover this driver in more detail in Chapter 6.

Customer-centric Cultures

 P&G has a strong and respected customer-focused culture: *"Every culture has a language and the corporate culture at P&G is rich in words and phrases that convey what it is trying to do. Of these, the most important is a phrase that sums up all its priorities: the consumer is boss."* A.G. Lafley, former Chairman and CEO, Procter & Gamble.[4]

 Tesco's culture has long been supported by its powerful brand idea *Every Little Helps* and the question *"What's in it for the customer?"* connects all business decisions back to the fundamental task of creating value for customers.

first direct
Member HSBC Group
First Direct has built its reputation for customer service in direct banking based on the idea of *Expect Respect*, a crucial belief that applies in the way its employees interact with each other internally as well as with their customers externally.[5]

Key Principles – *The Culture Driver*

- Once cultures become established they are notoriously difficult to change – this can work to positive or negative effect.

- Changing an established culture requires strong and determined leadership from the top. Everything must be done to align brand values with the delivery of the customer experience.

- A passion for customers should be at the heart of a company's organizational culture.

- A brand's mission or purpose can provide an important rallying cry for a company culture.

- Collaboration and teamwork are essential to ensure everyone is engaged in creating value for customers.

- Balance the need for strategic rigour with the need for impact, speed and action.

The value of an holistic approach

Each of the core drivers in *The Brand Learning Wheel* plays a key role in capability development. However, to create a world-class approach to marketing capability development, they need to be managed in a holistic and integrated way.

By focusing only on the *Skills Driver*, organizations can fall into the "training trap" mentioned earlier – building only superficial skills and not creating the tangible change in marketing capabilities needed to drive sustainable growth.

Any organization that is serious about building world-class marketing excellence should ensure its Marketing, HR and General Management leaders adopt a strategic and integrated approach to marketing capability development. And, because *world class* may mean very

"In hindsight, we focused a lot of our efforts on process and skills, but I think a couple of things were missing. I don't think we worked out early enough some of the strategy and the importance of the brand portfolio we wanted to build. Also, as a result, we hadn't fully worked through the relationship of the new processes to the organization structure. So we were building people's skills to carry out certain marketing processes, when in actual fact, once the implications of the tighter, more global portfolio became clear, we'd probably taught a few people to do things we didn't need or even want them to be doing any more!"

Kerris Bright, *former Chief Marketing Officer, ICI/AkzoNobel*

different things in different industries, taking the time to define a clear, tailored and aligned marketing capability strategy is highly advisable before starting out.

Practical Next Steps

So, in moving forward, what's the next step? How do business leaders work out which of the capability drivers to focus on to build the marketing capabilities and commercial performance of their teams and organizations? In the following chapters we will give practical guidance on how to transform marketing capabilities to drive growth by leveraging each of the core capability drivers and understanding the relationships between them.

To keep it simple, we will work through each stage of *The 3D Approach*. First, we will explain how to *define* a marketing capability strategy (Chapter 4), then how to *develop solutions* around the Process and Skills Drivers (Chapter 5), how to *develop solutions* around the Organization, People and Culture Drivers (Chapter 6) and finally how to *drive embedding* of new ways of working in practice (Chapter 7).

CHAPTER 3 – AT A GLANCE

- If an organization is to succeed in driving sustainable, profitable, demand-led growth, it needs world-class marketing capabilities.

- The word "capability" can be used at three levels: the ability of an *individual* Marketer to do their Marketing job; the capability of the *Marketing function* as a whole; or the ability of the *entire organization* to deliver better value to its customers.

- The *training trap* is where companies focus on individual skill development and fail to take account of the wiring into the Marketing function and the organization as a whole that is so vital for effective change management.

- *The Brand Learning Wheel* helps organize and prioritize the core drivers of marketing capability.

- At the heart of *The Brand Learning Wheel* are the *Business Objectives and Strategy* which define what the organization is trying to achieve and provide strategic direction for Marketing's functional activities.

- The *Process Driver* covers the best practice ways of working, systems and tools that Marketers use in their work.

- The *Skills Driver* covers the integrated learning solutions that equip people and teams with the attitudes, knowledge, skills and behaviours needed to perform effectively.

- The *Organization Driver* covers the effective structure of clear Marketing roles and responsibilities defined within and across each department, business unit and for specific job roles.

- The *People Driver* covers the attraction, development, motivation and retention of the right calibre of Marketer for each job role and of people capable of delivering a consistent brand experience to customers.

- The *Culture Driver* covers the values, beliefs and behaviours that drive the way things get done and decisions get made within the organization.

Notes

1   Aviva Annual Report and Accounts 2010.
2   "Aviva: making a difference with marketing", award submission for The Marketing Society Awards for Excellence 2011.
3   *Reorganize for Resilience*, Ranjay Gulati.
4   *The Game Changer*, A.G. Lafley.
5   "Successful employee engagement; beyond the rhetoric", CIPR event, 15th April 2010.

Part 2
How to Transform Marketing Capabilities to Drive Growth

Chapter 4

"*Marketing is too important to be left to the Marketers.*" That was one CEO's view of the importance of defining a marketing capability strategy, according to SABMiller's Group Marketing Director, Nick Fell. Nick has had extensive experience building global marketing capabilities at Diageo and Cadbury, as well as the South African brewer.

"*These three organizations never saw it as something to be delegated. Each has had very different orientations about the speed, the urgency and the scale with which they wanted to get behind building marketing capability. The biggest difference in the three programmes I've worked on has actually been the view of the CEO at the time – what it was that he wanted to get done and how important it was*", Fell reflects.

Given the acknowledged importance of marketing capabilities as a key growth driver within an organization, we believe that strong senior leadership and proactive development of a strategy to build marketing capabilities is essential. Yet this is often not the way capability development is managed in reality.

Some surprising research by the Chartered Institute of Marketing illustrates the haphazard way that marketing capability development is handled within many organizations. Just 15% of companies fully integrate marketing capability strategy with business strategy, and in only 22% of organizations

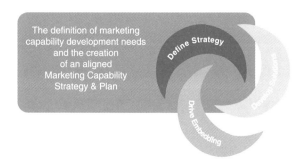

Figure 4.1: *The 3D Approach – Define Strategy*

was the management of marketing capability thought to be "embedded within Marketing".[1]

Equally revealing was the lack of clear functional leadership of the marketing capability development agenda. The agenda was set by the CMO in less than half of companies, HR or Learning and Development took the lead in many others, and as many as 30% admitted that there was no clear leadership for marketing capability development of any type.

In this chapter we will explore how to handle the first "D" in *The 3D Approach* to transforming marketing capabilities, i.e. *Define Strategy* (see Figure 4.1). We will address the key challenges that in our experience determine the impact and the effectiveness of capability development in equipping Marketers to create better value for customers and drive growth.

Key questions we will ask are: what kinds of marketing capability strategy do companies typically adopt? Who should lead the development of this strategy and how should it be approached? And what are the main elements of a strong marketing capability strategy and plan? We will also help readers benefit from the insights of those who have successfully defined marketing capability strategies for their organizations and show the crucial role of leadership.

Types of Marketing Capability Strategy

Defining a clear, aligned strategy for marketing capability development before embarking on the development of any programmes is a wise investment of time and money. It grounds initiatives firmly in the business strategy and ensures that marketing capabilities are being built where the organization needs them most, with the right level of resources to deliver results.

Marketing capability development initiatives come in many shapes and sizes. Important strategic choices must be made to determine the right approach for any specific organization and to guide the scope, breadth, depth and the ultimate impact of capability programmes and investments.

In our experience, there are five main types of change management intervention to build marketing excellence, each of which takes a different approach to the core Capability Drivers contained in *The Brand Learning Wheel* (introduced in Chapter 3).

1. Ad hoc skills training

First, as we described earlier, many organizations try to address skills gaps but languish in a situation where they persistently invest in ad hoc training programmes provided by a range of fragmented suppliers (the "training trap"). These programmes often focus on imparting *knowledge*, rather than truly building *skills*. They struggle to embed change because the initiatives are planned and implemented in isolation from business strategy and from the other core Capability Drivers described in *The Brand Learning Wheel*.

2. Task-focused learning support

In other organizations, the focus on the *Skills Driver* is strong and intentional, and *is* linked to business strategy. But the ambition is

"In the past, we didn't understand what true capability development looked like. So much of our view of training, and so much of the way we handled training, was sitting people in a room and talking at them. When I look back now it must have been painfully dull. Once you understand what true capability development looks like, you end up with a significantly higher on-boarding of the capabilities you're looking for, done in a way that is motivating, engaging and so life-changing to many people that you start a movement."

Mark Baynes, *Global Chief Marketing Officer, Kellogg*

Figure 4.2: *The Brand Learning Wheel – Skills Driver*

limited, focusing on addressing specific skills gaps, the skills of a specific team or a level of management when carrying out specific marketing tasks or activities. Provided they are "learner focused", such programmes can enable people and teams to assimilate new knowledge and skills, but they will be ineffective if insufficient attention is given to how new skills will be implemented back at work and integrated with other activities and teams (see Figure 4.2).

3. Pioneering leading-edge processes

Some organizations that already excel at marketing still strive to push the boundaries of their knowledge and understanding. These companies seek greater competitive advantage in the *Process Driver* by defining innovative, pioneering approaches in one or more key marketing areas (see Figure 4.3). This often involves a deep assessment of the current ways of working, capturing best practice internally and externally, and the development of new tools, systems and techniques.

Depending on the scope and leadership, they may also address changes in the other Capability Drivers such as the *Organization* (e.g. restructuring), *People* (e.g. buying in new skills) or *Culture Drivers* (e.g. culture change initiatives). Most commonly, however, they move directly to address the *Skills Driver* in a focused learning programme.

Figure 4.3: *The Brand Learning Wheel – Process Driver*

4. Integrated process and skill development

A strong and common choice for marketing capability development pro-grammes is to focus on a combination of addressing the *Process and Skills Drivers*. Common ways of working and new best practice tools are developed and then embedded via a cascade of launch workshops, learning events and support initiatives throughout, and in some instances beyond, the Marketing community. The most ambitious of these programmes aim to address many or all areas of marketing simultaneously, but more commonly there is a focus on one or more priority aspect such as Insight, Strategy & Planning etc. to aid the embedding of new ways of working (see Figure 4.4)

Figure 4.4: *The Brand Learning Wheel – Integrated Process and Skills Drivers*

Integrated Process and Skills Development

The recent merger of Friesland Foods and Campina has created a significant global dairy business with a turnover of 9 billion euros and sales and production locations in 25 countries. *"We have become a truly multinational company and we need to increase our marketing capabilities on this basis, as well as to create alignment across our organization"*, explains Franc Reefman, Marketing Director – FrieslandCampina.

For Reefman, this task extends far beyond sending people on a few training programmes. *"People that go through skill development exercises must come back and be confronted by the rest of the organization speaking the same language, especially the leaders of the business. Our approach is to make sure we train our people in a clear strategic framework and in the context of a common cross-functional process we call Integrated Commercial Planning. It is absolutely fundamental for us that we all end up speaking the same language."*

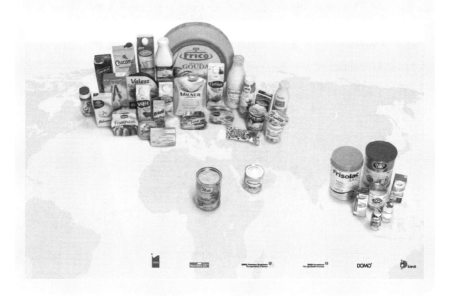

5. Customer-centric transformation

To carry out a complete transformation of an organization's marketing capabilities and to create a more customer-centric business, *all* of the core Capability Drivers around *The Brand Learning Wheel* need to be addressed and integrated. Initiatives of this type extend throughout and beyond the Marketing function to the whole business and include integrated high-level *process* redesign, *organization* restructure (with clarification and profiling of roles and responsibilities), enhanced *people* strategies (especially around recruitment and talent management), and investment in significant *skill* development and *culture* change programmes (see Figure 4.5).

It is usually not feasible on cost grounds for an organization to invest in addressing all aspects of marketing, across all core Capability Drivers, all geographies and in all business units simultaneously. However, in our experience, the remit for capability development is too often related more to the scope of an individual executive's department, job role or budget than to the strategic needs of the organization.

For organizations to build the marketing capabilities needed to drive growth, *active, conscious and continual* choices need to be made as to where to

Figure 4.5: *The Brand Learning Wheel – Holistic focus on all core Capability Drivers*

focus capability development needs and resources, in the context of what the organization is trying to achieve at any one time.

We will cover the detail of how to address each Capability Driver in turn over the next two chapters, but first let's share some key principles that underpin effective capability development.

The Golden Rules of Capability Development

In order to define the best marketing capability development strategy for any particular organization, it is vital that two *golden rules* are followed:

- **Marketing leaders must lead marketing capability development**
  Marketing leaders must assume *direct* responsibility for leading the change agenda, closely supported by HR and Learning & Development leaders. The CEO should also provide direct active support to ensure that Marketers, cross-functional teams and the organization as a whole are equipped with the marketing capabilities needed to help drive commercial performance and growth.

- **Marketing capability development must be planned strategically**
  The same core principles and intellectual rigour used in marketing strategy and planning must be applied to the planning of marketing capability development initiatives. If

> *"The momentum for marketing capability development at Pepsi is coming right from the top – from our global CEO; she is personally driving it. Her momentum is driven by strong growth focus – the need to drive a global agenda. And, global only makes sense if you can get economies of scale. With a common global branding agenda you have a common R&D agenda and suddenly the streams of work become harmonized and more efficient and you get scale – and that is essential when you are already a $63 billion business."*
>
> Simon Lowden, *CMO, Pepsi Beverages, North America*

organizations lack strategic planning capabilities this will naturally be a challenge, but we will give some practical guidance on getting started in this chapter. Let's explore the two golden rules in more detail.

Golden Rule #1 – Marketing leaders must lead marketing capability development

In our view, it is the direct responsibility of the Marketing leader and leadership team to drive the strategic marketing capability agenda since it is they who are ultimately accountable for Marketing's role in driving growth for the business. If they are to ensure the contribution of the function is in line with the requirements of senior management, they need to manage their expectations appropriately and build the capabilities needed to succeed.

In all the work we've done with clients over the years, *the single biggest factor that has influenced the effectiveness of marketing capability programmes* has been the extent to which senior management and marketing leaders see these programmes as a strategic means of driving business growth. They are not a "nice to have" or an "optional add-on" to the business agenda. They are an important driver of business results.

"The number one priority is commitment from the top – that is absolutely crucial. I've seen it in the past where both Friesland and Campina had similar initiatives before the merger, but in each case the board was hardly aware of what was happening. That doesn't work at all, because it is a serious investment programme, not only of money but also of time and the people who have to be part of it."

Franc Reefman, *Marketing Director, Friesland Campina*

"I would be hard pressed to believe any CMO would be looking at his or her business today, at consumers, at the market and not saying we have to evolve our structure, our capability. We have to work differently from how we did 2 to 3 years ago. We have to put in place a mechanism to develop our Marketers to flourish in the new environment."

Mark Baynes, *Global Chief Marketing Officer, Kellogg*

Inspiring Vision

The capability development of their people and teams is the most important and growing challenge facing senior Marketing leaders. To succeed, they need to create an inspiring vision of what role Marketing should play within the business and they must engage the leaders of the organization and their own colleagues and peers in that vision. Then they can agree where they are today, how they need to improve and together champion an effective, aligned capability development change management strategy and programme.

Stakeholder engagement

Although we recommend that senior Marketers take active ownership for the marketing capability development of their teams, they also need to involve and share the responsibilities with other stakeholders. This is particularly important when a re-orientation of the whole company is needed to focus on customers. The role of the CEO is crucial in driving an integrated cross-functional agenda in this regard.

Getting alignment in a large, complex multinational organization is time consuming. In a global business with multiple business units and where the Marketing directors report in to business unit managers rather than a functional CMO, the biggest challenge may simply be getting senior Marketers together to agree the issues, the objec-

> *It's not something to be undertaken lightly. You have to be single minded and determined that you want to bring a level of consistency across the globe and across the brand. I do think it is very helpful, maybe even critical, that you get a number of the functions joined up here because if people had seen The Diageo Way of Brand Building as just a Marketing thing, the opportunity to chip away at it would have been huge. But the fact that there are a number of people joined together that are really driving this is very important.*
>
> Nick Rose, *former Chief Financial Officer, Diageo*

tives and commit to shared goals.

So before an organization can address its marketing capability needs, it must first enable the Marketing leaders to meet across business units to agree a common agenda, coordinate and align with the global HR function and then get the multiple business unit heads internationally on side. Of course all of these different stakeholders will have potentially different priorities and objectives. We will return to this challenge and share some of the practical ways in which pioneering organizations have tackled this in Chapter 9.

"The biggest call in raising the bar for marketing competence in a complex environment is actually gaining alignment from people as to what we are trying to change round here, what problems we are trying to fix, what success looks like and how we're going to get there? Even if it takes you five months, it's worth getting alignment and buy-in around a clear programme scope and deliverables as it will save you time later. And I'm not talking here about sending out broadcast emails. I think you have to book one-on-one time with people and talk to them as experts."

Richard Davies, *Global Marketing Manager, Shell Bitumen*

Golden Rule #2 – Marketing capability development must be planned strategically

The second golden rule is that it is critical to apply the same rigour and discipline to the development of a *marketing capability* strategy and plan, as that which lies at the heart of effective *marketing* strategy and planning. As we will demonstrate throughout *The Growth Drivers*, there are many ways in which the approach to marketing capability development can draw from marketing disciplines, but this is one of the most important.

There are some useful guidelines about how to define a marketing capability development strategy which we will explore shortly. But it is important to understand that the development of a marketing capability strategy is not an ancillary process. If marketing is to be actively used as a lever to drive growth, then marketing capability development needs to be incorporated as a work stream within the organization's overall strategic planning process. This ensures that capability development is *directly* linked to supporting business objectives and strategy, sufficient resources are allocated and capability initiatives are integrated and sustained over time.

> *" A capability strategy doesn't have a life and soul of its own, it doesn't exist separately from the strategy of the business – it must be part of the business agenda. That's why it's important that everyone knows you're doing capability development for an express corporate strategic goal. "*
>
> Helen Lewis, *Consumer Insight and Marketing Strategy Director, Unilever Marketing Academy*

Key stages in strategic planning

The key stages in defining a marketing capability strategy are similar to the development of any other effective strategy (see Figure 4.6). Let's look at each of these stages in turn to explain how to go about building a strategy and plan to build the marketing capabilities needed to drive growth.

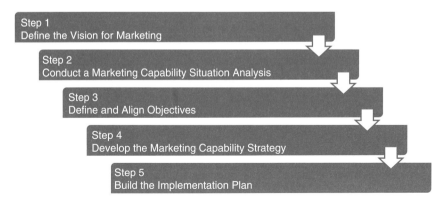

Figure 4.6: *The key stages in defining a capability strategy and plan*

Step 1 Define the vision for marketing

To lead a programme of effective change, the first step is to begin with a clear and compelling vision of the future which sets the ambition and the context, inspires people with a sense of possibility and engages them emotionally to commit their energy to making the vision a reality.

So, Marketing leaders wanting to drive change in the capabilities of their people, teams or organization need first to define an *inspiring vision for the role of Marketing* in the business. They need to then align other stakeholders in helping to shape that vision and establish the scale and scope of the marketing capability development needed.

T· ·Mobile· · · A Vision for Marketing

Phil Chapman, former CMO at T-Mobile, worked with his team to define a new vision for the role of the Marketing function – *"To anticipate and create everyday customer communication behaviours, driving profitable cross-functional delivery of T-Mobile experiences to make T-Mobile the UK's most considered network."*

This was supported by a detailed Marketing Capability Framework which defined the specific capabilities required to support the vision, from market and customer insight, through to innovation, communication and commercial accountability.

❝ *There's a tricky cross-functional leadership role. You have to get everyone behind one vision, explaining it to them and getting them engaged so they can contribute towards it. And people can sometimes be pretty uncomfortable with that culture shift. If you want to drive real organizational change, you must get the chief executive behind you and he must let people know that he's behind you – his backing and support are essential if you want to reorientate other functions towards a more customer-focused agenda.* **❞**

Phil Chapman, *former CMO T-Mobile,*
now Group Marketing Director, Kerry Foods

There is another reason why it is important for all companies to think hard about the role they see Marketing playing in future, even those in categories like consumer packaged goods where Marketing's role is generally well understood. This is due to the impact that digital technologies, social media and the networked world are having on the way Marketing is now working to influence the attitudes and behaviours of customers. These changes are significant and need to be reflected in the way companies approach their strategic development of marketing capabilities.

Traditional marketing approaches in areas such as insight generation, new product development, communication development and campaign implementation are all evolving rapidly. And the spirit behind marketing capability development initiatives is changing too. Greater emphasis is being placed on a "test and learn" philosophy with new ways of working being pioneered and then learning shared quickly throughout global marketing communities.

"In India, we generated 1.5 million Facebook friends on the back of one campaign around our sponsorship of the Cricket World Cup where we gave consumers the chance to get involved in the design of our packaging. In China, we have similar creative campaigns with millions of people submitting ideas, hundreds of thousands voting on those ideas, so the whole premise of getting creative ideas from consumers is coming to life all over the world. We can't control the output but it's such a powerful platform – there's no doubt we have to embrace it"

Simon Lowden, *CMO,*
Pepsi Beverages, North America

Define the Vision for Marketing – Practical Tips

- Create an inspiring vision of the future role of Marketing.

- Engage all key stakeholders in that vision.

- Consider the implications of social media, sustainability and CSR on the future marketing approach.

Step 2 Conduct a marketing capability situation analysis

Once key stakeholders have agreed on the vision for the role Marketing will play in driving organizational performance, the next step is to assess how well the Marketing function, and potentially the broader business, is equipped to deliver this vision in practice.

The Brand Learning Wheel provides a proven framework to help conduct this analysis.

Key Questions – Capability Situation Analysis

- Are effective, aligned marketing **processes** in place? Do the established ways of working, systems or tools need development or improvement?.

- How is the Marketing **organization** structured? Are roles and responsibilities clear, for example between global, regional and local teams or across departments? Are the main interfaces both within and outside the function working effectively?

- From a **people** point of view, is it clear how many Marketing people are in the organization, their profile, experience and locations? How engaged are they as employees? How well are attraction, recruitment, induction, development and career-pathing being handled for the Marketing community?'

- What is the status of marketing **skills**? How competent are Marketers in different roles and at different levels in the organization to handle the tasks that are expected of them? How equipped are people to progress to more senior roles over time?

- How well does the **culture** of the Marketing community (and of the organization as a whole) support effective brand and business performance? Are there clear, aligned values and behaviours? Is there the right level of customer focus, brand orientation, collaboration, agility and commerciality and any other relevant factors essential to driving business performance and growth?

Answers to these questions during the situation analysis can be obtained in many ways. At the most pragmatic level, stakeholder interviews can be highly illuminating. Even better is a facilitated workshop session for senior leaders to uncover the important capability issues, identify the drivers and generate alignment on the priorities for investment.

Where robust data is required, quantitative analysis can provide powerful information and insights into the perceived marketing capability strengths and weaknesses across the organization (see Chapter 8). When used in conjunction with a marketing capability framework (i.e. a structured summary of the key activity areas in which Marketers need to excel), this approach can also provide a deep dive assessment of the current and desired quality of specific processes and skills.

One important drawback with *internal* assessments of marketing capabilities is that they may not sufficiently challenge an organization that really needs to embrace *new* marketing capabilities to drive growth. They are also unable to provide an *external* benchmark of capability levels versus other organizations.

It was this challenge that led Brand Learning to develop an online service to enable the fast quantitative assessment, tracking and benchmarking of global marketing capabilities called *Brand Learning Radar*. The methodology is based on the core marketing activity areas defined in *The Growth Propeller* and has been developed in collaboration with research experts and the Oxford Retail Futures Group at Said Business School, Oxford University. (For further information, visit www.brandlearning.com.)

Marketing Capability Situation Analysis – Practical Tips

- Use *The Brand Learning Wheel* to help assess how well equipped the Marketing function is to deliver the business vision.

- Create a marketing capability framework to provide a structure for analysis and planning.

- Use stakeholder interviews, workshops and quantitative research (e.g. *Brand Learning Radar*) to engage and align influential leaders and end-users.

 **Marketing Health Check**

AstraZeneca launched a marketing capability "Health Check" for its new Global Marketing teams using a mountaineering analogy with powerful emotive and visual imagery. People were initially inspired with examples of world-class marketing from other industry sectors and then the teams worked together, led by their senior manager, to rank themselves on a five-point scale across the eight areas in AstraZeneca's own Marketing Capability Framework.

Using 'Mountaineering Spirit' To Describe The Assessment Levels

In The Foothills

Setting Up Base Camp

Scaling the Face

Reaching Great Heights

Peak Performance

Level One was described as the *Foothills*, Level Two as *Base Camp*, Level Three as *Scaling the Face*, Level Four as *Reaching Great Heights* and the ultimate aspiration at Level Five was *Peak Performance*.

It was good for us because there were new teams coming together and it allowed them to have really good discussions about what they do, how they do it and their ambitions for the future. It helped us identify key capability gaps and themes for our programme to focus on.

Tim Bailey, *Head of Marketing Academy, AstraZeneca*

Step 3 Define and align objectives

Having defined the main marketing capability issues facing the business, Marketing leaders must then establish a clear and ambitious view of the role they want marketing capability development to play and the related objectives and metrics.

Marketing Capability Mission Statements

At the highest level, it is helpful to start by crafting a clear statement of the overall goal or mission of the programme:

"To help build great hotels guests love by developing best in class skills and processes in hotel brand management, sales and marketing."

"Giving marketers the confidence to outperform."

Marketing capability *mission statements* define clearly and simply what a marketing capability programme is setting out to achieve. They help align other stakeholders and sharpen the focus of subsequent strategy and programme development. However, it is also important to drill down objectives to a more detailed level, defining specific, measurable targets and key performance indicators (KPIs) that can be used to set direction and track progress over time.

Objectives and KPIs

The ultimate measure of success of a marketing capability programme relates to its impact in creating better customer value and driving profitable business growth. However, to be meaningful, objectives and KPIs need to differentiate the unique impact of capability building activities from the other drivers of business performance.

Illustrative metrics around *The Brand Learning Wheel* could, for example, include changes in the numbers of Marketers in certain business units or levels of the *organization*, in the proportion of *people* promoted internally or brought in from the outside, or in improvements in attitude assessed through *culture* surveys.

In the *Process* and *Skills Drivers*, securing and embedding changes in the behaviour of Marketers on a day-to-day basis is the ultimate challenge, just as it is for Marketers trying to influence customer behaviours. For this reason a four-level measurement framework, based on the thinking first introduced by Dr Don Kirkpatrick, is a useful tool to plan and assess marketing learning programmes (See Chapter 8 for more detail).[2]

The choice of the objectives set will reflect the depth, breadth and scope of the required marketing capability development programme and the scale of investment needed to deliver tangible improvements in attitudes, skills and ways of working.

“To me the success of our insight capability programme relies entirely upon our ability to generate 'deep customer understandings'. We also need to demonstrate those deep understandings are supportive of driving business. If they're not, then quite rightly the question will come back 'well why are we doing it?' We need to be able to provide a link. If you don't do that, anything else you do is really rather irrelevant.”

Huw Jones, *Senior Director, Global Commercial Excellence, Novartis Pharmaceuticals*

Define and Align Objectives – Practical Tips

- Agree a mission statement for the marketing capability programme.

- Translate capability development priorities into KPIs.

- Find ways to measure the extent to which changes in the way Marketers work have been embedded.

Step 4 Develop the marketing capability strategy

Having defined and aligned clear, focused capability development objectives, the next step is to develop the marketing capability strategy.

Up to this point, there may be clarity on *why* a marketing capability initiative is needed, but not on what that initiative will comprise. From here, the focus needs to shift to decide *who* will be the target groups for the programme – levels, business units, geographies, etc.; *what* the programme will focus on – the priority content areas such as innovation, brand positioning, pricing, etc.; and *how* change will be driven – the main activities and channels that will be used.

The questions of *when* and *where* the programme will be implemented will be addressed when the focus shifts to building the implementation plan.

Underpinning the strategic decisions taken at this point are usually the guiding principles or beliefs that emerge in discussion with senior executives during the earlier stages of the strategy development process. Principles chosen may include, for example, "*We want learning to be connected to solving business issues*" or "*Process change must be owned and cascaded by senior management to embed new ways of working on the job.*"

   Marketing Excellence Programme

When Hewlett Packard's European Imaging & Printing Group embarked on a Marketing Excellence Programme, Philip Darnell, the VP of Marketing Operations, personally sponsored the initiative. He was deeply committed to the role of Marketing as a driver of business growth in their highly competitive category.

" *I passionately believe that building a world-class Marketing team requires a common language, best practice marketing processes and tools and efficient ways of working right across the business. Building future talent is critical – how can you do that unless managers in our B2B divisions build their marketing skills in just the same way as those in our B2C divisions. Our customers are most important here, not our internal business structures.* **"**

Philip Darnell, *VP Marketing HP, Imaging & Printing Group*

"The Marketing Excellence Programme has been a major catalyst to our business", says Philip Darnell.

Working closely with his colleagues in the global Learning & Development team, Darnell was adamant that the HP Marketing Excellence Programme should operate at two levels:

- Foundation level to establish a common language, common ways of working and common tools and techniques for managers at all levels and in all divisions in the European business.

- Advanced level to ensure that advanced process, tool and skill development was integrated in a way that would make the business more efficient, more effective and ultimately more successful in driving growth.

Kevin Kussman, Director Learning & Development, HP Imaging & Printing Group, who played a key role as HP's global head of Learning & Development, recalls, *"We needed to build marketing excellence in a more integrated and holistic way than previously. We conducted a rigorous diagnosis to define our issues, created an aligned marketing competency framework and then developed a Learning & Development strategy to guide the initiative with rollout to over 500 marketing managers worldwide, across over 70 in-market face-to-face and virtual workshops and events"*.

"Lifting the floor" or "Raising the ceiling"?

One vital consideration during the strategic planning stage is to clarify the fundamental role of marketing capability development. Is it designed to *"lift the floor"* of practices within the company by ensuring best practice ways of working are captured, enhanced, rolled out and embedded across the organization? Or is it aiming to *"raise the ceiling"* by stretching capabilities in priority areas that are particularly important to sustaining competitive advantage?

It is likely that most organizations will require a blend of these two approaches to reach world-class standards of marketing capability and commercial performance. Top marketing businesses often have core capabilities that enable them to stand out from the crowd – for example, Apple in the area of innovation and design and Nike in innovation and brand communication. But it is also necessary to attain acceptable base levels of competence in *all* areas of Marketing activity to avoid undermining these sources of competitive advantage elsewhere.

Marketing Capability Strategy – Life Stages Model

In our extensive work in this field, we have noticed an evolution in the way companies tend to develop their marketing capabilities which we have summarized in the *Marketing Capability Life Stages Model* (see Figure 4.7).

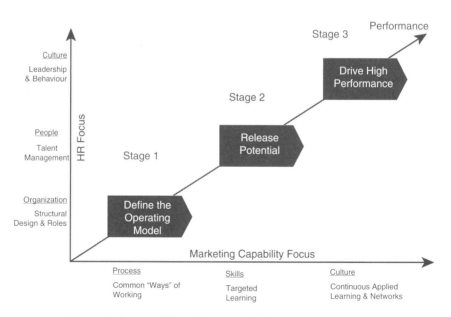

Figure 4.7: *The Marketing Capability Life Stages Model*

The *Marketing Capability Life Stages Model* explains how the different drivers in *The Brand Learning Wheel* relate to each other. It also clarifies the roles that the Marketing and HR functions each play in driving change.

Stage 1: Define the operating model

During the early stages of strategic marketing capability development, the first priority is to *"define the operating model"*. Initiatives frequently involve the design of a clear role and organization structure for Marketing (often led by HR), closely followed by the development and rollout of a "common way of marketing" with aligned processes and tools (led by Marketing). Learning programmes tend to be either inspiring launch events or foundation learning programmes aimed at embedding ways of working and tools.

Stage 2: Release potential

Capability development then extends to include targeted capability building for key groups or individuals. Typical activities include assessment and development centres, development planning, talent management initiatives, clarifying career paths, succession planning and the identification and development of high potential Marketing leaders (led by HR).

From a skills perspective, the focus moves to tailored skills development for those in different Marketing roles, across functions (e.g. Sales, Channel Marketing) and at different levels in the organization (often led by Marketing). The *training trap* we mentioned tends to occur when these programmes are put in place before the operating model has been established in Stage 1.

Stage 3: Drive high performance

The most advanced stage is when companies focus on strengthening the performance of *operational teams* on a live and ongoing basis. Significant emphasis here is placed on transforming the culture within the business and on establishing effective leadership through enhancing people's values, motivations and behaviours (led by HR). In parallel, internal networks and communities of marketing best practice are created in which the responsibility for learning and knowledge transfer shifts to the Marketing leaders and to the heart of the Marketing community (led by Marketing).

At this stage, skills development tends to leverage a blend of more advanced learning channels (i.e. knowledge sharing portals, webinars, virtual classrooms, e-learning, etc.). There is also greater use of "live action learning" in which coaching supports application to live business issues.

These three stages are not necessarily sequential and it is possible to work on all three at the same time. But in defining an effective marketing capability development strategy, it makes sense to ensure the earlier building blocks are firmly in place before moving on to the more advanced stages.

Develop Marketing Capability Strategy – Practical Tips

- Shift focus from the *why* of the programme to the *who, what* and *how*

- Decide whether to "lift the floor", "raise the ceiling" or to do both simultaneously

- Define your current and desired position in the *Marketing Capability Life Stages Model*

Step 5 Build the implementation plan

The final step in defining a marketing capability development strategy is to agree all the elements of the programme implementation plan. What will it look like in practice? What will be its scope, impact, timing and resources? What will be the key deliverables such as priority processes, best practice or mandatory tools, job role profiles and blended learning programme elements (e.g. workshops, virtual classrooms, online portals)?

There will also need to be a time plan showing key milestones and phasing of implementation across different business units and countries, a leadership plan showing key sponsors and decision makers and the budget scope and responsibility.

Another important component is a clear explanation of the internal roles and responsibilities for making things happen. This is particularly important in complex international businesses where the degree of commitment and involvement from people in different countries and categories is an important driver of success.

We will explore the organization of capability initiatives in Chapter 9, but at a high level the main roles are likely to be split across *The 3D Approach* that we introduced earlier:

Capability Strategy – Roles and Responsibilities

- **Defining strategy** – A senior leadership group will usually be charged with the responsibility for capability strategy, setting the key business objectives and priorities, approving the overall approach and allocating the necessary resources.

- **Developing solutions** – Small teams of internal and external experts will then be allocated the task of creating best practice process development, designing practical tools and developing learning initiatives and programmes.

- **Driving embedding** – The delivery and embedding process needs to be handled by teams of learning facilitators, IT systems experts, HR managers and, most importantly, line Marketing managers.

Investment and resource levels

A central requirement in any marketing capability strategy and plan is to make a strong, robust business case for the resources required, both in terms of people's time and financial budgets. In this respect it is vital that investment in marketing capability development is seen as a driver of top line value rather than simply a cost. As we explained earlier, this should *never* be approached from a "training cost per head" basis – if so, its effectiveness as a change-management initiative will be diminished before it even begins.

In simple terms, there are two approaches to justifying investment in marketing capability development. These involve making the case for:

- How capability development will improve the *effectiveness* of the Marketing function in creating superior customer value and helping to drive the top line growth of the business.
- How potential improvements in marketing *efficiency* will impact on costs and bottom-line profitability.

With significant resources invested in global brand innovation and communication campaigns, organizations are becoming aware that small improvements in the quality of these activities

"If people just perceive this to be about training, and not about business development in a broader sense, then they judge it by delegate cost per day and the metrics they have are on the cost side, not on the value side. You have to be able to point to the impact the programme can have on trading up on margin or attracting new customers. Ultimately, the only thing that persuades anyone is the incremental business that you can track from an activity. Once you can see the return, it becomes an investment decision, just like 'shall we build a new plant?'"

Richard Davies, **Global Marketing Manager, Shell Bitumen**

"Inside a business it's a war for resource. The CEO only has so much money and so many people, so either we get them in Marketing or the HR director gets them or Finance gets them. The person who ultimately succeeds in securing resource will be the person who is going to add most value to the bottom line. Profit is the common denominator; that is what you've got to learn to focus on."

Martin George, **Managing Director for Group Development, Bupa**

can make a big difference to the return on investment delivered from Marketing (see Chapter 8).

Communication plans

The final consideration in building an implementation plan is that of managing the *internal communications* needed to engage people to start to change their ways of working *in practice*. This takes us back to the theme of stakeholder engagement where we started this chapter. The involvement and buy-in of key stakeholders is a *critical* ingredient in the development of a successful marketing capability strategy and is one of the most important differences between successful capability-building initiatives and those which fail to gain any leverage.

The need for stakeholder engagement does not end at the point the strategy is approved. It continues at every stage of the subsequent development and delivery of a successful marketing capability programme. So an essential "must-have" is a well thought through plan for the ongoing alignment and engagement of different stakeholder groups to launch and sustain momentum, extending from senior management sponsors right through to the ultimate programme recipients throughout the Marketing community. We will explore this important topic in Chapter 7.

Build Implementation Plan – Practical Tips

- Clarify the key programme deliverables and timing milestones.

- Establish clear responsibility for defining strategy, developing solutions and driving embedding.

- Make a robust business case and create an internal communications plan.

In this chapter we have explored how to handle the first "D" in *The 3D Approach* to building marketing capabilities, i.e. *Define Strategy*. We will now move on to address the second "D", i.e. *Develop Solutions*, and as we do so we will expand and explore in turn each of the core Capability Drivers in *The Brand Learning Wheel*.

CHAPTER 4 – AT A GLANCE

- Defining a clear, aligned strategy for marketing capability development before embarking on the development of any programmes is a wise investment of time and money.

- Important strategic choices need to be made to determine the right approach for any specific organization and to guide the scope, breadth, depth and the ultimate impact of marketing capability programmes and investments.

- There are five main types of change management intervention to build marketing excellence – ad hoc skills training, task-focused learning support, pioneering leading-edge processes, integrated process and skill development and customer-centric transformation.

- To define the best marketing capability development strategy for an organization, it is vital that two *golden rules* are followed – 1. Marketing leaders must lead marketing capability development 2. Marketing capability development must be planned strategically.

- The biggest single factor influencing the effectiveness of marketing capability programmes is the extent to which senior management and Marketing leaders leverage capability development as a strategic means of driving growth.

- The key stages of marketing capability strategy development are similar to any other effective strategy process: define the *vision* for marketing, conduct marketing capability *situation analysis*, define and align *objectives* and set KPIs, develop the *marketing capability strategy* and build the *implementation plan*.

- A strong, robust business case should be prepared to secure the resources needed in terms of people's time and financial budgets.

- Internal communications and continuous stakeholder engagement need careful management to get people to change their ways of working *in practice*.

Notes

1   *The Future for Marketing Capability,* Chartered Institute of Marketing 2010.
2   *Evaluating Training Programs: The Four Levels,* Donald L. Kirkpatrick and James M. Kirkpatrick.

Chapter 5

Defining a marketing capability strategy and plan is just the starting point in terms of how to accelerate an organization's ability to deliver better customer value and drive growth. It helps to clarify objectives and build essential alignment to the scope and resources needed. But once that alignment has been secured, it's time to move on and develop capability solutions to bring to the Marketing community and business as a whole.

> "World-class marketing is not a one-off, it's not a brilliant tactic or advert; it is an integrated programme that really delivers value and inspires our stakeholders. And that makes it much harder to deliver. It's a journey, and the journey has felt very difficult at times."
>
> Nina Bibby, *Chief Marketing Officer, Barclaycard*

In this chapter we will explore the second "D" in *The 3D Approach* to marketing capability development – *Develop Solutions* (see Figure 5.1). We will look first at solutions that address the Capability Drivers in the "top half" of *The Brand Learning Wheel*, i.e. the *Process* and *Skills Drivers*, and their linkages with the *Culture Driver* – a key influencer across the whole "wheel" (see Figure 5.2).

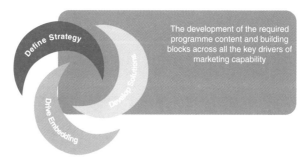

Figure 5.1: *The 3D Approach – Develop Solutions*

Figure 5.2: *The "top half" of The Brand Learning Wheel
The Process and Skills Drivers*

In our experience, the importance of this stage and the time required to develop marketing processes, capture best practice, develop aligned tools, and to develop the approach and content for learning programmes is least understood. People are under too much pressure to move on to the point where the outputs become tangible in the organization. They often seriously underestimate the amount of time and resources needed to complete this phase successfully. It can take 4–8 months, or even more in a complex, global business, depending on the scope of the task and stakeholder alignment needed.

This stage is also made difficult by the fact that processes and skills solutions which should be developed together are often under the leadership of two separate functions – the former by Marketing and the latter by Learning and Development or HR. This makes cross-functional integration essential and reinforces the golden rule we introduced in Chapter 4 – *Marketing leaders must lead marketing capability development.*

To help bring some clarity to this stage, we will answer questions such as what does process and skill development really involve? How do you develop processes and tools that represent best practice, are simple to understand and practical to use? What types of learning programme can be used? And what impact do digital technology and social media have on marketing processes and learning design?

InterContinental Hotels Group

Driving Growth at InterContinental Hotels Group

Back in 2007, Nina Bibby, then SVP Global Brands at Inter-Continental Hotels Group (IHG), was facing a problem on a positioning development project for Crowne Plaza, one of IHG's key hotel brands. "We had defined our target as the 'upscale business traveller' and we *had spent six months and a lot of money researching this group around the world. But we didn't discover anything new, nothing we couldn't have told you in the room before we started."*

The team realized they hadn't defined their target market precisely enough and therefore the questions they had been asking in their research lacked edge and penetration. *"Our brands tended to be quite mainstream, so it was very easy to define our positioning based on mass-market consumer target profiles"*, explains Bibby. *"But it's only when we sharpened the focus that we got to insights that could be a source of differentiation."*

So the Crowne Plaza team started asking deeper, more perceptive questions, about who their customers really were, what they enjoyed doing and what they  were looking for from a hotel experience. Through this challenge, a new insight was generated that opened up a very different positioning opportunity for the Crowne Plaza brand.

"We had previously been talking to business travellers in quite a negative way, about how business travel is really tough, the fact we know they've had a hard day and how we're going to look after them and help them relax. But actually there is an important group out there who don't think like this at all – they actually quite like business travel", adds Bibby.

This segment was termed the "stimulus seekers". *"Stimulus seekers enjoy staying in upscale hotels, they enjoy seeing places and when they come to the hotel they want to have some fun. That was the insight and it was one we'd never have got to if we had kept focusing on the 'upscale business traveller'"*, she continues.

As a result of this work, IHG created a new positioning strategy for Crowne Plaza based on the core brand platform of *Celebrate your Stay*. The team went on to use this idea to guide a new kind of guest experience incorporating more innovative and stimulating activities and opportunities.

Nina Bibby's insights went further. As the project had been unfolding, IHG had been developing some new tools and ways of thinking and trained its people to help them understand how to approach insight generation more successfully. These capability building efforts had enabled her team to handle the brand positioning challenge they faced in a new and more effective way.

"Between the time we did our first round of research and when we came back for the second time, we had done a lot of work with the team around how to develop insights. We looked to determine how to develop an insight, how to craft an insight, how to evaluate whether an insight is good. One of the things we introduced is what we call the 'problem fundamentals', a series of simple questions that help you get to the root of any issue you are facing from a customer perspective", she reveals.

It was this more rigorous approach to customer insight that helped unlock Crowne Plaza's positioning dilemma. As Bibby explains, *"You've got to be more precise in your questions and the issues you're trying to address. If you just go out and talk to consumers it's unlikely you're going to get anything useful back. You have to be clear about what your hypotheses are and, even if you're wrong, going out and trying to seek relevant information about them will help you get to something deeper."*

The new techniques have also been used successfully on other brand development projects, including for Intercontinental Hotels, Hotel Indigo and Priority Club Rewards (the world's largest hotel loyalty programme). And their impact has been even more far-reaching as they have been embedded within IHG's business.

In commercial terms, IHG's revenue grew by 6% to $1.6 billion in 2010, with profits leaping 22% to $444 million. Crowne Plaza performed particularly well, its total gross revenue (not all of which is attributable to IHG) increasing by 17% to $3.5 billion. During the 12 months of 2010, IHG's share price increased by 39%.

"We've made a huge jump in terms of the way the organization is run. The terminology and language is being used widely within the business. It's being used cross-functionally and insight is now at the core of our annual planning process. We have become an organization that embraces insight in a much bigger way than we did before and I think that will continue because of the tools and language we've introduced", concludes Bibby.

Integrated Process and Skill Development

The "IHG Way of Brand Building" is just one example of a marketing capability programme designed to drive commercial performance by enhancing the rigour of marketing *processes* and strengthening the *skills* of Marketers to put them into practice.

By leveraging both the *Process* and the *Skills Drivers* in *The Brand Learning Wheel*, the way people work across the organization, day to day, can be integrated and connected up with the skills development that Marketers need to enhance their performance. More effective processes help to clarify *what* it is Marketers need to be doing, *when* and *why*, but the focus of everyone involved in capability development should always be on linking that to *how* people do marketing, and even more importantly – *how well*.

Many organizations, however, still don't have any common marketing processes or marketing skills support programmes in place. They leave the choices of what to do and how to do it entirely up to individual Marketers, who, inevitably, are highly "individual" in the way they tackle those tasks.

While that may be fine in a start-up company, it can create havoc in any large organization that operates in a matrix structure, on a global scale or where Marketing roles are fragmented across different countries, teams or departments.

Empowered individuals can drive the business too far, too fast, in too many different directions. While this may drive short-term sales, it's also likely to add significant costs in terms of complexity, stock loading and system inefficiencies. This is especially true for a business seeking to build global brands and coordinate activities internationally. A heavy burden is placed on the Marketing leaders who need to engage, focus and "manage" the energies of their teams in such organizations.

The widespread habit of "hiring talent" from different organizations exacerbates efficiency challenges. People naturally import marketing thinking, tools and language from their previous employers, so they may *literally* struggle to "talk the same language". Resolving internal communication issues like this can slow decision making and divert business attention away from the far more important customer-focused agenda.

> **"***In one meeting, the people in the room had prior experience in 110 different companies and 30% had been in the business less than 5 years. On the one hand, that is fantastic from an energy and freshness of thinking point of view, but when it comes to trying to drive a level of common understanding, consistency to leverage scale and a PepsiCo way of doing things – it is very difficult.***"**
>
> Simon Lowden, *CMO,*
> *Pepsi Beverages, North America*

The benefits of common ways of working

- Marketers can focus on the content of the job, rather than on trying to understand the different marketing terms and concepts people may use.

- More efficient working – as Marketers don't need to reinvent the wheel and can leverage proven tools and techniques.

- Best practice ways of working, from both inside and outside the organization, can be captured, codified and evolved over time.

- Knowledge and insights are transferred more easily across brands, countries and business units.

- Easier for new recruits to get up to speed and make an impact.

Exploring the Process Driver

As marketing becomes increasingly specialized and fragmented, with responsibilities split by geography or business unit, it becomes essential to have processes and tools that enable Marketers to work more effectively and more efficiently across category, international and functional boundaries.

Process development does not, however, have to be complex or unwieldy. In fact the best processes and tools are simple to understand, easy to use and actively help Marketers make more effective business decisions. This enables them to better focus their time and energies on driving growth, rather than wasting effort reinventing the wheel.

 Creating the Sara Lee Way of Marketing

Nilgun Langenberg, former VP Talent Development & Learning at Sara Lee, describes how this challenge initially manifested itself at Sara Lee: "We have been more a buyer than a developer of people and we bring a lot of people in from outside to work for us, from Unilever and P&G and other businesses. We didn't have a common language or common templates. It was very inefficient. In fact it was this inefficiency that was the initial driver for us to start building something different."

However, Sara Lee soon realized the opportunities for a marketing capability development programme extended well beyond addressing these initial concerns. "As we built the programme, we achieved better effectiveness, not just efficiency", continues Langenberg. "As we built our team from across different businesses and started to benchmark and build the content of our processes internally and externally, we quickly saw that not only did we need to create a common language, but we also needed to be more effective in our marketing capabilities – so we raised the bar."

She continues, "The marketing capability development programme actually helped us with a lot of business alignment, as every time we looked at a process we streamlined that process and globalized it – so creating the Sara Lee Way of Marketing was much bigger than creating a training programme", she says.

Sara Lee's approach to building marketing capabilities has been characterized by a number of strategic choices made by the Marketing Leadership Team to ensure it was most appropriate to business goals and objectives, as well as to culture.

Strategic Choices

First, they decided to focus on a single process area at a time, developing, launching and embedding each new process, set of tools and common definitions over a period of 1–2 years before moving on to the next topic. Over the past seven years, they have successively covered capability areas such as brand positioning and communications, brand activation, innovation, shopper marketing and commercial effectiveness.

Each initiative has been driven by an international team of Sara Lee Marketing and HR Learning and Development leaders with external capability development experts in support. They took on the responsibility, on top of their normal day jobs, for leading both the development and internal alignment of the Sara Lee processes and tools and then championing their launch and embedding. Skill development saw the introduction of the new ways of working cascaded through large scale workshops, initially for the international marketing leadership team in global conferences, followed by regional rollout workshops and supported by online learning materials. Sara Lee's agency partners have also been invited to participate, where appropriate, to familiarize themselves with the company's ways of working.

The active leadership of the CEO and HR, who provided the budget, were also critical. *"We had strong leadership endorsement and strong empowerment"*, explains Langenberg. *"At the time, the CEO of the international business said this is how we will approach it. He appointed a core team to work on it and empowered them to make it happen. The budget was held centrally by HR which helped all the businesses come to the table, particularly since we did not have a global Marketing organization."*

"Looking back on it, the approach and the programme has served its purpose very well for us", she reflects. *"From an employee's perspective, they know that there is a structured Marketing curriculum, something that is very important in attraction and retention. From a manager's perspective, they have a vehicle to support their teams with frameworks, knowledge and platforms that they can leverage. From a business perspective, looking at the specific topics we have worked on, we can measure that our communications are better, our business planning processes are stronger and our internal conversations are much more effective. We are spending less money and doing a better job in the communications area."*

BUPA's Marketing Way

After reviewing internal and external best practice, Bupa defined a set of eight key marketing areas including *"Customer-led Strategy and Planning"*, *"Leveraging Insights"* and *"Designing Customer Propositions"* and the inter-relationships between them. Each process area was defined with key principles, core process steps, a common language and core tools and the emphasis is now on embedding changes in ways of working across the organization.

❝ *I want people at Bupa to approach marketing from first principles, so we can better understand and solve customer needs and be effective Marketers, rather than just follow established marketing processes and activities.* **❞**

Fiona McAnena, *Global Brand Director, Bupa*

Levels of process development

There are three levels at which processes can be developed to help Marketers improve their capability to drive business growth: the *overall* end-to-end process framework for marketing, the *individual processes* (e.g. innovation, strategy and planning) and the practical support tools and examples *within* each process. Let's briefly look at these differences before we move on to describe how to develop processes and tools in practice (see Figure 5.3).

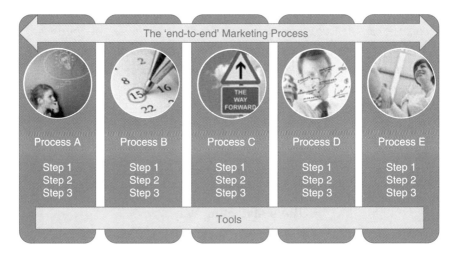

Figure 5.3: *Levels of process development*

1. End-to-end process framework

The creation of an overall "end-to-end" marketing process framework involves identifying the core marketing activities needed in an organization, and identifying how they connect to each other and to the other processes in the company.

Executives often overlook the importance of this high level thinking, but if marketing processes are not developed in an integrated way it can lead to costly and time-consuming complexity later. For example, there is no point designing brand innovation and communication strategies if their implementation doesn't take account of the lead times involved in selling new propositions to customers. Nor is there much value in developing a longer-term brand plan if there is no aligned view as to the role the brand plays in the overall company portfolio.

2. Individual process design

The second level can be very time and resource intensive as it involves the definition of the key strategic principles and stages involved within each prioritized marketing process. Examples at this level may include some or all of the marketing capabilities defined in *The Growth Propeller* such as Marketing Strategy & Planning, Innovation and Communication Development.

"What programmes like The 'Diageo Way of Brand Building' do, in my view, is bring structure and framework and a consistency of language which is important to a global, very diverse organization. All functions had to participate and we made it a 'have to do', i.e. it was not optional because we wanted everybody talking the same language and going in the same direction."

Nick Rose, *former CFO, Diageo*

Marketing processes can be tackled at a topline level or can be drilled down to a detailed process map using analytical systems and tools to increase efficiency and reduce costs as well as enhance effectiveness.

3. Practical support tools

The final level involves the development of the more detailed steps and a set of practical tools to help Marketers work through each process area in practice. The challenge is to clarify the language, explain how the tools work and provide practical examples and tips to support marketers back on the job.

The resulting toolkits may include templates, frameworks, checklists, screening criteria and online support systems. They are developed based on a combination of internal and external best practice to help Marketers work through each process step as effectively and efficiently as possible. They should not be too rigid, with the focus being on support and prompting Marketers to ask the right questions at the right time with the right mindset and behaviours.

Balancing creativity and rigour

Having highlighted the role of process development in supporting improved marketing capabilities, it is important to acknowledge that there are some important "watchouts". "Process" for some has connotations of slow decision making and inefficiency. Too much "process" is seen by others as the "enemy of creativity", at odds with vision, inspiration and flair, a sluggish and inefficient overlay that can bog Marketers down in red tape and waste precious time and energy.

These perceptions may result from the fact that many organizations are genuinely struggling under the burden of unwieldy processes that

" We took every process, every element, the staging of brands and redesigned everything – the planning cycle, segmentation capabilities, how we evaluate our brands strategically, the innovation process, communications process. All our internal documents and process calendar planning – everything was rewritten from the bottom up. We have taken it apart, turned it upside down and put it back together again – that took two years to align the whole organization. "

Mark Baynes, *Global Chief Marketing Officer, Kellogg*

have evolved over time or are based on overly complicated principles. These often require complex and costly software solutions simply to make the processes manageable. Typically they have been introduced without any practical understanding of the simple realities of what people need to do, in their jobs, day to day, and of what practical support they need.

The challenge here is to get the balance right, to provide Marketers with helpful structure and guidance to build their capabilities, but without cramping their style – leaving plenty of room for creativity and experimentation.

In our experience, in order to help companies operate successfully, and especially across geographical, business unit and departmental boundaries, it is essential that the energies of Marketers are aligned and organized, and that all parts of the company are clear about what needs to be done, when and by whom.

66 We're on a big drive to balance all the creativity and artistry of marketing with a lot of the rigour and more analytical discipline. We're after a more strategic understanding of where the opportunities are and really 'sweating the data'; committing to more measurable objectives. 99

Helen Lewis, **Consumer Insight & Marketing Strategy Director, Unilever Marketing Academy**

66 To be a great Marketer you have to be comfortable with both the art and the science, with the creativity and the structure. Marketing is about being logical, being structured, but then within the limits of that structure to allow yourself to be completely creative. You have to be comfortable with both aspects. 99

Phil Chapman, **Group Marketing Director, Kerry Foods**

Developing support tools in practice

The structure, resources and budgets needed for process development vary according to the ambition and scale of the task, but there are 5 key questions to ask at this stage.

Developing Process Solutions – Key Questions

- Have we got the right mandate?

- Who is on the steering group?

- Who will supply best practice content?

- Who will be on the development team?

- How will tools be brought to life?

Getting the right mandate

Success in developing practical new tools and ways of working depends largely upon their quality, accessibility, and ease of use from the perspective of the end user. But that does not mean they are simple or easy to develop. Significant amounts of time and money can be involved and resources can be wasted if process development is not set up with a clear mandate, with the right people engaged in development and with the right stakeholders.

The starting point is to make sure there is strong alignment and buy-in among senior managers about the need for a common way of working (see "Define Strategy" – Chapter 4). There also needs to be a willingness among leading Marketers to contribute

"** In the past we, as an organization, have been focused on operational basics, so it was mainly about cost, volume and price which are important fundamentals. But the growth and longevity of your business performance ultimately comes down to your customers. You've got to be in tune with them, meeting new and emergent needs. Thankfully I think we're past the point where processes are seen as a hindrance to good marketing. If a process is going to help us deliver results, let's not argue, let's just do it. You have to hardwire it into the business. Everyone is focusing on real delivery, numbers, this is a hard environment – so anything that makes marketing simpler and easier to do is accepted. **"

Mel Lane, *General Manager UK Retail, Shell UK Oil Products Ltd*

their own best practice expertise, time and experience to help develop new tools and practical examples across the organization.

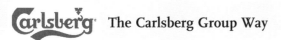 **The Carlsberg Group Way**

Julie Blou, Senior Manager, Carlsberg Group Way, has been leading a capability initiative focused on developing marketing processes and skills in the beer company's international business. *"Creating the ownership and input to the development process is essential for a change programme to work; it is the backbone of change. With senior management ownership you can change the world. Without it, you can have the best toolbox in the world but it won't matter because they won't believe in it and neither will their people."*

To embed new ways of working, new processes have to be hardwired into the way everything else is carried out within the business, and this will only happen if top managers believe in it. Blou elaborates: *"You can only get people to implement marketing capability programmes if they own it and they are more likely to own it if they are part of the development process. Our Marketing Directors have made change requests, helped prioritize, given examples and helped shape the tools. Upon implementation, they can further tie it into their processes to make sure it fits perfectly in their world – then we together realize the Carlsberg Group Way, a common way of working."*

Defining the steering group

To address these challenges, we advise setting up a senior management "steering group" to provide strategic guidance, allocate resources and to agree on process recommendations for capability development initiatives. This should also include relevant representatives from other functions – HR and Learning and Development teams and, where relevant, aligned functions such as Finance, Sales or R&D – to make sure marketing processes are joined up with those in other parts of the organization.

Developing best practice content

Once the development of process solutions gets under way, the next challenge is to ensure any new tools take into account the best possible insights and experience of the leading Marketers and internal *subject matter experts* (SMEs). External agencies and capability development specialists are frequently used to challenge thinking and to provide leading edge content and tools. But the key challenge is to ensure that new knowledge, content and tools are integrated into the way that Marketing works in the organization as opposed to fragmenting ways of working.

"** You need a guiding coalition – you need your leadership team to collectively buy in to create and be able to powerfully articulate the need for change. Unless you can get that it's a painful and difficult process. You have to have the support of the organization. You have to have a champion at senior executive level because it's difficult to change within and you have to have a strong raft of subject matter experts. **"

Mark Baynes, *Global Chief Marketing Officer, Kellogg*

Building the development team

In a small business or organization, process development may be a highly focused task, managed "part-time" by one person with the support of external specialists. Whereas in a large global organization, a dedicated capability team including specific project leaders will need to work in partnership with lead subject matter experts for each process area. Regional or business unit champions may also be involved to help drive embedding, along with a team of external specialist consultants and facilitators supporting the in-house resources.

The core project team will also need to build up support, engagement and alignment among key Marketing leaders from each part and level of the organization that will be called on to implement the new process.

Bringing tools to life

The most important deliverable of a process development initiative is the way it is brought to life and shared to support behaviour change. And the most tangible way in which this can be achieved is with a set of practical desktop tools. These consist of accessible guidelines and resources that guide Marketers through the key process stages and decisions.

Desktop tools

Desktop tools typically take the form of online toolkits and resources, sometimes supplemented by hard copy published materials. They usually include:

- Clear "process frameworks" – to explain and guide people through marketing processes and tools.

- "Templates" – to guide provision of the right data at the right point in the process.

- "Checklists" – to help people assess and screen the inputs and outputs needed.

- Both internal and external case studies and examples of good and bad practice.

- Online performance support tools – which e-enable marketing activities (e.g. innovation approval documents).

In general, desktop tools differ from academic or theoretical tools in that they are specifically designed and *tailored* to the organization and its processes. They enable Marketers to benefit directly from the business experience of all those who have contributed to their development. They have the additional benefit of being crafted using a "common language" that is understood, makes sense in the context of the organization and integrates seamlessly with other processes and tools.

When new marketing tools are going to be introduced or even mandated in an organization, it is crucial that they are accessible, robust and practical. To gain alignment, the principles and assumptions behind key tools will need to be debated by senior leaders and decisions made about the way the new tools should be configured. But the rigour of the intellectual process must not complicate or overshadow the practical guidance that is provided to Marketers in using tools in their everyday work. The more complex and unwieldy a management toolkit becomes, the less likely it is to be used in practice!

Businesses should mandate a maximum of 2–3 core tools for each process; the rest should be developed as "helpful support" tools. If a business tries to mandate more than this it will find that adherence becomes patchy and the value of the tools in saving time and effort becomes overwhelmed by the energy needed to "police" their implementation, defeating the whole object of the exercise.

> *There are areas where we know perhaps we created things where the principle was fine, but the practice of it was too complicated, the tool was too complex or we just hadn't thought it through well enough. It's not the content that gets resisted, it's the quantity of things and the time and place to absorb them. The tools people talk about are simple, impactful and require everyone to change.*
>
> Helen Lewis, *Consumer Insight and Marketing Strategy Director, Unilever Marketing Academy*

The impact of social media

One monumental new challenge facing organizations as they seek to strengthen their marketing processes is the transformation taking place in the networked world of social media – particularly the control customers now have, the contributions they are willing and able to make and the ways in which customers and organizations interface with each other.

There is now the unprecedented opportunity to engage large numbers of customers directly in the creation and sharing of brand innovation and communication. Innovation can now be opened up – customers can actively help shape new products and services. Creative content is no longer produced only by the brand and its agencies – customers are keen to contribute. The change is extraordinary and organizations and their marketing teams and agencies need to learn how to operate differently – and learn fast.

Kraft – Real Women of Philadelphia

Kraft's "Real Women of Philadelphia" campaign in the US is a good illustration of the role social media plays in brand communication and promotional campaigns. What started as a one-year promotional campaign, to increase awareness of Philadelphia's versatility as a cooking ingredient by getting 400 women to share videos of recipe ideas online, blossomed into an ongoing social community of 40,000 women, with over 5,000 video submissions and over 30 million recipe views.[1] Unit sales of Philadelphia cream cheese increased by 5% in the year up to August 2010.[2]

The site's focus is very much on user generated content rather than on communication by the brand. Interestingly, the content of community discussions has extended well beyond food, with members sharing issues and ideas with each other on a much broader social basis. Kraft has let this dynamic unfold, allowing the community to shape the development of the site.

So what are the implications of the social media revolution? Brands are increasingly thinking of themselves less as distributors of messages *to* customers, and more as facilitators of engaging conversations *with and between* customers. They are finding ways to develop more engaging creative platforms and to build greater responsiveness into their campaign management. They can then amplify and reinforce elements that capture people's imagination and influence their attitudes and brand choice behaviours.

Together, these factors mean that the nature of brand communication has changed – so the processes and tools used by Marketers to generate and manage it must move forward too. These capability challenges are most apparent in the area of brand communication development, but there are significant implications for other marketing disciplines too. The growth of social networks has opened up a whole new dimension of potential sources of consumer and customer insight, leading to many new forms of market research technique. It has also created new opportunities to engage customers earlier and more thoroughly in the development of new products and services.

The organizations that build the capabilities needed to navigate these new waters successfully, and use process and skill development programmes to capture and share learnings most quickly, stand to gain *significant* competitive advantage.

The Process Driver – Practical Tips

- Define a joined-up end-to-end overview of the main marketing process activities and align this with related functions, e.g. Sales.

- Scope out for each individual process an agreed definition, a set of guiding principles and key process stages.

- Develop practical desktop tools to help Marketers work more effectively on the job and keep them updated.

- Balance creativity and rigour, keeping processes and tools simple so they enhance great marketing, rather than constrain it.

- Develop a set of terms to provide a common marketing language for everyone in the business.

- Engage business leaders and subject matter experts to ensure they agree with and believe in the new ways of working.

- Reflect the changes being brought about by digital technologies and social media in the way marketing processes are designed.

Exploring the Skills Driver

Up to this point, we have focused on the development of new ways of working – processes and tools that help define *what* Marketers need to do. But, no matter how well designed these may be, there is no guarantee that the best possible activities and decisions will be taken by Marketers when they put them into practice on the job. That's where skill development comes in – the learning support people need on *how* to do marketing better. It is the *integration* of process and skills development that starts to differentiate world-class marketing capability development programmes.

The role of skill development

Skills are the capabilities of individual marketers to carry out their roles effectively in the organization. They are built through a wide variety of experiences ranging from on-the-job practice, experience and coaching, to more formal learning interventions like training, workshops, virtual classrooms, toolkits and e-learning. Skill development programmes play an influential role in strengthening the quality of people's decisions and actions in driving overall brand and business performance.

The *Marketing Capability Life Stages Model* we introduced in Chapter 4 is worth expanding on here as it provides a useful framework to describe the types of learning programme that can be used to build marketing capabilities (see Chapter 4).

Stage 1: Define the operating model

The most essential level of learning is to explain the company's core ways of working in marketing and any language, processes and tools that are mandated in the organization. This kind of learning experience is often introduced when a new "way of marketing" has first been developed and typically takes the form of face-to-face launch workshops or events, with follow-up support via line management coaching, online reference materials, e-learning modules and desktop tools.

The value of this kind of learning programme is that it helps establish a common marketing mindset and language and helps Marketers get a better understanding of the tasks expected of them.

Stage 2: Release potential

The next level of skills development solution is to develop targeted learning programmes that meet the needs of particular employee segments. These can include, for example, foundation marketing training programmes for graduate recruits or non-marketers, coaching or leadership programmes for senior managers and advanced programmes for technical specialists. It is here that the risk of fragmentation begins to emerge, so a careful balance must be struck between the top down capability development priorities of the business and the bottom up skill development needs of individual managers.

Stage 3: Drive high performance

The most advanced level of skills development covers advanced learning solutions designed to enhance the performance of operational teams as they work to implement marketing strategies and activities, on the job. It is at this level that knowledge sharing communities and networks are built and "live action learning" (i.e. building skills at the same time as addressing business issues) and coaching support for teams can be introduced.

Many organizations are now applying the 70/20/10 concept in the planning of their learning strategies. The original source of this model is unclear, but it suggests that learning occurs in the following ways:

- **70%** linked to real life and on-the-job experiences, tasks and problem solving

- **20%** from feedback and from observing and working with role models

- **10%** from formal learning programmes and activities

The dilemma inherent in the model is that the most important contributor to learning – informal, on-the-job experience – is also the most difficult to influence and manage. Many capability programmes focus their attention on formal learning programmes because they are relatively easy to deliver. But in our experience, expert solutions that enhance on-the-job learning, embed change and leverage line management coaching support, reward mechanisms and career paths can have a highly effective, long-term impact on skills development.

Supporting High Performing Teams

Skill development at AstraZeneca uses a lot of real-time capability development solutions to support Marketers as they do their jobs.

"Everyone fills in their personal assessments against our marketing and leadership capabilities, loads their development plans on to the system and they are then given advice about the support they can receive. We use a 70/20/10 approach in which 70% of skill development support is built around on-the-job interventions including live-action learning, 20% through coaching relationships with others and just 10% from formal training interventions."

Tim Bailey, *Head of Marketing Academy, AstraZeneca*

Social media technologies also offer significant new opportunities for enhanced workplace learning. Just as consumers are connecting, communicating and creating things together, there is also a growing trend for online knowledge sharing, collaboration and learning in the workplace. A leading-edge example is BT's highly successful *Dare2Share* initiative where employees upload self-created video learning content using a tool similar to YouTube.[3]

The parallels between marketing and learning

While much has been written about the "war for talent", the impact of skill development for *existing* employees is often underestimated in terms of the impact it can have on brand and business performance. The central challenge is to make sure that learning programmes are planned and developed in a way that *drives* business results.

For this reason, we believe the task of effective marketing capability development is very similar to that of effective "marketing", i.e. both seek to drive improvements in business results by influencing people's attitudes and behaviour. The only difference is that marketing focuses on *customers* whereas marketing capability development focuses on the *executive, manager* or *'learner'*.

As we will explore in Chapter 7 (when we cover the third "D" in *The 3D Approach – Driving Embedding*), we have found the most effective results are delivered when the core principles of effective *marketing* are applied to marketing capability programmes – a focus on the needs of the learner, the use of segmentation and insight to target learning effectively, clarity on the benefits offered and smart use of learning media channels.

The Skills Driver – Practical Tips

- Link learning programmes to internal processes and ways of working to make it easier for people to apply their new skills back on the job.

- Remember that most learning takes place around on-the-job experiences and interventions.

- Leverage line manager objectives and rewards, career pathing and online resources for a more sustained impact on skills development.

- Use an innovative blend of learning channels to provide appropriate learning support at all key stages – including experimentation with social media.

- Adopt "live action" learning to influence on-the-job performance and maximize impact on business activities and results.

- Develop targeted learning programmes to support skill development in priority areas.

- Apply the principles of effective marketing when designing learning programmes.

Exploring the link with Culture

The way process and skill development is handled in a business can have an important influence on the *culture* of the organization, one of the other core drivers of marketing capability. We will cover this more fully in the next chapter, but it is worth mentioning here that culture is a very important consideration for the way processes and skills are developed and received in an organization.

 Driving Culture Change

Kerris Bright's observations from her time as CMO of ICI were that, "*Through the 'Advance' marketing capability programme, our profile as a department was raised. The programme was very clearly branded – it had energy and a pace to it that really brought about degrees of cultural transformation in the Marketing community.*"

Reflecting on ICI's subsequent merger with AkzoNobel, she continues, *"We were suddenly integrating two very different cultures and two very different businesses. We had this big cultural issue about who is taking over whom, imposing ways of working, whereas the way we designed the marketing capability programme it felt like we were together creating ways of working. We used the marketing capability programme to massively accelerate the integration of the business and it's been incredibly successful in integrating and starting to create one Marketing community, one language, one new way of doing things that has really energized people."*

Karen Jeffery, AkzoNobel's Global Marketing Capability Leader, agrees, *"It is interesting that in some ways our work on capabilities has helped to establish the Marketing department as the functional pioneers in the company. Many of our initiatives, including the auditing of processes, the creation of the Advance Academy and the development of job profiles, have all been modelled, and in some cases replicated, by other functions. As a result, the status of Marketing in the business is very different now from a few years ago."*

The organizational culture is a critical factor when designing capability programmes, for example the balance between hierarchical and consensus-driven decision making, the levels of centralized versus decentralized ways of working and the passion for embracing innovation and ideas versus the status quo. Either capability programmes have to be designed to work within the prevailing culture, or senior management need to be actively engaged – hearts and minds – to deliver culture change.

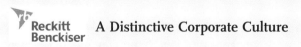

Reckitt Benckiser   A Distinctive Corporate Culture

Reckitt Benckiser is a company whose unique corporate culture is closely linked to its approach to marketing process and skill development. The household, health and personal care multinational has set the pace in the consumer packaged goods sector, quadrupling its value in just 10 years to £20 billion. Its impressive growth performance continued during the recession with like-for-like revenues increasing by 6% and adjusted net income by 15% in 2010. Reckitt Benckiser owns brands such as Dettol, Nurofen, Cillit Bang, Gaviscon, Finish, Strepsils, and its recent acquisition of SSL has now brought Durex and Scholl into its market-leading portfolio.

"*There is a mentality to make things happen here*", explains Victoria Coe, Global Brand Marketing Manager at Reckitt Benckiser. "*We're empowered to make decisions, so we don't have to produce a thousand page report to get approval for something. We have small teams and we're not given bucket loads of money, so you have to really prioritize and focus.*"

She continues, "*It's a sink or swim culture – if you fit, you are fine, you swim. If you don't, you sink and you don't last. We don't have a lot of layers, so you get a lot of exposure to the way the business is working and how things are managed at a very senior level, even when you are a junior person.*"

An example of the effectiveness of this culture is provided by the development and launch of Reckitt Benckiser's Air Wick Freshmatic brand, an innovation that provided a longer lasting air freshening benefit. The product went from initial concept to launch in just eight months and was rolled out globally to 60 markets in under a year. This extraordinary speed of execution helped Air Wick establish a new premium market segment, which now accounts for 15% of global air care sales.

Its focused "*just get on with it*" culture is reflected in Reckitt Benckiser's approach to skill development too. Reckitt Benckiser has moved over the past 10–15 years from a company that used to recruit people who had already been trained in marketing from other FMCG businesses, to one that brings on board graduates and develops people more from within.

Coe comments, "*Learning is mainly done on the job and is a lot about self-motivation, taking the opportunities to learn from your peers and your managers. There are more formal training courses now in place, but they're put there very much on the basis of business needs. The focus on business needs is always blatant; it drives across every part of our business."*

The culture at Reckitts is well illustrated by the rollout of "Ideactive", a live action learning marketing capability programme designed to balance the rigour and discipline of innovation activities by building stronger creative insight and idea generation skills within brand teams. *"The head of our Category Development Organization saw the need for innovation training across the business. He was the sponsor and it was mandatory, 'people need this training now, get this rolled out, just do it,' – typical Reckitt Benckiser style!"*

In this chapter, we have highlighted the fact that integrating initiatives around the *Process* and *Skill Drivers* can have a powerful impact on culture and in building marketing capabilities to drive growth. However, it is only when organizations develop solutions around all five capability drivers around *The Brand Learning Wheel* that they can be confident of developing a truly "world-class" marketing capability development programme

So let's now move on to look at the *Organization* and *People Drivers* of marketing capability and more directly at initiatives aimed at addressing the *Culture* Driver.

CHAPTER 5 – AT A GLANCE

- Developing solutions to address the Capability Drivers that sit in the "top half" of *The Brand Learning Wheel* – the *Process* and *Skills Drivers* – helps integrate improvements in day-to-day marketing ways of working with the skills Marketers need to enhance their performance.

- More effective processes help to clarify *what* it is Marketers need to be doing, *when* and *why*, but the focus of everyone involved in capability development should always be on linking that to *how* people do marketing and even more importantly – *how well*.

- There are three levels at which marketing processes can be developed: the *overall* end-to-end process framework for marketing, the *individual process areas* and the supporting tools *within* each process.

- The best processes and tools are simple to understand, easy to use and actively help Marketers make more effective business decisions.

- When developing new processes, some key questions to ask include: Have we got the right mandate? Who is on the steering group? Who will supply best practice content? Who will be involved on the development team? How to bring the tools to life?

- The growth in customer control and impact due to advances in digital and social media is extraordinary and organizations, their Marketing teams and their agencies need the capabilities to operate differently – and to learn fast.

- Skills are the capabilities of individual Marketers to carry out their roles effectively in the organization and they are built through a variety of experiences ranging from on-the-job experience and coaching to more formal learning interventions.

- There are three main types of learning programme – defining the operating model, releasing individual potential and driving high performance teams.

- The way process and skill development is handled in a business can have an important influence on the *culture* of the organization, one of the other core drivers of marketing capability.

Notes

1   Marketwatch.com, 4th April 2011
2   *Advertising Age*, 26th October 2010.
3   BTtoday, www.btplc, 13th July 2009.

Chapter 6

Having looked at the Capability Drivers in the "top half" of *The Brand Learning Wheel*, let's stay with the second "D" in *The 3D Approach – Develop Solutions*. We'll now explore solutions addressing the Capability Drivers in the "bottom half" of the wheel – *Organization, People and Culture* (see Figure 6.1).

In many organizations, these Capability Drivers are the primary responsibility of the HR function and of general managers. So senior Marketing, HR and other business leaders have to collaborate in order to build marketing capabilities effectively.

"In a service business, it's fundamental for Marketing to engage and support the whole team. Our responsibility is not just for the advertising, it's the brand; it's the organization and how well it works to meet customers' needs; it's the 30,000 people who manage the service British Gas offers its customers and it's the culture we create to ensure we deliver value to our customers – day in and day out."

Chris Jansen, *Managing Director, Services and Commercial, British Gas*

In this chapter we will share further insights and practical examples as we ask – why is "developing solutions" around the *Organization, People* and

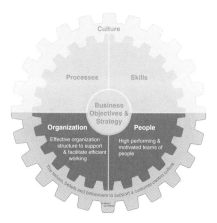

Figure 6.1: *The "bottom half" of The Brand Learning Wheel The Organization, People and Culture Drivers*

Culture Drivers so important to building marketing capabilities? What is the value of creating aligned role profiles for Marketers? How could Marketing work better with HR on capability initiatives? What does a great Marketing leader look like? And how can Marketers inspire a customer-focused culture across the organization?

 **Driving Transformation at British Gas**

To say that British Gas has undergone a whirlwind trans-formation over the past few years is an understatement. In 2007 British Gas set out on a *"journey back to great"* by placing customer satisfaction at the heart of its business per-formance ambitions. A transfor-mation programme was put in

place with three key building blocks – restructuring the business around the customer, setting a clear direction to lead the industry and empowering the front line. The culture of this utilities giant gradually came to respect, then to actively embrace, the power of delivering superior customer value.

2009 saw the first growth in customer numbers for nine years and across 2010 the business built on this momentum and increased product holdings and customers by an additional 500,000. By 2011 challenges remain, but the metamorphosis of British Gas into an organization that places customers at the centre of its business has been remarkable.

Customer complaints have fallen by 90%, customer churn has fallen by 50% and profitability has improved. The growth and adoption of online services has been significant with 18 million service transactions now taking place annually. Critically, for every £1 invested in communications there was a three-fold return in customer value. Customer satisfaction has increased to such an extent that British Gas is now the most preferred energy and services provider in the market.

Exploring the Organization Driver

The *Organization Driver* of marketing capability covers the way in which marketing resources are structured to facilitate effective and efficient ways of working. The importance of an effective organization can never be underestimated as it supports the flow of marketing knowledge and communication, as well as the decision making so essential to creating better customer value to drive sustainable, profitable growth.

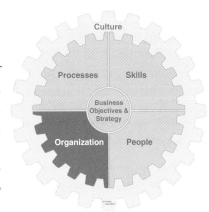

Levels of organization development

The organization of Marketing is changing radically. In a recent study, Forrester Research found that 75% of CMOs plan to rearrange their teams in the next 12 months.[1] Given the pace and scale of change faced by most businesses and the impact of the transformation in digital technologies, organizations appear to be on an almost constant search for

> *I used to believe that if you got the right people with the right spirit and the right talent, you could achieve anything and structure was not that relevant. But I have now realized that if you change structure and you get that right too, then some unbelievable things can happen.*
>
> Amanda Mackenzie, *CMO, Aviva*

more effective and efficient ways to organize their marketing resources. However, the upheaval that results is causing a widespread lack of clarity in Marketing roles and responsibilities that is at the heart of some of the confusion in the function highlighted earlier.

There are two main levels at which the structure of resources needs to be considered in order to create an effective marketing organization.

- **Overall company organization** – Is the *company as a whole* organized to focus on creating better value for customers?

How well is the company organized in its marketing efforts (i.e. marketing with a small "m")? What is the role and remit of the Marketing function and the scope of the responsibilities of the CMO? How does Marketing interface with the rest of the organization such as Sales, HR, Finance? How does it connect with the business unit reporting structure, with other functions and departments and with external third parties (e.g. Communications, Digital and PR agencies)?

- **Marketing department organization** – Is the *Marketing department* itself organized effectively to create better customer value and drive growth?

Is the department structure fit for purpose based on the role defined for the Marketing function? How should roles be split between global, regional and local Marketers and between Marketers in different teams within the department? To what extent should specialist functional teams be established in areas such as insight, digital, pricing or promotions? And how should the responsibility for brand development (the more "upstream" activities identified in *The Growth Propeller* like portfolio strategy, brand positioning and innovation), be handled relative to brand activation (the more "downstream" activities like pricing, promotions and channel marketing)?

Let's explore these challenges as we present some answers to these questions, taking each level of organization in turn.

1. Overall company organization

If companies are to succeed in creating value for their customers, marketing activities have to be organized in a way that makes them focused and responsive to the needs of those customers. In Ranjay Gulati's book *Reorganize for Resilience* (Harvard Business Press), he argues that businesses need to embrace an "outside-in" customer-centric perspective. This requires them to break down organizational structures that are traditionally based on "standalone silos that revolve around products, functions and geographies".

"The vast majority of enterprises talk the customer talk, while failing consistently to walk the customer walk. This failure results from not only how companies understand (or don't understand) customers, but also – far more importantly – how they structure their internal organization."

Ranjay Gulati, *Professor of Business Administration, Harvard Business School*[2]

This is both true and very difficult to implement in practice. As evidence of the major issues faced, one executive operating in a leading multinational candidly admitted to us, "*As an organization we haven't been focused on customers, we've been focused on operational basics. So it's all about volume and it's all about price. I would say the customer mindset doesn't exist; we don't bring the customer into the boardroom; we don't have customer meetings. The customer service centre has been located offshore and we don't have any idea what our customers are saying. So there is a pressing need to bring that customer focus back into the heart of what we do.*"

Creating a customer-centric business

To change organizations of this type is complex and difficult to achieve. It usually requires a fundamental restructuring of the business. But, it also demands a radical shift towards more collaborative ways of working that ensure everyone contributes towards delivering the customer experience in a seamless and integrated way.

The responsibility for bringing about this kind of change ultimately lies at a CEO level, but senior Marketers need to do all they can to influence the agenda if they are to succeed in their own task of creating better customer value to drive growth.

 **Back in Time**

In 2006, before Centrica's finance director Phil Bentley took the helm as managing director of British Gas, the energy provider had more than 80% of the industry's customer complaints, despite having just a 33% share in the gas and electricity market. It was not a "customer-focused" business, being engrossed with its own internal business operations and issues.

The biggest issue facing British Gas at the time was the huge number of errors in its new IT system designed to manage customer billing. British Gas's billing process was impacted to such an extent that the energy supplier had to hire hundreds of extra staff and invest millions to make the system work. The errors caused immense operational problems for frontline staff, and more importantly for customers. They switched to competitors, damaging market share and denting revenue. British Gas has since fixed the system and complaints have subsequently fallen by 90%.

Another major strategic step in the company's transformation was to restructure the organization of the business around its core customer segments, identified through extensive market research and analysis. The three key divisions that resulted were "Pay As You Go Energy" (for lower income customers), "Premier Energy" (for high value customers who buy both their gas and electricity from British Gas) and "Energy First" (mainstream British Gas customers).

The role of the CMO

The increasing profile of the Chief Marketing Officer in large organizations has been an important development in recent years. Over 47% of Fortune 1000 companies now have a senior Marketer in the CMO role, to create a focal point through which the Marketing function can translate the voice of the customer and engage with the rest of the business at a strategic level.

" There was no point having brilliant advertising when customers' bills were consistently wrong, prices were too high and customer service was not working. We needed to transform the business from the inside out – it's been a customer-led transformation."

Phil Bentley,
Managing Director, British Gas

Some organizations are going one step further. An article in the *Harvard Business Review* called 'Rethinking marketing'[3] reported that a new senior management role has emerged worldwide, with over 300 companies now possessing a *chief customer officer* rather than a *chief marketing officer*, including Chrysler, Hershey's, Oracle, Samsung and Sears. This represents a shift from traditional "Marketing departments" to what can best be described as "Customer departments". Within the remit of these more broadly defined departments fall a wide range of customer-facing functions, including, in some cases, Customer Relationship Management (CRM), R&D and Customer Service.

In these cases, a broader range of the activities that we have captured in *The Growth Propeller* are being brought into the remit of one business function focused on creating customer value. However, there is also an important risk worth highlighting from such moves, that Marketing in these organizations may be seen as both everything and nothing as a result.

Even where changes aren't this radical, many businesses are now extending Marketing's influence into areas such as customer relations, call centres and corporate communications to ensure that brand communications are integrated and consistent with the overall stance of the company.

Despite this growth in influence, the average tenure of CMOs is unusually low compared to other leadership positions. A recent study by the executive search firm Spencer Stuart found that CMOs averaged just 26 months in their job, versus 36 months for chief information

"In the role of CMO, I believe you have one central challenge. Ultimately the only way for Marketing as a function to succeed is to make sure the whole company works as a marketing organization. You therefore have to shape the whole organization so that it focuses on the consumer and you have to ensure that the commercial business model is integrated with the way you are building and developing your brands."

Phil Chapman, **Group Marketing Director, Kerry Foods**

"I remember when I was at BA we had a really positive culture in Marketing, but we couldn't always leverage our expertise or knowledge effectively in the wider business; on occasions it proved a challenge to persuade others about how we were enhancing profitability. Many people are conflict averse – they are happy in the function but less engaged with the rest of the business. The ability to engage effectively with the wider business and galvanize your arguments to influence the business to be customer focused is absolutely critical to success."

Martin George, **Managing Director for Group Development, Bupa**

officers, 39 months for chief financial officers and 44 months for chief executive officers. So, the pressures on CMOs to secure quick wins in organizational and business transformation can be considerable.

"My role was created to bring all of communications and marketing together – to set up a global function which hadn't existed before, define what it might mean and how that might operate. Our goal was to become internationally known as Aviva in 28 markets – so the big markets, UK, Ireland and Poland, all had to change their name."

A critical success factor for any CMO is to make sure they align their agenda for change with their CEO; aligning their vision for the role of the Marketing function in helping to create

Amanda Mackenzie, CMO, *Aviva*

an organization that is more effective in creating better customer value, and as a result one that is better equipped to grow.

2. Marketing department organization

The structure of the Marketing function, particularly in complex service organizations, has moved a long way beyond the brand management system prevalent in the packaged goods businesses during the 1980s and 1990s. Driven by the need to capitalize on global market opportunities and economies of scale, splits in responsibility between global brand building and local activation/implementation teams are now widespread in most consumer goods organizations.

Different Marketing organization models

Unlike the old "brand manager" role, which in the best marketing organizations had clear line of sight and responsibility for the entire brand (including the P&L), marketing responsibilities are now commonly fragmented among specialists operating across complex geographical, business unit or departmental structures.

The growing power of retail and digital channels has also stimulated massive integration challenges for brand development and communication.

This is having a transformational impact not just on the way Marketing and the wider business is organized, but also right across the agency network.

In industry sectors beyond consumer goods, even more complex structures have evolved, resulting in many different approaches to organizing Marketing resources. In "mono brand" companies, the responsibility for strategic brand positioning and communication may lie with a central brand team while the product and service propositions are managed by separate business units.

Such companies may also have specialist, stand-alone teams in key Marketing areas such as customer insight, digital and social media, propositions, pricing, promotions, customer relationship marketing, PR and sponsorship, giving rise to complex challenges of alignment and integration of the customer-facing teams. Meanwhile customers are quite rightly oblivious to these internal barriers and are increasingly vocal in demanding a more holistic "joined-up" approach to their interface with brands and businesses.

> *"We have changed our entire organizational design. We created a centre of excellence first in the US for bringing in valuable digital and media capabilities to support the organization. We've now done this for all the regions. We consolidated our agency network. We went from 27 digital agencies in Europe to one. We consolidated our creative agencies. We weren't hiring agencies because of what they thought they could do. We were hiring agencies for what we wanted them to do – taking specialist capabilities and knotting them together to collaborate and bring integrated ideas through to the organization."*
>
> Mark Baynes, *Global Chief Marketing Office, Kellogg*

Global versus local marketing structures

The decision about how best to allocate responsibilities between global, regional and local Marketers is a particularly tough one for multinational businesses across all industries. In the words of one Unilever SVP, "*What we do best globally we must do globally, what we do best regionally we must do regionally, what we do best locally we must do locally.*"

British Gas — Changing the Role of Marketing

British Gas Marketers had previously played a more limited role with their main focus on brand communications, believing that integration of brand activities with the front-line call centre staff and the rest of the customer-facing business operations were not in their remit. It wasn't just the wider business that needed to change; the Marketing department too had to embrace a broader role in driving growth.

" It was a 'communications department' not a 'strategic Marketing department' and it had little rigour or discipline, no clear marketing or customer plans and no robust and insight driven testing of ideas. It was disconnected from the realities of the customer's experience of British Gas and, like the rest of the business, it was too inward-looking. That needed to change "

Chris Jansen, *Managing Director,*
Services and Commercial, British Gas

At a practical level this reinforces that it is essential to be clear which specific aspects of the marketing role are best done at each geographical level and then to structure the business accordingly.

Some businesses, particularly US-based corporations, tend to be more familiar with a centralized approach based on the strategy and scale built up within their domestic US business. International markets are treated like satellite sales regions and the core development of brand strategy, products and advertising is handled at a global level. Companies like Apple, PepsiCo and Gillette are illustrative of this approach.

However, sometimes in the US and other large markets, the concept of "global" gets misinterpreted as the "rollout of US activities" and "international" gets viewed as just one more region outside the domestic market, rather than the complex collection of discrete markets with very different languages and cultures it is in reality. As such, the organizational challenges of global marketing and the leadership required can be underestimated.

Other businesses, such as Unilever, SABMiller and AstraZeneca, have a more decentralized heritage and in categories such as food, where local tastes are strongly influential and manufacturing and distribution efficiencies less obvious, there is much greater regional and local variability in the marketing mix.

Whatever the prevalent model, the key challenge is to avoid the extremes and the pendulum effect whereby the organization finds itself in a constant state of chaos as it seeks to obtain equilibrium. Best practice experience would reinforce that it is important to get the balance right between both the efficiencies of centralized working – leveraging big ideas, driving economies of scale, harmonizing customer communication, *and* the benefits of local market responsiveness – connection with the attitudes, values, behaviours and income levels of local customers.

Defining job roles and responsibilities

We have outlined some important considerations when making decisions about the high level role and structure of the Marketing function. But, once these are made, it is just as critical to clarify and define the specific roles and responsibilities for individual Marketing jobs within the structure.

Global/Local Dimension

SABMiller's Nick Fell has had to grapple with the issue of global/local focus in the beer market. SABMiller has strong global brands like Grolsch, Peroni, Pilsner Urquell and Miller Genuine Draft. But even then, there are questions about how much of their marketing should be handled at a global level.

❝ Brewing is an intensely local business and the vast majority of our business sits in local, mainstream brands. The first question you have to ask yourself is, 'what role should global brands have in the portfolio?' Nobody wants a global brand that doesn't sell anywhere. Given a choice between a brand that is global but that's executed in 15 different ways in 15 different markets and growing by 20%, and one that is executed in the same way everywhere but static, I know which I'd prefer!❞

Nick Fell, *Group Marketing Director, SABMiller*

Without this rigour and discipline, Marketers will lack clarity about what it is they are supposed to be delivering in their everyday activities. This is typically managed by creating detailed role profiles that specify the main tasks and degrees of marketing expertise required of people doing each key job based on an aligned "Marketing capability framework".

Role profiles usually work up from a foundation level through to more advanced skill levels, though in practice we don't recommend more than 3–4 levels to avoid complexity.

Marketing Role Profiles

Marketing role profiles serve a number of useful purposes:

- To ensure marketing processes and organizations are designed in an integrated way, with clearly defined roles and responsibilities for key marketing activities.

- To serve as a means of clarifying and communicating what is expected of individual Marketers and teams.

- To provide a recruitment tool by defining the specification for the profile of skills needed to fill each role.

- To provide a framework for the analysis of skill development needs as part of employee personal development plans.

Role profiles also provide clear functional direction and signposting to guide the HR processes and practices needed to attract, recruit, motivate, develop and retain great marketing talent. As such, they form an important link to the next driver of marketing capability we will cover – the *People Driver*.

The Organization Driver – Practical Tips

- Listen to customers and to the frustrations and complaints they have and commit to solve any issues being caused by internal organizational barriers.

- Canvass opinions as to how well the organization as a whole, and the Marketing department in particular, is working to create better value for customers.

- Set up a cross-functional leadership team to collaborate and integrate marketing initiatives so that customers experience a seamless service or experience.

- Create role profiles for key Marketing jobs so that people's responsibilities are clear and aligned.

Exploring the People Driver

The value of people

Having an aligned vision for Marketing, a clearly articulated functional remit, an effective organization structure, and well-understood roles and responsibilities are all important drivers of marketing effectiveness. But the right people are obviously also key to building the marketing capabilities needed to create better customer value and drive sustained, profitable growth. Just as in the area of organization, the *People Driver*  works to build marketing capability at both the departmental and the entire organizational level.

Any organization seeking to drive customer demand-led growth needs to invest in talented Marketers for its Marketing department with the skills, experience, mindset and personality traits needed to excel in specialist and demanding Marketing roles.

British Gas   Attracting Marketing Talent

As part of British Gas's radical transformation, a high powered team of Marketing experts were hired, many from leading consumer pack-aged goods business. It was initially headed by Chris Jansen, ex-P&G, who had previously led the British Airways global loyalty programme. *"The business at the time didn't respect that customers have choices, that they need reasons to stay with us and reasons to choose us",* reflects Jansen. He subsequently focused on extending the capability, discipline and effectiveness of the Marketing team, which was expanded and rebuilt with specialist Marketers from British Airways, Mars, American Express, Lloyds TSB, P&G and O2 amongst others.

But, the impact of great marketing is even more evident when senior Marketers influence the recruitment and motivation of people throughout the organization as a whole. This can help to create a customer-focused culture where people in all functions live the brand values and collaborate to system-atically deliver integrated brand promises to customers.

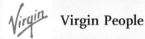

Virgin People

A company that appreciates, more than most, the value that employ-ees bring to a business is Virgin. As founder Richard Branson says, *"Convention dictates that a company looks after its shareholders first, its customers next, and last of all worries about its employees. Virgin does the opposite. For us, our employees matter most. It just seems common sense to me that, if you start off with a happy, well-motivated workforce, you're much more likely to have happy customers. And in due course the resulting profits will keep your shareholders happy."*

The emphasis is all about recruiting the right kind of *Virgin people* who build the brand in everything they do. Virgin's internal brand guidelines bring this philosophy to life. This is superbly illustrated by the *"Do It Yourself"* booklet used to communicate their approach. This is not a typical "how-to" manual on running the Virgin brand, but a refreshing and inspiring call for people to take personal responsibility in making the brand live.

"We don't have a strict brand book or anything like that, and you won't find a brand 'onion' or a 'pyramid' tool in it. There really is a focus on getting the right team make-up within Virgin. A huge emphasis is placed on people's emotional intelligence and whether they are going to fit the bill here", explains Mark Gilmour, Brand Director for South East Asia, Virgin.

The primary focus in the Virgin brand book is on helping people recruit successfully: *"Virgin people are easy to spot. They act in unusual ways as it's the only way they know how. But it's not forced – it's natural. They are honest, cheeky, questioning, amusing, passionate, intelligent, restless…Virgin people are smart."*

A marketing approach to people

Evidence from the global companies we work with suggests that despite headcount pressures from heavy cost-cutting, the challenge of attracting, recruiting, motivating and developing talented Marketers to fill key roles remains as difficult as ever. This creates significant pressure for senior HR and Marketing executives to work together to "get it right" and to build the talent needed to enable Marketing to act as a *growth driver* for the organization.

The quality of the people in the company is critical to marketing effectiveness and we believe Marketing leaders should take active responsibility, working with HR leaders, to shape all the "briefs" that determine the talent pool for customer facing roles. They must also be actively involved at key stages in the HR processes that influence the capabilities of the Marketing department. This includes activities such as attraction and recruitment, talent management, compensation and benefits, performance management and learning and development.

Moreover, the benefits of closer collaboration between HR and Marketing benefit not just the Marketing function, but the whole organization. While *direct* responsibility for the *People Driver* and budget usually sits in HR, Marketing disciplines, processes and tools can also be leveraged by HR professionals. This has proven to be highly effective in giving corporations a competitive edge in winning talent.

Just as Marketing seeks to attract and retain people in the form of *customers*, HR faces the same kind of challenges in attracting and retaining people in the form of *employees*. In our experience, HR professionals can step-change their performance by leveraging marketing tools and techniques to create and manage the "employer brand", to be more relevant and differentiated in attracting great candidates.

Leveraging Marketing Techniques in HR

Shell has experienced great success in adopting marketing disciplines for the attraction and recruitment of new talent right across its business, not just in Marketing. Back in 2006, Shell's HR team faced a challenging target – the need to recruit 14,000 new employees globally by 2008, a significant increase versus the total of 4,151 in the previous three years. This overall target covered a complex range of multifunctional roles extending from engineers in Aberdeen to lawyers in Malaysia.

Navjot Singh, an experienced Marketer, was brought on board to help transform Shell's approach to attraction and recruitment globally:

"The gap I saw was that the ability of people to understand their market and do some basic marketing planning in the recruitment sphere was non-existent. Our strategy was to avoid everyone trying to invent their own new approach and introduce a consistent and best practice way of planning attraction and recruitment activities and budgets globally", he explained.

Singh went on to lead a global marketing capability programme for Shell's Attraction and Recruitment (A&R) team. The initial focus was on establishing a standard marketing planning process designed with the recruitment candidate at its heart. Three stages were defined – Situation Analysis, Strategy Development and Action Plan Development; with focused tools introduced at each stage.

"Our view was that we didn't want to explain in 'marketing speak' what a marketing plan was", explains Singh. *"We translated it into what we called a 'Talent Plan' and explained how it could benefit HR professionals and company chairmen in each of the*

countries in which Shell operates. We created our own distinctive approach, using marketing tools but expressed in HR speak."

The next step was to develop a relevant and differentiated Employee Value Proposition (EVP) based on insights into the attitudes and motivations of prospective employees. In the past Shell had focused primarily on salary and benefits, but research showed that target candidates were looking for a broader spectrum of attraction points like personal development and work/life balance.

Once the EVP was in place, powerful creative techniques were introduced to help Shell's A&R team find new and impactful ways of connecting with candidates. They sought to better understand all stages of the "candidate journey" (from awareness of Shell to joining the business) and used this to inform their communication strategy and execution.

The results were dramatic. Shell's recruitment targets were exceeded between 2006 and 2008 with 14,722 new employees being brought on board. Most impressively, the cost per recruit fell to just 41% of the original level in 2006 and the candidate experience improved with the average length of the recruitment journey for Shell cut from 81 days to 39 days. Shell was also awarded The Marketing Society's Award for Excellence in Marketing Capability for its work.

&& The reputation of recruitment in Shell has changed and become more positive. And it had an impact on perceptions of our 'recruitment brand' and reputation. Most impressive of all, at the same time as we have become more effective, our average marketing costs per employee are now much lower. Whereas marketing costs used to be 70–80% of total recruitment costs we have managed to get that down to 8%. &&

Navjot Singh, *Global Marketing Manager, Recruitment & Global HR Communications, Shell*

The challenge for the Marketing function

Both Virgin and Shell provide excellent examples of how Marketers can influence the capabilities of their organizations by using their functional expertise to support HR to attract and retain the right people, enhance the cultural fit of employees and bring brand values to life. But how can organizations leverage the *People Driver* of capability to ensure they build the right profile of people *within* the Marketing function?

The role of Marketing in many organizations is too narrowly defined at a functional level. Marketers often don't appreciate the broader role they could be playing to be effective at a more strategic level. But whose responsibility is that? In part, it is the responsibility of HR to open up new opportunities and to encourage Marketers to gain broader functional insights to other functions or specialist departments.

> *"People who come into Marketing tend to be pretty bright. If I think about all the departments I deal with from an HR perspective, Marketers tend to be among the quickest, sharpest and smartest – so you typically get good raw material. But a lot of Marketing people tend to have a restricted vista because of the way the profession works. The ways in which their careers get managed and the way they manage themselves tends to be a bit narrow which means it is hard to break out.*
>
> *If I look at the really good Marketing people I have met over the years, they have an outward focus into the world and a genuine curiosity in what is going on and why. They then bring this back into the organization and respond to it, finding ways to make money from what they see and learn."*
>
> Jon Harding, *Head of Organization Development, Barclaycard*

But it is also the responsibility of the Marketers themselves to be more proactive in their career development and to better understand the contribution made by experts in other functions to delivering customer value.

Excellent Marketers have a palpable passion for customers and for marketing and they need to transmit that passion to everyone they come into contact with.

Five Star Marketing Leaders

Research conducted by Brand Learning among senior marketing leaders from top multinational organizations including Sony, SABMiller, Virgin, Honda, Aviva and Unilever confirms perceptions that the role of Marketing should not be too narrow. Instead, it has a unique and important role to play in leading the whole organization to create better value for customers to drive growth.

However, this does not necessarily mean organizations need to be "Marketing led". In fact, there are many companies where the predominant function is made up of technical or financial experts. However, if an organization aspires to drive growth by being more *customer focused*, then the Marketing function has to climb out of its "communications and promotions" box and make its voice heard. It should be able and equipped to confidently act as the *focal point* for customer insights and for engaging the rest of the organization to act on those insights to create better customer value.

Marketers cannot, however, develop and deliver successful brands, product and service propositions by themselves. And they should never be held uniquely accountable for the performance of the *entire* organization. As we covered earlier in *The Growth Propeller*, Marketers need to engage people in other functions and external partners across the organization to help create better customer value and drive growth. For this reason, Marketers cannot be

"The one thing Marketers should be able to do better than anyone else is to bring the outside in – what's happening with consumer needs, with the competition, with the general market dynamics. You have to be confident enough and capable enough to keep your hand on the tiller and your antennae open and attuned to what is going on in the outside world. They are Marketers, not just at work, but 24 hours a day, seven days a week – walking around Sainsbury's thinking what am I seeing here that is relevant to my job? Watching TV thinking what here is relevant? It's something you dedicate your life to because you love what you do. "

Martin George, *Managing Director for Group Development, Bupa*

recruited and developed on purely "technical" marketing terms and emphasis should also be placed on their potential as future brand and business *leaders*.

Much has been written on the importance of building leadership skills as they are a vital consideration for any organization committed to drive growth (e.g. Steve Radcliffe's excellent book *Leadership Plain and Simple* published by FT Prentice Hall). But it is helpful here to include a summary of the main skills and attributes we see as relevant to Marketing in particular.

Our own marketing leadership research shows that there are some common behavioural attributes that tend to be shared by what we call *"Five Star Marketing Leaders"*:

> ❝ *In life we go along with our same old routines and there's a bit of our human nature that likes comfort zones. And the trouble is if we stay in our comfort zones, guess who is going to be moving beyond us – 'our consumer'? And that's the real issue for us as Marketers. Unless we create an environment where we are constantly re-evaluating and thinking ahead, we're going to get stuck. Consumers will move ahead and someone will come in to the gap we leave. So our role is to be constantly refreshing and thinking of ways to disrupt. You come to realize that the greatest marketing is achieved when you have a compelling, single-minded vision and you drive it through an organization. And sometimes you really have to put your head above the parapet to keep it going.* ❞
>
> Mark Gilmour, *Brand Director for South East Asia, Virgin*

1. Restless customer obsession

Five Star Marketing Leaders are constantly challenging and looking to the future as the "customer advocate". They are restless with the status quo and curious about what makes customers tick. They are always looking for new and interesting ways to better meet customer needs and wants.

2. Bold and inspiring vision

Once they have spotted an opportunity, *Five Star Marketing Leaders* translate it into an inspiring future vision for people across the wider business by linking it to and communicating the big strategic picture. They excite and motivate people with a compelling, customer-focused sense of possibility and as such they have a powerful asset – the ability to galvanize action and get things done that are beyond their reach alone.

The strongest Marketing leaders are confident, bold, brave and passionate, willing to fight for what they believe in and to champion the customer's voice.

3. Humble

While a passionate vision is a powerful starting point, in today's complex matrix organizations, it is not enough. *Five Star Marketing Leaders* also need the humility to appreciate the limitations of their role and the areas where they rely on other functional or geographic experts. More than ever before, effective corporate team work is a prerequisite for business success and effective Marketers need the skills to listen to and engage others in delivering their customer-focused vision.

4. Honest

Five Star Marketing Leaders are challenging and lean into issues, but they behave consistently with a spirit of honesty, integrity and humility. They listen to other people, not just to respond to their views, but to understand their concerns, genuinely appreciate what issues and challenges need to be addressed and adapt plans accordingly.

> *"Don't do the politics or be Machiavellian. Just be honest. Don't be tricky, because it will catch you out. Be straightforward. Make sure people know where you're coming from and why you come from there."*
>
> Amanda Mackenzie, *CMO, Aviva*

5. Attention to detail

Finally, *Five Star Marketing Leaders* are rigorous in their attention to practical and commercial details. They balance their passion for creative ideas with a rigorous financial and analytical orientation, demonstrate sound commercial judgement and make the right decisions when it matters.

Being a *Five Star Marketing Leader* is tough. When added together with the functional capabilities we outlined in *The Growth Propeller*, it is a formidable list of capabilities and attributes for any one person to possess. But an effective leader is also extremely conscious of their strengths and weaknesses, thereby enabling them to balance their personal capabilities with those of others they bring into their immediate team.

"All of the leaders I've really admired have got fantastic judgement about details. These are people who engage at a big picture level, but also today, on this piece of work, this brief, they are also able to engage in a very physical and practical sort of way."

Helen Lewis, *Consumer Insight and Marketing Strategy Director, Unilever Marketing Academy*

The People Driver – Practical Tips

- Challenge the brief for the people being recruited into specialist Marketing roles and for those tasked with bringing the brand to life at all customer touch-points.

- Build a talent management strategy for marketing at both a big "M" and small "m" level to build the talent needed to enable marketing to act as a growth driver.

- Identify and nurture *Five Star Marketing Leaders* – they are a valuable asset to any organization.

- Apply marketing techniques in HR to build more competitive recruitment strategies and *create better value* for candidates and employees.

- Ensure Marketers build practical experience in other functions and vice versa to enhance organizational awareness and experience.

Exploring the Link with Culture

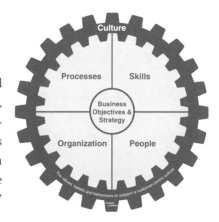

Having reviewed the *Organization* and *People Drivers* of marketing capability, we will conclude this chapter by returning to the *Culture Driver* that surrounds *The Brand Learning Wheel*, to reflect on its important role in supporting the Capability Drivers in the "bottom half" of *The Brand Learning Wheel*.

If one factor above all others marks out a world-class marketing organization, it is having an organizational culture which is obsessively focused on creating better value for customers.

Definition of Culture

Culture is the prevailing set of attitudes, values and behavioural norms that build over time to shape the way things get done in an organization.

There are a whole series of factors which influence the culture of an organization and the effectiveness of the Marketers within it. These include recruitment profiles, reward mechanisms, management structures, myths and taboos, even the physical office environment. Culture change of this magnitude is a major task for the whole management team – and particularly for the senior leadership team.

Since culture is shaped strongly by the values and behaviours of current or historical leaders in the organization, the CEO and senior leadership team have a disproportionate impact on the existence or not of a customer-centric culture, and they need to be aware of their own possible blind spots as regards customer focus. Many senior executives get drawn into their strategic and operational responsibilities and lose touch with customers – as evidenced by the many "customer-connect" programmes springing up globally.

So, building a customer-focused culture in a complex matrix organization historically focused on technical, operational or financial excellence is a major challenge. But solutions successfully addressing the *Culture Driver* can have a major positive influence on effective marketing capability development and vice versa.

The key challenge for organizations seeking to establish a customer-centric culture to drive growth is to look not just within

❝Our marketing capability programme was like offering water in the desert. It made people feel proud to be part of this bigger global organization and very excited to get exposed to best practice from all over the world. It was enormously energizing for people because they could understand how their bit of the jigsaw fitted in to the whole.❞

Jan Gooding,
Global Marketing Director, Aviva

the Marketing department, but throughout the whole organization so that at every customer touch-point, operations are reoriented to provide customers with an integrated, consistent experience of the product, proposition or service. The more complex that service, the more critical is the role of the prevailing culture and the more damaging its impact if neglected.

In our experience, organizations with a customer-centric culture put customer goals at the heart of their corporate strategy and ensure they are firmly articulated and embedded throughout the organization. They place customer segmentation at the core of their market assessment and portfolio planning, build brand positioning based on insights into what customers need or want and develop innovative value propositions that address unmet customer needs. They go on to develop engaging communications that connect with customers' hearts and minds and ensure they consistently deliver a valued customer experience.

But a customer-centric culture also needs *all* functions to be engaged and aligned in working towards the common goal of anticipating and meeting customer needs – which is where the unique role of the Marketing department comes into play. Without the focus provided by expert Marketers, an organization can easily get pulled in different directions by reactions to competitors, channel partners, emerging technologies, commercial pressures, stakeholder demands and political policies.

Marketers need to be equipped to synthesize and distil the constant stream of customer data arriving from all angles. And then equipped to translate this mass of complex data into powerful insights, platforms or strategic thrusts capable of "engaging" other specialists in the organization. This thought is at the heart of *The Growth Propeller* we introduced in Chapter 2 and explains how both marketing as a discipline and Marketers as professionals can act as growth drivers of the organization.

In our view, Marketers should not be held accountable for every customer-facing issue or responsibility in the organization, but they should be enabled to provide *"unifying customer energy"* – generating and applying insights and engaging other specialists in the organization to create better customer value to drive growth.

An organization with marketing edge is not necessarily "run" by the Marketing department, but it is underpinned by a deep spirit of collaboration in which people from different functions, business units, geographies and teams work towards meeting customer goals effectively and constructively and where the impact of their efforts becomes evident in tangible brand and business results.

 **A Customer-focused Transformation**

When taking over as managing director at British Gas, Phil Bentley's first task was inspiring his new leadership team and aligning around a clear vision of the transformation journey they planned to lead. A huge amount of time was then spent visiting all units across the country, listening to people at all levels from British Gas's 30,000 staff.

" *Staying as we were was not an option in my view or that of our board. The organization needed a major transformation to get it back to growth and to reignite pride and passion for meeting our customers' needs. We surveyed over 5,000 people in the business and as a leadership team, we met the entire organization in groups of 100 to listen to concerns, share the new vision and to explain why becoming a customer-centric business was so essential. The entire organization then contributed to and voted on a new set of values for British Gas*

– 'Wear our customers' shoes', 'Keep it simple', 'Take pride in what we do' and 'Keep our promises'.**"**

Phil Bentley, *Managing Director, British Gas*

Industry Recognition

British Gas has been recognized by a plethora of industry and marketing awards including the Marketing Society Awards for Excellence – Brand Revitalization in 2010. It was awarded 14th place in *The Sunday Times* Best Companies Awards in 2011 and accredited by Best Companies.

British Gas is now unrecognizable from its old self and while there are many remaining challenges and the leadership team are not complacent, the business has restructured its operations and engaged its customers and front-line colleagues alike. The British Gas "Services" company (boiler repairs and installations) has now been merged with British Gas Energy to create "one" British Gas with over 30,000 employees. United, it has emerged as the UK's leading energy and home services provider, looking after half the homes in Britain.

Inspiring brand ideas

There is one final aspect of creating a customer-centric culture where Marketers can make a real impact.

Their role is to ensure the mission, vision and values of the organization, business unit or department is fully integrated with customer needs and brand promises. One powerful way to do this is by developing inspiring, motivating brand ideas that can galvanize the organization into delivering customer value at every touch-point. Such inspiring "brand ideas" bring to life an organization's promise to its customers, and in so doing provide a unifying, energizing purpose that guides people's values and shapes an aligned way of working.

For a "mono-brand" business, big brand ideas are the platform to engage and inspire the whole organization to come together to deliver customer value to drive growth. But they can be just as powerful in multi-brand businesses too, providing there is a remit for those working on each brand to work in a way that respects and is true to the customer-centric brand values, as opposed to being force fit into a

"Marketing now is seen in its broadest sense. At its core, the Marketing team have all the customer data and understanding. If Marketing is defined as just communications, it's hard to influence the rest of the business. We have a strong commercial team with Marketing at its core. The easiest thing a Marketing team can own is advertising and promotions; it's much harder to take customer data, build insights and link it with business strategy."

Chris Jansen, **Managing Director, Services and Commercial, British Gas**

"Boots has re-energized its retail business using the idea 'Feel Good'. It's about people feeling good about themselves, looking good and having confidence. The idea has captured that internal sense of 'that's what we stand for'. In an organization with so many thousands of people who are themselves really passionate about the business, giving them a clear sense of purpose has been transforming."

Torvald de Coverly Veale, **International Brands Development Director, Alliance Boots**

corporate culture that is distant from the concerns and day-to-day lives of their customers.

Unilever has enjoyed great success in recent years by finding engaging emotive causes on which to base many of its brands' positioning such as Omo's crusade to encourage children's learning and development under the "Dirt is Good" banner and Dove's "Campaign for Real Beauty", designed to overturn conventional attitudes towards beauty and glamour.

By generating visionary brand ideas, Marketers can have a huge impact on the culture of an organization and by inspiring and aligning the people in the company around a customer-centric mission, the main and most important task of a strategic Marketer will have been achieved.

The Culture Driver – Practical Tips

- Assess the key elements of the culture – understand which elements support or detract from the creation of better customer value.

- Encourage senior executives to experience a customer-connect initiative to build confidence and to open an ongoing channel of insight and awareness of customer issues.

- Put customer goals at the heart of the corporate strategy and ask customers how well you are doing in delivering against those goals.

- Use inspiring brand ideas to create a customer-focused purpose for the organization.

As we close this chapter, we have explored how marketing capability solutions need to be developed that go far beyond *training* to leverage the core Capability Drivers right around *The Brand Learning Wheel*. We will next move on to the final "D" in *The 3D Approach* – *Driving Embedding* of changes in people's attitudes and skills into improved activities and behaviours on the job. Only then can capability solutions have an impact in driving marketing performance and business growth.

CHAPTER 6 – AT A GLANCE

- Developing solutions to address the Capability Drivers in the "bottom half" of *The Brand Learning Wheel* – the *Organization, People* and *Culture Drivers* – helps create a more holistic and effective approach to marketing capability development.

- In many organizations these Capability Drivers are the responsibility of HR or of general managers, so senior Marketing, HR and other business leaders need to collaborate on capability development.

- The *Organization Driver* covers the way in which marketing resources are structured to facilitate effective and efficient ways of working throughout a business.

- Creating a more customer-centric company requires an "outside in" perspective that breaks up traditional "siloed" ways of working to achieve seamless integration in the delivery of customer offerings.

- CMOs must align their vision for the role the Marketing function will play with their CEO and with other functions, to help to create an organization that is more effective in creating better value for customers.

- The structure and role of the Marketing function is changing dramatically, which makes it vital to spend time rethinking the organization internally and externally and defining clear role profiles to enhance marketing effectiveness.

- The *People Driver* of capability works to build marketing capability at both a big "M" (functional) and a small "m" (company) level.

- Marketing and HR leaders must work closely together to build the Marketing talent pool and leverage the key HR processes that influence marketing capabilities.

- *Five Star Marketing Leaders* share some key attributes – a restless customer obsession, they create bold and inspiring visions and they are humble, honest and have great attention to detail.

- Brand ideas can bring to life an organization's promise to its customers and provide a unifying, energizing purpose for everyone in the business.

Notes

1 "Gambling on the future" by Lucy Handley, *Marketing Week*, 10th March 2011.
2 *Reorganize for Resilience* by Ranjay Gulati, Harvard Business Press 2010.
3 "Rethinking marketing", Roland T. Rust, Christine Moorman and Gaurav Bhalla, *Harvard Business Review*, January–February 2010.

Chapter 7

DRIVING EMBEDDING

Many organizations express ambitions to be "world class" at marketing, but few really grasp what that means in practice. Many more seriously underestimate the enormity of the task of driving real changes in the attitudes, skills and behaviours, not just of Marketers, but potentially the organization as a whole, if the stated strategy is to become more "customer centric".

"We want to be world-class, not just best in class. In the past, people focused on the day job whereas now there is definitely a new vision – things have changed, people see there are capability gaps and that the organization needs to change to be successful."

Tim Bailey, *Head of Marketing Academy, AstraZeneca*

As we have outlined *The 3D Approach* to marketing capability development, we first addressed how to *Define Strategy*, then how to *Develop Solutions* – covering the *Process* and *Skills Drivers* and then the *Organization, People* and *Culture Drivers*. Let's now move on to focus on the last "D" – *Driving Embedding* (see Figure 7.1).

In this chapter, we will share insights and practical examples about the challenges of *embedding* tangible changes in the attitudes, skills and behaviours of Marketers, Marketing teams and of organizations as a whole. It is only through achieving this goal that companies will be able improve their marketing effectiveness in ways that create better customer value and drive growth.

Figure 7.1: *The 3D Approach – Drive Embedding*

We will ask some important questions including: what does embedding changes in attitudes, skills and behaviours really involve in practice? What is the right blend of activities to secure that change? How do you make the right choices to balance channels and budgets? How do you sustain changes in behaviours and ways of working over time? What lessons can the discipline of Marketing itself offer to capability development and change management?

 **Driving for World Class Marketing**

AstraZeneca helps treat a wide range of serious illnesses globally with R&D centres in 8 countries, manufacturing sites in 16 countries and sales across over 100 countries. Its sales revenues in 2010 were $33 billion and its profits $11 billion. AstraZeneca's customer base is complex, with large national health and private health procurement teams, medical practitioners, pharmacists and nurses all potentially involved before their products reach the patient. And like other big pharmaceuticals companies, it is facing some challenging market developments.

Andrew Bailey, AstraZeneca's Vice President of World Class Marketing, explains, *"The old pharma model was all about selling. In the past you*

*would launch a new drug
and your sales reps would
battle it out in the marketplace. How good you
were came down to your
salesforce effectiveness
and your time in front of
the customer."*

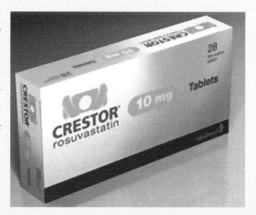

A number of factors
have undermined this
model in recent years.
These include fewer, truly
differentiated drugs coming through the pipeline, tighter legislative
controls on marketing claims, and the growing influence of "payers",
the people in the health services that manage the budgets. Andrew
Bailey continues, *"There are so many checks and balances on what
you can do in the pharma world. You have to find smarter ways of
getting your product to market, get smarter about who you are talking
to, what you want to say to them and how you connect with them."*

As a result, Marketing's role in
shaping the design of drugs earlier in the
emerging development pipeline has
become more influential. *"It is very
much about working closely with R&D,
picking your winners early and making
sure you're generating real world evidence, through the design of your scientific trials, to prove you're providing
a product that meets your customers'
needs"*, explains Andrew Bailey.

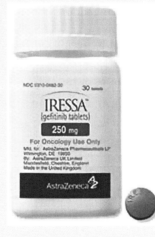

AstraZeneca's employees tend to
come from scientific backgrounds and
excel at scientific innovation, but marketing concepts like brand building or customer insight-driven initiatives were not established in its

corporate culture. It has traditionally been an R&D-led business and in order to effect its transformation, some core strategies and behaviours were going to have to change.

Towards a new marketing model

In the autumn of 2007, the new chief executive David R. Brennan announced a strategic review of the entire business to ensure AstraZeneca could better serve patient needs. An initiative was launched called *Fast Forward* to make sure each of the company's functions was "fit for the future". The role of Marketing in the organization was a particular focus.

"It wasn't clear where the global Marketing teams were adding value to the organization. They weren't providing strong enough commercial input into R&D's development. There were a lot of activities going on but they were more tactical than strategic. People were spending more time deciding what would be on the exhibition stand for the conference next week rather than on strategic positioning", recalls Tim Bailey.

Driving embedding

To begin its marketing transformation, AstraZeneca had to "rewire" the underlying mindset about what Marketing could and should contribute to the growth and performance of the business. It also had to move beyond defining strategy, beyond process and tool development, to work out how to embed changes in the way Marketers worked across the global organization.

“This time a year or two ago, people weren't even talking about world-class brand ideas or engagement. Now they are and our capability initiative has already established ways of working that didn't exist before. It's having a real impact across the organization.”

Tim Bailey, *Head of Marketing Academy, AstraZeneca*

The Challenge of Embedding Change

It is relatively easy to launch a marketing capability initiative into an organization. It is much more difficult to make it stick and really make an impact. Embedding *sustained* changes in people's attitudes, skills and behaviours and in the way Marketers and Marketing departments work in large, complex organizations is a tough, challenging task.

The reasons why embedding change is such a challenge lie in

> *❝The challenge for any organization is making change happen because everyone is just so damn busy. There's also a fear that change can be a threat to people, particularly if you're seen as coming in to assess them. You have to show people the journey and that there is some sort of personal reward at the end of it.❞*
>
> Andrew Bailey, *Vice President, World Class Marketing, AstraZeneca*

a number of areas. The culture, organization and people systems surrounding Marketers may perpetuate long outdated ways of thinking and operating. The attitudes of line managers are also critical, as are the ingrained mental models Marketers accumulate based on the experiences they have encountered over many years.

The sheer scale and complexity of large multinational organizations is another hurdle. We have seen cases where global Marketing leaders have not known how many Marketers they have working for them, let alone known all the jobs they do or the profile of their experience and capabilities.

The rapid turnover in Marketing departments exacerbates this problem, making it very difficult to bring about the lasting improvements in marketing capabilities needed to drive growth. In our consultancy business, we encounter client reorganizations, promotions, new hires, overseas moves, cross-functional moves, transfers and resignations on almost a daily basis in the field of international marketing.

And while change can be highly beneficial for personal development, this high degree of organizational turmoil comes at a substantial cost in terms of diminishing capabilities and wreaks havoc with the stable teams needed to establish common understanding, knowledge, skills and behaviours.

To drive more efficient ways of working there is a continuous need to refresh content, evolve learning and to sustain new ways of working if the organization is to attain, and then maintain, *world-class* marketing capabilities.

Even assuming a strong senior management will and commitment to change, a clear capability strategy, the availability of excellent data, processes and capability solutions, the most frequently quoted practical obstacle to the uptake of new capability solutions is simply people's lack of time.

" You have got a lot of inertia to deal with. You've got an environment where you're having to say goodbye to things that have governed you and provided meaning and purpose for many years. It is easy to go into cliché mode here, so you start talking about creating a 'learning organization' and 'celebrating failure' and all that sort of stuff people talk about but never really believe in. The fact is that changing how people approach their jobs and then following that up with changes in what they do in practice is just really hard. "

Jon Harding, *Head of Organization Development, Barclaycard*

Moving Forward – a Powerful Insight

So, acknowledging there are big challenges in embedding new marketing capabilities, how can you change the way people and teams work in practice? How do you move from developing new content solutions (e.g. new processes, new tools and new systems or ways of working) to *embedding* them so that Marketers are equipped and enabled to create

" One of the biggest challenges is encouraging people that this is a worthwhile use of their time and they are going to get value out of the programme. We worked really hard; we met every brand leader, talked about the concept, tried to get them interested. We've done a lot of internal communication – trying to share from team to team. "

Tim Bailey, *Head of Marketing Academy, AstraZeneca*

better customer value to drive profitable, sustained growth?

As any experienced Marketer knows, the definition of a challenging issue is the best way to start searching for an insight to unlock the problem. And we have uncovered a powerful insight in our work with our clients that we believe has major implications for the way that marketing capability development should be approached, particularly where embedding new ways of working is a significant challenge.

> *" There are only so many hours in a day and there are 20 million things that can't get done today because there are just too many other priorities on the list. The irony is that you could argue the time when you are at your busiest is also the time when you most need stronger capabilities. "*
>
> Ian Armstrong, *European Communications Director, Honda*

Marketing Capability Development – Core Insight

Business leaders who want to build the marketing capabilities of their people and teams need to influence the attitudes and behaviours of those *employees* in the same way that Marketers seek to influence the attitudes and behaviours of *customers*.

We believe that effective marketing capability development, at its core, is like marketing itself – because it is all about changing people's attitudes and behaviour to help drive growth.

For this reason, in our experience, the principles and practices of marketing can also be applied *internally* to transform the effectiveness and efficiency of marketing capability change initiatives. To be effective, marketing capability development needs to be planned, developed and driven just like the best marketing initiatives – with energy and passion, an "employee-focused" mindset, a balance of rigour and creativity, emotional engagement, benefit focus and with rigorous measurement of impact.

The Embedding Arrow

So how do you apply core marketing principles to drive successful capability development?

" You can have the best ideas in the world but if you don't find a way to get them embedded, they won't happen. It's about helping people to translate a principle, an idea which no one can disagree with, into a different action for themselves. "

Fiona McAnena, *Global Brand Director, Bupa*

To help business leaders drive the embedding of marketing capability programmes, and provide inspiration and guidance throughout the process, we've developed a useful tool called *The Embedding Arrow* (see Figure 7.2).

The Embedding Arrow outlines the key steps needed for Marketing and other business leaders to plan and implement capability development initiatives in the right way – so they embed changes in the ways Marketing people and teams work in practice to deliver better customer value.

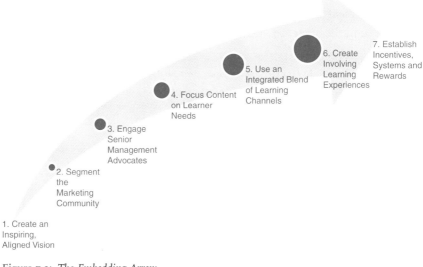

Figure 7.2: *The Embedding Arrow*
The practical steps to follow in embedding new ways of working

Step 1: Create an inspiring, aligned vision

In the previous chapter, we asserted that creating a "bold and inspiring vision" was an essential attribute of a *Five Star Marketing Leader*. These leaders have the ability to create a clear and compelling vision of the future and know how to share it to engage and inspire other people in the organization. They create an exciting sense of opportunity which is essential to galvanize the organization to pull together to create better customer value and drive enhanced business performance.

Leaders of marketing capability initiatives need exactly the same leadership ability – which is why in many organizations the role of a specialist Marketing Capability Director or VP has been established to lead marketing excellence programmes and to create a bridge between the Marketing, HR and general management leaders.

As we've consistently argued, capability development is far more demanding than delivering a "training programme" or a set of "workshops". The ability of capability development leaders to communicate a clear, engaging and compelling vision for marketing excellence is vital to creating the right context and conditions for success.

" Make sure you know where you are today and where you want to get to, point A to point B. Quite simply, in Shell we wanted to be number one in the recruitment space. We wanted to get to the top of our game in terms of costs and in terms of our attraction and recruitment marketing activities to become the 'candidate's choice'. "

Navjot Singh, *Global Marketing Manager, Recruitment & HR Communications, Shell*

" We had the big reorganization and the big refocusing on what Global Marketing was all about and we agreed what the remit for capability development was and our vision to be world class. That was the starting point for everything – that really helped to focus on what needed to be done. If we hadn't had that new remit and the vision as the starting point, it would have been a lot more difficult. "

Tim Bailey, *Head of Marketing Academy, AstraZeneca*

Only then will capability development initiatives be able to cut through the clutter of operational demands. An inspiring vision can lift and focus the energy of Marketers and other executives, enabling them to learn, to practice new skills and to demonstrate excellence in the new ways of working in practice.

Lifting people's energy

The "mindset" of Marketers towards a change initiative has a significant bearing on its impact. The best change initiatives are driven when Marketers feel inspired, enthusiastic and committed to making changes. In this case, new ways of working are seen as helping them to do their jobs better and faster and Marketers are therefore willing to make the effort to change their attitudes and behaviours and enthusiastic to learn new skills.

By contrast, initiatives that fail to get established usually do so because they don't engage and connect with Marketers, so they remain sceptical about the organization's commitment to change, struggle to see the value, or simply feel weighed down by the new demands coming their way.

When Marketers appreciate that a capability programme links directly to the key issues and strategic priorities facing the organization, their function and their own team, it builds their active support – which is critical for change. This commitment is further enhanced if the programme is championed publicly by senior management.

A key "watch out" in creating an inspiring vision is to make sure that the benefits of the capa-

❝ In many cases, people were literally meeting each other for the first time through the programme. It was incredibly energizing for people to discover how much they had in common as opposed to what was different. I think that what you have to deal with is the fear of change, the fear of being made to do things in a different way. But what quickly takes over is people's sense of a common vision and agenda and how incredibly helpful it will be to have common frameworks and common ways of having conversations together. ❞

Jan Gooding, *Global Marketing Director, Aviva*

Bupa ⁀ᴧ⁀ Board Level Inspiration

At Bupa the desire for a step change in marketing capabilities and performance started at board level.

❝ One of the executive board members created huge momentum around a whole strategy initiative and out of that came the focus on the role of the brand and how Bupa should be one business around the world and how powerful an asset that is. It takes energy, courage and perseverance to overcome the inertia. I think historically Bupa was a bit passive. If you didn't initiate things nobody really minded, but now if you do take initiatives to change you can really make a difference, if you have the energy to keep behind it. ❞

Fiona McAnena, *Global Brand Director, Bupa*

bility development programme are not limited to benefits from the organization's perspective. The opportunities for Marketers and other executives to build their personal experience, marketing skills and career prospects must also be embraced.

If new ways of working are positioned as an opportunity for people and teams to develop their personal skills in marketing, to help them do their jobs better *and* to benefit the organization, it will have a significant beneficial impact on employee pride, motivation and satisfaction.

❝ People now have a greater understanding of why we are investing in marketing capabilities and what it's leading to. Now it's all coming together and it links together really well – it's a lot easier for people. It addresses a lot of the issues we've had this year and people support it because it's important for their own personal development. ❞

Tim Bailey, *Head of Marketing Academy, AstraZeneca*

Step 2: Segment the Marketing community

At the heart of any strong marketing strategy is a clear definition of the market and target segments – an essential foundation for the development of relevant propositions that address customer needs and motivations. And exactly the same discipline is needed when planning marketing capability programmes. The two key questions to ask are:

1. What is the target group for the programme?

Is it aimed at Marketers only or will the new thinking, processes and tools also need to be extended to other functions like Sales, R&D or HR who interface with Marketing, or like Guest Services, Brokers, etc. who play key customer-facing roles?

2. What are the key subgroupings or segments?

Is it aimed at *all* Marketers – from board level right down to the latest new hire? Or is it more targeted at a specific job level, specialist function (e.g. Trade Marketing, Insights teams, etc.), location (e.g. global, regional, local teams) or business unit?

❝ It's not always appropriate to create a blanket framework for everyone. We've got different levels of experience, different levels of job grade, guys that are junior, guys at exec level. We need them all to have a level of capability that is appropriate to their job, but they don't all need strong strategic thinking. ❞

Ian Armstrong, *European Communications Director, Honda*

AstraZeneca's Use of Segmentation

AstraZeneca has used segmentation smartly to drive embedding of its global marketing capability development initiatives. At a high level, it has structured its extensive programme to reflect differences in the roles Marketers play at different stages of brand development across the drug lifecycle and also in different geographic regions.

"The trick for us has been in segmenting our audience", explains Andrew Bailey. *"The capability needs of our US business, for example, compared to some of our emerging markets are very different. You're dealing with different types of people and levels of experience."*

AstraZeneca has also taken into account the different levels of Marketers in the business, with targeted foundation, advanced and leadership programme components.

From the employee's personal perspective, AstraZeneca has also developed a capability assessment tool which Marketers use in discussion with their line managers to enable them to identify their personal skill development priorities. As AstraZeneca's Tim Bailey explains, *"The tool contains job descriptions and the target capability levels for every job in Global Marketing. Everyone then goes in and fills in their profile online with evidence of where they are on each dimension. They discuss and agree it with their line manager. They also have access to resources and suggested activities to help them build their capabilities on the job."*

This aggregated data gives Bailey invaluable global capability profile information to enable him to plan programme development and embedding. *"It means we can do an analysis report looking at all our marketing capabilities, looking at where things are versus target across different brand teams, job levels and lifecycle stages. It means we can pinpoint where the needs really are and plan things accordingly."*

Step 3: Engage senior management advocates

The most critical group to engage during the embedding phase of a capability development programme is the senior Marketing leadership team. For a capability build initiative to be successful, they must shift from being passive observers to being actively engaged as the programme's most passionate champions and advocates. To do this in practice requires engagement, alignment and active co-creation behind the priority elements of the programme. Public commitment is essential to focus their own and their peers' attention behind the key decisions needed for successful embedding and measurement.

Senior managers must also commit to coach and embed new ways of working on the job and take steps to question, challenge and inspire Marketers to stretch performance. They need to ensure that new processes and tools result in better decision making and ways of working in practice, leading to measureable improvements in capabilities and business results.

DIAGEO CEO Endorsement

When Diageo launched the global "Diageo Way of Brand Building" (DWBB) capability initiative, it actively leveraged its senior management team to cascade and help embed its new ways of working. The initiative was sponsored at the very top of the organization, evidenced by board and cross-functional participation and Paul Walsh, Diageo's CEO, personally engaged all employees in a letter saying:

" The first phase of Diageo's evolution is behind us. Part of the next phase is to implement new ways of working around brand building, building talent and delivering superlative performance. Diageo now needs swift, market-based execution that will drive profitable growth. This in turn requires empowered, energized, management teams who are passionate about growing our brands by continually serving the needs of our customers. The Diageo Way is what the key thought leaders across Diageo feel is imperative to realizing our goals, i.e. a common language, common behaviours and common processes. "

He ended with an impassioned personal plea to all Diageo executives, "*I ask each of you to embrace these new ways of working, because I believe this is the only way we can start to realize the promise we have made to our colleagues, our shareholders and ourselves.*"

Step 4: Focus content on learner needs

As we will cover later in Chapter 8, the concept of "payback" is central to the success of any marketing capability programme. This applies *both* in the form of a commercial ROI from the perspective of the business leader *and* personal achievement, development, reward and career progression from the perspective of each individual Marketer. Programmes must therefore be planned and constructed in ways which focus on learners' needs and directly enable Marketers to do their jobs more effectively.

 Capability Insight

When Unilever set up its global Marketing Academy in the late 1990s, a core insight was defined as the basis for the positioning of its activities: *"For managers to invest time and money in marketing learning, they need to see a payback in terms of improved business and personal performance."*

This insight was used to guide the practical development of its early marketing capability programmes, from Unilever's Global Marketing Foundation programme for graduate recruits, through to the comprehensive overhaul of its Brand Positioning and Communication processes. The focus was on providing capability solutions that would make a real difference to a Marketer's ability to do their day job, rather than providing them with isolated academic or theoretical learning support.

Learning materials should always be designed from the end-user's perspective. They should be simple, focused and practical – not too academic, impenetrable or theoretical. Examples and case studies should be accessible and relevant, not just to the learning objectives but to the industries, categories, brand and business issues Marketers are working on. And programmes should make full use of *all* the best internal communications channels available to reach employees at every relevant "touch-point".

Live-action Learning

One of the key elements in AstraZeneca's global marketing capability strategy has been to successfully use "Live-action Learning" modules, where Marketing teams are given active support to build their capabilities at the same time as solving current business issues. *"In one case recently, the team said it had enabled them to make progress that would normally have taken six months to achieve. In another, a team was really struggling to understand the different disease areas and how their particular product should be targeted. They had physicians role-playing as if they were diagnosing a patient and this helped them generate some extremely useful new insights and ideas"*, explains Tim Bailey, Head of Marketing Academy, Astra Zeneca.

Step 5: Use an integrated blend of learning channels

Just as marketing campaigns which rely solely on a 30-second TV ad are a thing of the past, so too are marketing capability programmes which rely solely on traditional training courses.

In marketing, as technology has progressed over time, the focus first shifted away from TV-dominated campaigns organized in "bursts" to multi-channel ongoing campaigns. The explosion of social media has now enabled "social marketing" campaigns, creating two-way dialogue, co-creation and crowd-sourcing. While TV still plays an important role, it is just one component within an integrated blend of communication channels.

A similar development has taken place in learning, with courses and workshops being supplemented with a wide range of e-learning techniques to create "blended" learning programmes. Social network channels are also starting to impact learning programmes, enabling employees to connect and learn from each other more readily than ever, i.e. "social learning". The result is an opportunity to shift even further towards continuous, "fluid" learning support for people as they do their jobs (see Figure 7.3).

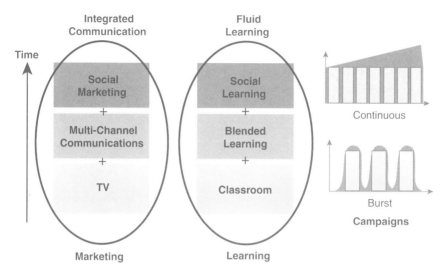

Figure 7.3: *Evolution in marketing and learning channels*

In our experience, the effective planning of more innovative capability development channels benefits from exactly the same disciplines used by Marketers for effective media and channel planning.

Decoding Social Media

AkzoNobel have experimented successfully with social learning channels in their *"Decoding Social Media"* programme. AkzoNobel's chairman, Tex Gunning, made an impassioned challenge to the Marketing team to embrace and step change its utilization of social media channels. To embed changes in ways of working, the programme aimed to build a common level of awareness and understanding about the social media landscape throughout the global Marketing community. Tex Gunning was highly supportive throughout, reinforcing his view that *"a better connected team will go on to create better connections with our customers."*

The programme was run virtually over a six-week period, with a community for discussion established on LinkedIn to enable people to share and reflect on their learnings. *"The big risk with a programme of this sort is that people might not bother to get involved because they are too busy"*, reflects Karen Jeffery, Global Marketing Capability Leader at AkzoNobel. *"But the engagement levels have been fantastic, partly because people can't fail to recognize the ever-increasing importance of social media and partly because we've been able to set the right context for the programme with senior management leadership and commitment. One of the interesting things to emerge is that discussions on the networks created by the programme have extended beyond the immediate programme tasks."*

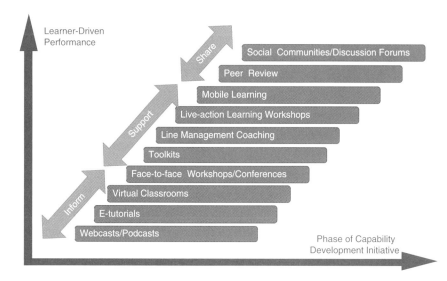

Figure 7.4: *The key learning channels*

Key learning channels

There are multiple face-to-face and online learning channels available. Programmes can be planned by looking at the role each plays in "informing" people with new knowledge, "supporting" them as they do their work and helping them in "sharing" their learning and experience with others (see Figure 7.4).

Face-to-face channels

Facilitated face-to-face channels such as workshops, conferences and events provide highly valued group-learning opportunities for Marketers

The fact is, that for us, physically getting together is very important. There's a tension here because sparing a day or two out of the office is difficult, so you have to use other learning channels too. But for a Marketing Director to get their team together to do some capability development, and at the same time have conversations about what they're doing as a team, has an incredibly powerful impact on people's spirit and engagement.

Jan Gooding, *Global Marketing Director, Aviva*

to meet up and work together to learn, share and align knowledge, generate ideas and build relationships. Well planned and facilitated sessions to build team spirit and commitment help to create the energy, excitement and momentum needed for change initiatives.

The type of face-to-face events used by companies for marketing capability development varies widely. Some companies have a powerful cultural belief in management capability development and use *international workshops* to help actively engage groups of Marketers across different geographies and product categories. A suite of workshops is typically available for people at different stages in their careers, each focusing on a skill area set as a strategic priority for the business. The workshop content is designed to balance the embedding of core skills with inspiration from "cutting-edge" marketing thinking and techniques.

Other companies prefer *large scale conferences* where entire international teams and their agencies, where relevant, come together from around the world.

Sara Lee Global Capability Cascade Events

Sara Lee has launched a number of process and skill change initiatives over the past five years, each focused on a priority marketing capability area such as "Great Communications" or "Great Innovation". Each initiative is launched with a global conference for Marketing leaders, before embedding the new ways of working by cascading with regional events for the rest of the Marketing community. While quite costly and complex to host, this approach achieves significant organizational focus and impact.

A growing and effective format for face-to-face group learning is that of *live action learning*. This kind of learning is designed using advanced learning techniques to embed new ways of working that apply to specific operational teams. It involves expertly facilitated sessions designed to build team capabilities and solve current business issues at the same time, delivering marketing business solutions, such as new marketing plans or innovation concepts, as a specific output.

Individual coaching

The most influential channel of learning for any Marketer remains their on-the-job experience and the coaching provided by their line manager, together with that of other accessible internal and external experts.

Focus should therefore be given in any marketing capability initiative to engaging line managers and clarifying their role and objectives. Tools and guidance should be provided to coach them in how to embed new ways of working. Unfortunately, time pressures and the scarcity of resource in today's organizations can make it difficult for the most experienced managers to offer ongoing consistent professional development, but its value should not be forgotten.

More formal *applied coaching* should also be provided to support Marketers with particularly important capability needs. It tends to be a resource-intensive channel and is therefore usually used in a focused way in one of two situations:

- When an executive is taking on a senior Marketing role without previous functional experience; for example, a senior Sales manager building up cross-functional experience by taking on a Marketing or general management role for the first time.

- When an individual is leading a critical business team to deliver a key project and needs support to build marketing capabilities at a specific point of time.

Online Channels

For global organizations, pressure on time is so intense and both financial and environmental costs of travel are so high that companies need to evolve ever more effective and efficient ways to embed capability programmes. Given the massive advances in technology, in computer hardware, software applications and bandwidth, increasing use is being made of a variety of online learning solutions, though there are some important watch-outs to bear in mind.

Online *e-tutorials* offer flexible, self-paced learning to build management awareness and knowledge levels, though this channel can be limited in its ability to establish depth of engagement.

Webinars and *virtual classrooms* are similar in many respects to face-to-face workshops, but Marketers log into online virtual space. They differ from e-tutorials in that they are scheduled at specific times and involve a facilitator. Technology and telecommunications companies such as HP and BT have been at the forefront of adopting this channel.

We have already highlighted the growing importance of social learning techniques. Other new developments likely to have value

" Remote learning has been a great success in BT because it has enabled us to reach Marketers globally, even when people may be home-based. Innovation in learning delivery is important as it helps generate buzz, interest and engagement. "

Lesley Wilson, *Head of the Marketing Community & Brand Operations, BT*

for embedding marketing capabilities in future include co-creation forums, the delivery of learning through mobile devices, game-based learning, augmented reality and even gesture-based computing. Virtual worlds can already be used to create immersive, remote, interactive experiences. As these technologies develop, online learning is evolving from being primarily an interaction between a "producer" and a "consumer" of knowledge, to a virtual world where people are supported to work and converse in social communities to co-create and enhance their capabilities.

Desktop tools

Another valuable way to embed marketing capabilities is to enable Marketers on the job by capturing core learnings about new processes, tools and ways of working in the form of accessible online and hard copy learning guides or toolkits. Marketers can use these to guide them through the steps in new processes at the point when they need to implement the new ways of working on the job.

The value of toolkits is in helping to capture, define and embed a common language for everyone in the organization. They also make accessible a set of practical templates, checklists and tips that means that each Marketer does not have to "reinvent the wheel" every time they approach a marketing task.

Desktop toolkits can take many forms, but the two most commonly seen are hard copy booklets and online portals or learning areas located on company intranets. Many companies have built their own proprietary sets of marketing tools and organizations as diverse as Diageo, AstraZeneca and HP have all defined and communicated their own "way of marketing" in this way.

The benefit of flexible online tools and support materials is that they can be regularly updated – a key consideration for ongoing knowledge management. They can also link to other internal and external online resources, such as e-learning programmes, community knowledge sharing forums and the organization's other operational processes and systems.

Step 6: Create involving learning experiences

Successfully embedding new ways of working requires that *all* the possible learning channel options are considered, before being selected and blended in an integrated manner to reach people across the best available touch-points. Each specific element of the programme must then be designed to maximize the engagement and involvement of participants.

Just as Marketers strive to influence positively every aspect of their customers' brand experience, world-class capability development programmes give a high priority, time and effort to the design of engaging learning experiences.

The presentation of masses of charts, information and data is not engaging, motivating or inspiring to most people and there is no correlation between

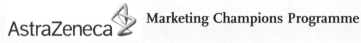

AstraZeneca — Marketing Champions Programme

AstraZeneca's 'Marketing Champions Programme' was designed to support the Global Marketing Leadership Team's mission to become a world-class marketing organization. The theme of "being a champion" was introduced ahead of time and Marketers were briefed with preparation work. The kick-off workshop was held at Manchester United's football ground, so pre-workshop invitations started to build the energy and excitement.

Over three days, focused sessions prompted discussion, reflection and action planning. Videos of interviews with senior Marketing leaders from other companies introduced new perspectives and best practice, and inspiring leadership ideas and challenges were put forward by a top leadership coach. A blend of syndicate work, plenary debate and paired discussions on more personal leadership issues was used to vary the dynamics throughout the workshop. Further interest was added by an evening session, featuring Sir Clive Woodward, coach of England's World Cup winning rugby team.

To maintain momentum, a follow-up video conference engaged Marketing leaders internationally to review their progress. The key principles and learnings were rolled out a few months later to the entire Global Marketing team.

Feedback on this learner-oriented programme design provided by participants highlighted its positive impact: *"I most liked the fact we were not 'taught', but led to reflect and to learn from real life examples of world-class Marketing leaders"*, and *"I found it extremely valuable with a number of 'aha' moments which I believe will have a lasting impact"*.

"The feedback we received from the champions programme was stunning", comments Tim Bailey. *"If you go into people's offices, they have still got materials up on the walls reminding them of what they learnt there."*

the number of charts presented and the effectiveness of learning experiences! So our advice is that, just as in marketing where the most effective brand experiences are designed around the customer, so learning experiences must be oriented around the needs and motivations of the learner.

Step 7: Establish incentives, systems and rewards

Finally, to drive the embedding of marketing capability programmes it is essential to look beyond the delivery of learning to the role other influential supporting HR systems, mechanics and incentives can have on people's behaviour.

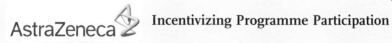

AstraZeneca **Incentivizing Programme Participation**

Once the skill development programme had been established for Global Marketing in AstraZeneca, it was agreed that most of the specific learning solutions would not be made mandatory, but that people would *opt in* to them based on their personal or team development needs. This approach, while logical in principle, caused some practical issues.

"We weren't initially getting the uptake of the learning programmes we were expecting", explains Tim Bailey. *"There was no incentive for people to do it. So we looked at the whole range of options, some more 'carrot', some more 'stick' and now we can see who has done their assessment, who has signed up for the programmes, how many have done them. We can send out reports to each of the team leaders to show how happy their teams have been doing the virtual classrooms, and how many hours they've done. We've done a lot of communication around that so people can see how other teams are doing and the benefits they are getting."*

The conclusion AstraZeneca came to about incentives, as Bailey explains, was, *"We wanted to do it through good, open, transparent development planning rather than having, for example, points for programmes which affect rewards. We shied away from that. It is done through proper, rigorous development planning and then we track that to make sure it is being done."*

Learning incentives, systems and rewards

The best incentive techniques are related to the characteristics and issues of any given company. Here are a few examples we have seen used successfully:

- **Personal development planning** – linking learning programmes and resources into the assessment of personal capability development needs, defined as part of the HR performance management system.

- **Reward mechanisms** – basing every Marketer's appraisal and reward on their performance in building the business and the organization, with the development of people being a key component of the latter.

- **Award schemes** – awards involving an expert judging panel giving global prizes across a range of marketing categories, thereby raising the profile of best practice and inspiring teams to reach new standards of performance.

- **Peer reviews** – senior Marketers from different operating companies invited to share their most recent brand development projects and tap into the expertise and experience of their colleagues.

- **Business systems** – hard wiring the use of standard best practice innovation proposal documents through the rollout of a global online innovation process management system.

- **Stakeholder involvement** – asking communications agencies to give ratings on the quality of briefs being received from Marketing teams following the rollout of a campaign management learning programme.

We began this chapter by illustrating the challenge of driving real changes in the attitudes, skills and behaviours, not just of Marketers and of the Marketing department, but potentially of the entire organization. We then explained why *driving embedding* of sustained changes in people's ways of working is such a difficult yet critical part of building marketing capabilities.

Our experience confirms that only when marketing capability development is "hard wired" into the way people work *in practice* can it generate the changes in attitudes and behaviours needed to enhance marketing performance and drive growth. In the next chapter, we will move on to look at the important issue of how to *measure the impact* of marketing capability programmes – setting measurable targets and key performance indicators (KPIs) and tracking these over time.

CHAPTER 7 – AT A GLANCE

- Many organizations express *'world-class marketing'* ambitions but seriously underestimate the enormity of the task of driving real changes in the attitudes, skills and behaviours, not just of individuals, but of an entire Marketing function or organization.

- *Driving Embedding* of new skills and behaviours means securing sustained changes in attitudes, skills and behaviours and in the way people, teams and organizations work in practice.

- Business leaders who want to build the marketing capabilities of their people and teams need to influence the attitudes and behaviours of those employees in the same way that Marketers work to influence the attitudes and behaviours of customers.

- The principles and practices of world-class marketing can be applied internally to transform the effectiveness and efficiency of marketing capability change initiatives.

- *The Embedding Arrow* is a practical tool to embed changes in the ways Marketing people and teams work in practice to deliver better customer value. It has seven core steps: 1. Create an inspiring, aligned vision; 2. Segment the marketing community; 3. Engage senior management advocates; 4. Focus content on learner needs; 5. Use an integrated blend of learning channels; 6. Create involving learning experiences; 7. Establish incentives, systems and rewards.

- Only when marketing capability development is "hard wired" into the organization will it generate the changes in attitudes and behaviours needed to enhance business performance.

Part 3

Sustaining Growth in Practice

Chapter 8

Up until now in *The Growth Drivers*, we have focused on understanding the main challenges in marketing capability development. We have worked through each of the stages in *The 3D Approach*, from defining a capability strategy and plan, to developing solutions, then driving embedding of new ways of working. In this chapter, we will now look at some of the challenges in *measuring the impact* of marketing capability development and how they relate to those of measuring marketing itself.

As we do so, we will ask some key questions including: Why is measuring marketing so difficult? What are the levels at which marketing effectiveness and efficiency should be assessed? How can you measure the impact and ROI of marketing capability strategies and programmes? And how should organizations set the right mix of objectives and KPIs?

"When you try to reduce brilliance and flair to logic and analysis and ask 'how are we measuring our success?' and 'how do we know if what we are spending gets a return?', people talk about the search for the 'holy grail'. But it's just a constant process of 'how do we find more value for what we spend?' I have a constant ask of Marketers, 'seek the growth drivers, wherever they are' – not where we think they should be or where we would like them to be – in the most efficient way."

Nick Rose, *formerly Diageo's Chief Financial Officer*

DIAGEO Measurement Approach

Diageo has invested millions over a period of more than ten years to launch, embed and strengthen its world-class "Diageo Way of Brand Building" capability development programme. In giving his commercial perspective on the challenge of measuring the impact of that marketing capability development, Nick Rose, formerly Diageo's CFO, is in no doubt why, *"We looked more at the outcome. The ultimate answer is 'did the top line grow faster?', 'are the brands in better health?', 'did we produce more innovation?' Yes. Yes. Yes. And, in a relative ranking versus the other consumer goods companies we admire, 'did we move up that ranking?' Yes."*

If the aim of building marketing capabilities is to help organizations to create better customer value, which in turn drives demand-led growth, it's clearly important to understand how that impact can and will be measured by the organization.

So before we explain our approach to measuring the impact of *marketing capability development*, we need first to give a brief overview of how the impact of *marketing* itself is assessed. This is a complex area and it is not our aim to cover it comprehensively here, but it's important to explain our perspective since there are some key principles and challenges involved in the measurement of marketing that also apply to the measurement of marketing capabilities.

Measuring Marketing

"Senior management is losing patience with marketing over the lack of marketing results measurement."[1] This is the warning recently given by Philip Kotler, Kellogg Professor of International Marketing at the Northwestern University Graduate School of Management in Chicago.

The thorny issue of measuring marketing has been hotly debated for many years and there is a lot of confusion and uncertainty surrounding the topic. A certain level of apprehension is prevalent amongst Marketers and their agencies. Marketing budgets tend to be relatively large, visible and are increasingly being put under the microscope by Finance and General Managers. There is rarely a shared understanding of where the real value of marketing investment lies.

Advances in digital technology, however, are adding important new dimensions to this debate, creating new opportunities and new challenges for Marketers to contend with. The availability of real-time digital customer data is transforming the speed and extent of metrics available to measure the impact of marketing, right down to the level of individual customers. This is opening a door to a new world of powerful information and with it far greater board level appreciation of the tangible value of marketing activities in driving growth.

“Marketing used to be an 'act of faith' discipline; now it's becoming a measurable, scientific discipline and for companies who do that well, then marketing is clearly, demonstrably, the engine of growth and the engine of development of new markets.”

Dan Cobley, *VP Marketing, Northern and Central Europe, Google*

But the widespread availability of extensive data does not necessarily make the challenge of measuring the overall impact of marketing any easier in practice. Indeed the pace of technological change and the sheer weight, complexity and immediacy of data can obscure, rather than enhance, clarity on the customer impact of marketing investments.

A further challenge is that the decision-making behaviour of customers is changing significantly in the digital world. Instead of the simple 'funnel' used by Marketers to understand and measure how customers move through from consideration to purchase, more complex and iterative customer journeys are becoming the norm.

In his *Harvard Business Review* article entitled '*Branding in the Digital Age*', McKinsey's David C. Edelman describes how "*Touch points have changed in both number and nature, requiring a major adjustment to realign marketers' strategy and budgets with where consumers are actually spending their time.*"[2]

When you boil it right down, fundamentally, Marketers have to move along with the digital wave to get the most efficiency out of their spend. We want top line growth and therefore we have to go where our customers and consumers are. The more digital you go, the more you can track individual consumer behaviour and the more you get access to real time data.

Nick Rose, *former CFO, Diageo*

I think it is still quite tough to measure the effectiveness of spend in the digital and social space. You get great pockets of information looking at promotional awareness and participation, and linked sales are possibly easier, but in terms of overall brand health metrics we're still finding it quite hard to understand how to measure success.

Simon Lowden, *CMO, Pepsi Beverages, North America*

Leading companies are developing sophisticated new customer journey tools to help better understand customer behaviour and set a new framework for planning and measuring channel and media investment. Daryl Fielding, VP of Marketing in Kraft Food Europe gives one example, "*We've invested in creating a proprietary, bespoke tool that will help us understand where we can best place our marketing investment, where are the 'off ramps' and 'on ramps' on the*

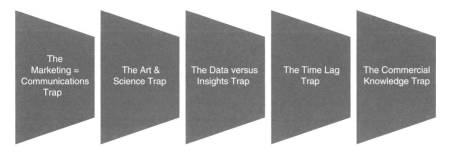

Figure 8.1: *The Measurement Traps*

path to purchase and where we might lose consumers and where we might gain them."[3]

Developments of this type are undoubtedly enhancing the measurement and impact of marketing in certain businesses, but in our experience, the common challenges that people, teams and organizations face in measuring the impact of marketing stem from five issues which we call *The Measurement Traps* (see Figure 8.1).

The Measurement Traps

1. The marketing = communications trap

For many years there has not been a clear and universally understood definition of what marketing is and does, which has made it almost impossible to establish a common approach to measuring its effectiveness and efficiency.

As we explained at the start of *The Growth Drivers*, the discipline of marketing is widely misunderstood by many CEOs, CFOs, by executives in other functions such as Sales and Finance, by many in creative agencies, and even by some Marketers themselves. Marketing is often believed to relate solely to the brand communications and promotions used to generate customer demand.

This has resulted in too much attention being paid to the return on investment of communications and promotional campaigns, and not enough to the more strategic, brand building aspects of marketing in *creating better value for customers*, such as portfolio management and innovation, as outlined in *The Growth Propeller* (see Chapter 2).

2. The art and science trap

Great marketing is acknowledged to be a balance of both the "art" of creativity and imagination and the "science" of analysis, discipline and rigour. The best Marketers and agencies are strong in both fields, but many have historically been more comfortable and familiar with the world of creative ideas and concepts and less so in the commercial world of robust analysis and financial accountability.

The key point is that, given the transformation in digital data, Marketers can no longer operate successfully without strong commercial and analytical skills. But equally, it is vital that organizations do not allow their Marketers to get so enmeshed in data and analysis that they lose sight of the fact that customers have powerful emotional influences on how they assess which brands, products and services offer them the best value.

Somewhere between the two is a sound commercial view that if the core role of marketing is to create better value for customers to drive demand-led growth, then getting sucked into either of the extremes of creativity or analysis is equally unhelpful. A balanced perspective taking both dimensions into account is what is required.

3. The data versus insights trap

Customer buying behaviour, leading to today's sales data, is relatively easy to measure. But it is far more difficult to get behind those revenue numbers to build insights into what *drives* the customer buying behaviour that, ultimately, Marketing and others in customer facing and support roles across the organization need to influence.

Isolating the specific impact of marketing activities from other external influences on customer behaviour and business performance, and

> *"If I cast my mind back before The Diageo Way of Brand Building, Marketing was in the world of intuition more than anything else. Many of the Marketing guys thought their mission was to produce the ad item to win the next Golden Globe, as opposed to influencing our customers and consumers to choose our brands more of the time."*
>
> Nick Rose, *former CFO Diageo*

predicting future likely behaviour and results, is extremely challenging. Customer data is also hard to distil, analyse, track and action when multiple levels of customer data are involved, e.g. the trade or channel customer, the buyer/shopper and the end-user or consumer.

The root issue for many organizations is no longer how to obtain robust data – most organizations have data overload. The issue has become instead how to synthesize and explore that information in a way which generates *actionable insights* that can be used to drive marketing effectiveness and growth.

4. The time lag trap

While sales data is relatively easy to access and analyse, the impact of investment in new propositions, innovation and brand communications to build enduring customer relationships and brand equity takes time to work through to commercial results.

Powerful brands can take time to build as successive waves of communication, word of mouth and customer relationship-building activity combine to form

❝The mindset you bring to this is critical. You can throw up your hands and say 'I'm overwhelmed with data', or you can say 'Wow, I have an incredible opportunity to understand things better.' It's like anything in life – you have to look for the patterns. You have to continually ask the question 'so what does this tell us? The great thing is that the ability to test and to segment is reaching the potential levels that those of us who have been working in Marketing for a while have always hoped for.❞

Barry Herstein, *CMO, HP Snapfish*

❝The marketing investment is to make sure we've got a revenue stream in six to twelve months, or even three years' time, because the legacy of how brands change and how people's perceptions of brands change is not something that happens overnight. If I want to double my business tomorrow, then it is probably going to be a sales mechanic that is going to do that, not a marketing mechanism. But we'll be here in three years' time because of what we are doing today in Marketing.❞

Ian Armstrong, *European Communications Director, Honda*

the perceptions that exist, both positive and negative, in people's minds. The relationship between marketing activities, the measurement of customer attitudes and behaviours and brand sales performance is often poorly understood. As a result, insufficient focus is given to understanding the underlying drivers, not just the apparent outcomes.

5. The commercial knowledge trap

We hear a common complaint that there is a lack of basic commercial knowledge among many Marketers and agency staff about what drives profit and loss and the financial concepts and methodologies involved in assessing the effectiveness of marketing activities. Les Binet and Peter Field wrote a revealing report for the IPA (Institute of Practitioners in Advertising) analysing the data from the 880 case study entries submitted since 1980 for its prestigious marketing effectiveness awards.[4]

They discovered basic errors in many submission papers, such as miscalculating incremental sales effects, treating revenue as profit and using the wrong profit margin. Some papers used financial terms such as ROI incorrectly to refer to non-financial measures and many did not seek to measure financial payback at all. These IPA case studies are likely to be at the higher quality end of the body of evaluation work done by Marketers and their agencies, so the implications for more general standards of practice are worrying.

So we have established that that there are some "traps" to catch the unwary when evaluating the impact of marketing effectiveness. But there is no doubt that significant improvements can be made in the way Marketers approach the measurement of their impact and effectiveness. The question is, how?

In our view, the impact of *marketing* should be measured at

❝ Since most people on executive boards have some financial background, it's crucial to be able to demonstrate to them how marketing is not just logos and fluff but has rigour and quantitatively robust insights. It's about demonstrating how Marketers make choices, about how we spend the money. ❞

Fiona McAnena, *Global Brand Director, Bupa*

two levels. First, at an overall strategic level, to assess the way Marketing contributes to the organization's *overall* business objectives. Second, at a more micro and operational level, measurement should take place of the contribution made by *specific* marketing activities and investments. So let's look briefly at each area in turn, before we move on to consider what implications this has on the measurement of *marketing capability development*.

The Value of Marketing

In order to measure the value created by the Marketing function at a strategic level, we need to return first to our definition of what its role is all about – *creating better value for customers, by building salient brands and innovative propositions that people find relevant, appealing and distinctive, to drive sustainable, profitable, demand-led growth.*

This definition identifies the core indicators by which the measures of Marketing's strategic contribution to driving brand and business growth need to be assessed, i.e. growth in sales revenue, growth in profit margins, enhancement in brand equity and growth in customer perceptions of value relative to competitors.

And by drilling deeper into the key activities that Marketing involves, as outlined in *The Growth Propeller* (see Chapter 2), several important measures emerge which play a key role in *driving* performance against these strategic goals (see Figure 8.2).

Marketing measures and metrics

The range of marketing measurement options is extensive, but there are two key priorities to bear in mind in selecting the most appropriate measures.

First, the chosen metrics should focus on the areas that are most important in driving the growth of the specific brand, business unit or organization. As Professor Tim Ambler, Honorary Research Fellow in Marketing at London Business School, points out in his book *Marketing and the Bottom Line* (FT Prentice Hall), some of these will be similar whatever the business – degree of brand salience, penetration and loyalty levels, customer preference and satisfaction levels, and availability. But others will be tailored to its particular

Figure 8.2: *Illustrative marketing measures and metrics*

strategy, for example shifts targeted in particular brand image ratings or an increased sales contribution from new products.

The challenge for Marketers is to understand the *drivers* of both customer behaviour and business performance and to link metrics with their strategies to drive improvements in both. In this respect, econometric modelling is proving a valuable tool providing significant rigour regarding customer metrics as a predictor of future success.

The second priority is to ensure that the most important customer objectives are built into a balanced scorecard of metrics at the overall organization level.

To enable the sustainable delivery of profitable, demand-led growth and meet the needs of all

❝What defines a successful strategy in driving growth is when Marketers understand the business drivers and the customer dynamics, prove we have done the analysis, have really listened to customers and have developed a deep, meaningful understanding of the market. We have all got to get better at talking the language of business – be as close as possible to what impacts the bottom line.❞

Martin George, *Managing Director for Group Development, Bupa*

stakeholders involved in an organization's sustained success, key performance dimensions should always extend beyond the financial measures to include customer, employee, environmental and operational factors.

It is crucial in this respect that Marketers encourage the organization to assess its performance against customer measures, not just financial or operational metrics. Changes in customer attitudes and behaviours today are the leading indicators for the performance of the business tomorrow – it is vital these get adequate focus and attention at board level.

Marketing activities and investments

Having covered how to approach the measurement of Marketing at an overall *strategic level*, let's now look at the more operational challenge of assessing *specific marketing activities and investments*.

Nick Rose describes how, in Diageo's top markets, more than 80% of the marketing spend now goes through a detailed pre-launch and post-launch filter. But not all organizations are as diligent in insisting that evaluation is done to estimate the value delivered by competing activity choices both before and after the event.

It is essential to think through the commercial case for decisions *before* they are taken, using the retrospective analysis and lessons from previous experience and with econometric input where available. The need for more robust commercial assessment of marketing activities is not just about holding Marketers *accountable* for what they do *after* the event – the point is for them to take sound commercial decisions in the first place. So how can Marketers best assess the commercial impact of their marketing activities?

"Sometimes Marketers don't use quantitative data at all, it tends to be qualitative and that risks turning half the audience off. People who are not marketing literate, or for whom it's not their primary function, can't always make the leap between improvements in, say, customer advocacy and improvements in the bottom line. Whereas if you can say that if we spend x and deliver y improvement in the bottom line, then they tend to be more supportive. At the end of the day, profit is the language of business."

Martin George, *Managing Director for Group Development, Bupa*

TESCO Tesco's Steering Wheel

The Tesco "Steering Wheel" is an excellent example of a balanced scorecard with its focus on measures of Customer, Community, People, Operations and Finance.

Tesco describes the role of its Steering Wheel in its Annual Report for 2010:

"Its prime focus is as a management tool for the company so that there is appropriate balance in the tradeoffs that need to be made between the main levers of management – such as operations measures, financial measures or delivery of customer metrics. It therefore enables the business to be operated and monitored on a balanced basis with due regard to the needs of all stakeholders."[5]

Financial measurement techniques

There are several techniques for determining the financial impact of marketing activities such as communications or promotional campaigns.

Two of the most widely used are return on marketing investment (ROMI) and discounted cash flow (DCF) analysis. Both have their merits, but as Binet and Field's report illustrated, the methodologies and the way they should be used are not always well understood by Marketers and their agencies. Tim Ambler reinforces this point, highlighting, in particular, some pitfalls with the use of ROMI.[6]

The measurement of marketing activities does not have to be complex and some of the best techniques focus on the actual or estimated *net value*

Financial Measures – Examples

ROMI

Return on Marketing Investment (ROMI) is determined by dividing the incremental profit resulting from marketing activity by the cost (i.e. level of marketing spend), and then multiplying by 100. As a result, it is not a ratio that companies should try to maximize since if targets for ROMI are set in isolation, the simplest way to achieve them is by slashing marketing spend levels. And while this might not impact short-term sales, such action can seriously impact longer-term measures of customer loyalty and brand growth.

Discounted Cash Flow

Discounted Cash Flow (DCF) analysis determines the estimated future cash flows from marketing activities and then discounts these by the interest rate over the investment period to determine what future cash flow streams would be worth today – the net present value (NPV) of the investment. This figure can then be used to compare alternative investment opportunities to decide which generates the best value.

generated by marketing activities, based on both short-term impact (i.e. immediate sales uplifts) and longer-term effects (e.g. reflecting the impact of longer-term changes in customer behaviour) less the costs of each activity.

However, whichever methodology is chosen, they all rely on forecasts of the likely incremental revenue streams from future marketing activities. These are calculated by making assumptions about anticipated customer buying behaviours and, as Ambler points out, these can be "highly conjectural". So Marketers need to do all they can to make their forecasts empirically robust and as accurate as possible.

One important way of addressing this challenge is leveraging the advances in data availability and econometric modelling to determine the statistical relationships between known variables such as sales, prices and marketing spend levels. This can provide very compelling predictive data to support the marketing investment proposals most likely to drive growth and should be a key building block of analysis.

Another way of challenging thinking in the area of marketing effectiveness is to look at the work of external organizations such as the Marketing Science Institute and the Ehrenberg-Bass Institute. There is substantial cross-category data now available which can be of genuine value to Marketers as they look for empirical data on which to base their forecasting assumptions.

By being better equipped to assess the estimated financial

We had a conversation with our CEO as part of the budget process this year based on some econometrics about our communications spend. We were able to show, over the past 12–18 months, where we had spent money and the effectiveness of different channels in terms of building sales and in growing brand equity. This kind of work enables you to start informing a qualitative conversation with data, on the basis of which you can play forward into a 'so therefore we should . . .' discussion. Suddenly you have the chief executive's attention. You have a common language, and the common language, quite frankly, is data. The closer that data relates to profit the better.

Martin George, *Managing Director for Group Development, Bupa*

impact of planned marketing activities, and being clearer where resources are being invested and why, Marketers will be able to invest their budgets more effectively and efficiently. Better decisions will be made and valuable learning will accrue about the inter-relationships between marketing activities, customer attitudes and behaviours and business results in the longer term.

"If you can demonstrate that marketing is something that drives your brand and is an ingredient cost in your sales process then you've got twice the leverage and impact on a business. And, if Marketing is much more measurable, accountable and scientific, then it has a much louder voice in the organization."

Dan Cobley, **VP Marketing, Northern and Central Europe, Google**

Measuring Marketing Capability Development

Having shared some perspectives on the main issues and approaches concerning the measurement of *marketing*, let's now move on to explore how the impact of *marketing capability development* can be measured. The issues involved mirror those for measuring the effectiveness of marketing, yet the challenge is even more difficult since capability development is one step further removed from the point of customer impact. This makes it even harder to determine cause and effect in generating value.

We believe that as with measuring marketing, the impact of building marketing capabilities should be measured both at an overall strategic level – in the way that capability development contributes to the organization's overall business objectives, and also at a more micro, operational level – by assessing the contribution of specific capability programme activities and investments.

The Value of Marketing Capability Development

The ultimate business objective for marketing capability development is the same as that of marketing itself – to drive sustainable, profitable, demand-led growth. And to reach meaningful metrics that allow measurement of the most relevant *capability growth drivers*, it is helpful to use the framework of *The Brand Learning Wheel* which defines the core drivers of organizational marketing capability.

Marketing capability measures and metrics

The range of potential capability measurement options is just as extensive as that for marketing itself, but again, at a more strategic level, metrics should be selected to focus on the areas that are most important in driving growth.

Illustrative Marketing Capability Measures and Metrics

- **Organization Driver**, e.g. if the strategy is to move to a more central-ized global structure, metrics might include a reduction in Marketing department numbers in local operating companies.

- **People Driver**, e.g. if the strategy is to move from hiring experienced Marketers from outside the business to start growing more talent from within, metrics may be set for graduate recruits, for internal promotions, or for retention levels.

- **Culture Driver**, e.g. metrics here might include employee engagement scores like com-mitment to the company, opin-ions on the quality of people development programmes, or understanding and commit-ment towards the organization's values and customer proposition.

- **Process Driver**, e.g. if a new common way of working has been intro-duced, metrics could relate to the awareness, adoption and embedding of new processes and tools.

- **Skills Driver**, e.g. metrics need to be set to assess the knowledge, confidence and ultimately the performance and behaviour of Market-ers in priority marketing capability development areas.

Once selected, capability metrics relating to the delivery of the organization's business objectives and strategy should ideally be built into an integrated scorecard that can be assessed and tracked over time.

One of the most difficult areas to measure however, and perhaps the one
that matters most, is the behaviour of Marketers on the job. This relates particularly to the measurement of the *Process* and *Skills Drivers* and was the focus
of the previous chapter on *Driving Embedding*.

Measurement of Marketing Excellence Programme

At the start of its Marketing Excellence Programme, ICI (now
AkzoNobel) established a rigorous approach to measuring on-the-
job Marketing practices and behaviour to assess and track progress
over time. The starting point for its activities was to define clear business objectives as a central focus for the initiative: To turn round
business performance and achieve an average growth rate of over
4% per annum, together with an improved profit margin, over a three-
year period. ICI exceeded these targets in the original three-year time
frame.

Having now rolled out its capability programme as part of the
integration with AkzoNobel, their joint business has since moved on
to achieve sales growth of 9% and profit growth of 13% in 2010.

As CEO David Hamill said when ICI's marketing capability programme was launched, "*In the end our business is about profitable
growth and ultimately the success of the programme will be determined by its impact on growing the business above market rates, with
an incrementally higher rate of profit than rate of sales.*"

To deliver against this challenge, Kerris Bright, CMO at the time,
addressed the need to measure the standards of marketing processes
and skills across the company by creating a "Process Capability Audit
Tool" (PCAT) – since renamed the "Decorative Capability Roadmap".
By defining a spectrum of marketing practices, from "ad hoc" to

"world class" in each key area of marketing activity, teams were assessed and set tangible targets for improvement.

Kerris Bright explains, *"We defined nine critical marketing processes and skill areas – marketing strategy, insight, etc. And we articulated for each of these process areas what "world class" looks like, doing our best to benchmark across other best practice businesses, not just against those in our own categories but against the best in the world."*

That data was aggregated to provide a single metric to indicate and track the overall standard of marketing practices. Over the course of a three-year period, AkzoNobel saw this rise from a level of 3 out of 10 to 5.5.

Having quantitative measures of capability provides a vital link between business objectives and the behaviours of Marketers. Bright describes how the tool is used. *"If we decide that in India we want one and a half times market share leadership and very strong Dulux brand performance against certain equity measures, we can then work out where we stand against this business requirement."*

"The Marketing team then has a very active dialogue about the big things getting in the way of reaching these objectives. Organizationally, in terms of process, what can we improve? Let's say we're 4 out of 10 on a certain dimension, we then put an action plan together to focus on two or three critical elements – getting better at brand equity development and innovation, for example – to raise our practices to say 6 out of 10. These then become set in people's personal targets and action plans and we review them at board level."

As in the case of AkzoNobel, some organizations tackle the challenge of capability measurement by creating bespoke tools to audit marketing behaviour based on internal marketing capability frameworks. Another way is to set up robust quantitative measurement by leveraging an external benchmarking tool such as *Brand Learning Radar* (see Figure 8.3). This has the benefit of being more standardized and therefore allows organizations to benchmark themselves against other companies and to assess performance against the aspiration of achieving 'world class' marketing standards.

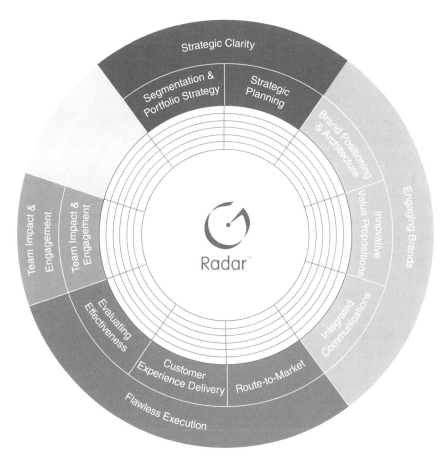

Figure 8.3: *Brand Learning Radar*
Online quantitative tool to assess, track and benchmark marketing capabilities

The Brand Learning Radar

The Brand Learning Radar (see Figure 8.3) is an online tool that enables the fast quantitative assessment, tracking and benchmarking of marketing capabilities, facilitating quantitative comparison across brands, categories, business units and geographies. The methodology is based on the core marketing capability activity areas defined in *The Growth Propeller* (see Chapter 2) and has been developed in collaboration with research experts and the Oxford

Retail Futures Group at Said Business School, Oxford University. (For further information visit www.brandlearning.com)

Marketing capability activities and investments

The same techniques used in marketing (e.g. ROMI or DCF analysis) can, of course, also be applied for the financial assessment of specific marketing capability initiatives.

However, a broader case for investment in marketing capabilities is usually constructed on the basis of either an improvement in marketing effectiveness (i.e. improved top-line growth rates), or improved marketing efficiency (i.e. reduced spend levels or headcount). By working through the discipline of these calculations, the commercial impact of marketing capability development can be assessed, shared and captured for future analysis.

Just as we stressed in the case of marketing activity, however, measurement should not be left until after the event. The advance setting of objectives and metrics is central to the way a capability programme is designed to maximize its chances of success.

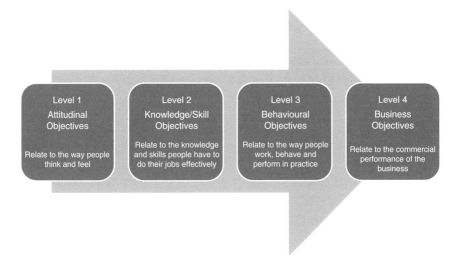

Figure 8.4: *Four Level Measurement Framework*

When designing and assessing specific marketing capability initiatives aimed at the *Process* and *Skill Drivers*, securing and embedding changes in behaviour is the ultimate challenge. With this in mind, it can help to break down the contributing factors behind those behaviour changes by digging down even deeper to assess people's knowledge and attitudes.

The Four Level Measurement Framework in Figure 8.4 is a very useful tool to help set learning objectives as part of a capability programme. It is based on the four-level learning evaluation model first introduced by Dr Don Kirkpatrick.[7]

Measuring Capability Development – Practical Example

To illustrate the use of the four measurement levels in planning a programme, let us assume a need has been identified to improve the quality of a Marketing team's brand communication skills and performance.

- **Level 4: Business Objectives**
  As a context for the programme, what are the *Business Objectives* – the current and future targets for business performance? And if those results are to be achieved, what changes in customer attitudes and behaviours are required, e.g. to improve the conversion of customers from "awareness" to "consideration" or to turn "consideration" into "trial"? What role could communication play in bringing these changes about?

  By clarifying the role that brand communication needs to play in driving business performance, the capability programme can be designed to equip the Marketing team with the specific communications tools and skills needed to improve the effectiveness of campaigns and meet the business objectives.

- **Level 3: Behavioural Objectives**
  How does the way people work, behave and perform in practice need to change? For example, issues may be apparent in the ways Marketers brief their agencies, assess and screen creative proposals, or integrate 360 degree engagement plans with creative idea development.

- **Level 2: Knowledge/Skill Objectives**
  What changes need to take place in the knowledge and skills of Marketers to enable them to perform better? Are they aware of the company's best practice tools? Have they had enough experience and practice in writing creative briefs?

- **Level 1: Attitudinal Objectives**
  Which core individual attitudes need to change that influence the way people think and feel about the creation of brand communications? Do Marketers need to be braver when approving creative work? Or perhaps they need to be more experimental in their use of media channels?

By clarifying the role that brand communication needs to play and the capability development goals at each of the four levels, a much tighter brief for the individual capability development project or initiative can be defined, with appropriate metrics.

Capability development programmes that are planned, developed and measured in this way will be better able to influence the way people work in practice and to connect with the practical challenges and issues that drive broader business issues. They are therefore far more likely to be effective in helping Marketers create better customer value and drive growth.

Setting capability programme investment levels

One key question facing leadership teams is how much should the organization invest to build its marketing capabilities? This is a tough question because marketing capability programmes vary considerably in scope, ambition and scale. At one end of the spectrum are the global organizational change initiatives like the Unilever Marketing Academy and the Diageo Way of Brand Building which cost millions with sustained activities over many years. At the other are highly focused programmes that target specific skill gaps in small teams of people with far more modest budgets.

There are many ways in which budget decisions are approached in practice. How much was spent last year? How much budget is available? What needs to be achieved, by when, and how much will it cost? What's left in the Marketing or HR "pot"?

However, we recommend that the best way to set a marketing capability development budget is for the Marketing, Human Resources and Finance leaders to meet and jointly address the following questions – all of which should ideally be discussed when defining the Marketing Capability Strategy and Plan in the *Define Strategy* stage of marketing capability development (see Chapter 4).

Capability Budget Parameters – Key Questions

- What marketing capability improvements are needed to deliver the business objectives and strategy?

- Is focus needed on all aspects of *The Brand Learning Wheel* or just specific aspects of it (i.e. on processes, skills, organization, people and/ or culture)?

- What scale of programme will best deliver these improvements?

- What is the level of investment cost?

- What resources are available or can be secured?

- Who is (or should be) the budget holder?

- What can be achieved for the amount invested?

- What will be the estimated net value generated?

This chapter has covered some of the many different approaches to measuring the impact of both marketing and marketing capability development. One final point deserves particular emphasis. By adopting a more rigorous approach to measurement and bringing measurement to the *start* of the marketing capability development process – as the strategy is defined, rather than after the initiatives have been implemented – the impact of *marketing*, *marketers*, and of *marketing capability development* as the core *growth drivers* will all be considerably enhanced.

In the next chapter of *The Growth Drivers*, we will now move on to how companies can mobilize their resources to build the marketing capabilities needed to drive growth in practice.

CHAPTER 8 – AT A GLANCE

- The measurement of both marketing and of marketing capability development is changing with advances in technology, but ultimately the key issue is their impact in creating better customer value and driving profitable growth.

- The challenges that hold people, teams and organizations back from being able to demonstrate marketing effectiveness stem from five key pitfalls – we call these *The Measurement Traps*: the *marketing = communications* trap; the *art vs. science* trap; the *data vs. insights* trap; the *time-lag* trap and the *commercial knowledge* trap.

- Marketers must select metrics that relate to the drivers of profitable business growth and ensure that customer measures are included in the overall company balanced scorecard of measures.

- The best measurement techniques focus on the actual or estimated *net value* generated by marketing activities based on both short-term and longer-term impact.

- By being better equipped to assess the estimated financial impact of planned marketing activities, Marketers will invest their budgets more effectively and efficiently.

- The ultimate business objectives for marketing capability development should be the same as those for marketing itself – business growth and profitability.

- *The Brand Learning Wheel* can be used as a framework for marketing capability measurement because it captures the core marketing capability drivers of business performance.

- Specific marketing learning programmes can be planned using measures at four levels: Business Objectives, Behavioural Objectives, Knowledge/Skill Objectives and Attitudinal Objectives.

- Investment in capability initiatives can be justified either by an increase in marketing effectiveness (i.e. increased top-line growth) or an increase in marketing efficiency (i.e. reduced marketing spend or headcount).

- By adopting a more rigorous approach to measurement and bringing measurement to the start of the marketing capability development process, the impact of *marketing, marketers,* and of *marketing capability development* as growth drivers will all be considerably enhanced.

Notes

1 "Ending the war between sales and marketing", by P. Kotler, N. Rackham and S. Krishnaswami, *Harvard Business Review*, July 2006.
2 "Branding in the Digital Age", by David C. Edelman, *Harvard Business Review*, December 2010.
3 "Kraft data tool part of new marketing approach", by Rosie Baker and Lucy Handley, *Marketing Week*, 8th August 2011.
4 *Marketing in the Era of Accountability* by Les Binet and Peter Field, Institute of Practitioners of Advertising.
5 Tesco Annual Report 2010.
6 *Marketing and the Bottom Line* by Tim Ambler, Financial Times/Pearson Education
7 Evaluating Training Programs: The Four Levels, by Donald L. Kirkpatrick and James M. Kirkpatrick.

Chapter 9

Driving growth is not a one-off task – it is an *ongoing* imperative. It is an essential means of sustaining the support of shareholders, creating value for customers, expanding opportunities for employees and making an important contribution to society as a whole. We believe that one of the best ways to drive that growth is mobilizing resources to build, embed and drive improvements in marketing capabilities.

So far in *The Growth Drivers*, we have explored the nature of the growth challenge, how marketing drives growth and what building marketing capabilities involves in practice. We have explained how to *define strategy* in capability development, how to *develop solutions* to address the core drivers of capability around *The Brand Learning Wheel*, and how to *drive embedding* of new processes, skills and ways of working. And we have looked at some of the challenges of *measuring impact*, both of marketing and of marketing capability development.

“We are well aware of the need to create sustainable top and bottom line growth. Responsible, profitable growth is at the root of long-term value creation.

The success of any organization is a function of the strength of its people. If we aspire to more than double the size of this company, we need to be sure we have the skill set and capabilities to deliver.”

Paul Polman, *CEO, Unilever*

But there remains one important area to address in this penultimate chapter: how should companies *mobilize resources* to build the marketing capabilities they need to drive growth in practice? What's the best way to build a dedicated Marketing Excellence team or 'Academy'? What about options for organizations with more modest ambitions or limited resources? How can capability development be sustained over time?

Mobilizing for Growth

There are many different ways in which companies can mobilize their resources to enable Marketers, and the organization as a whole, to work more effectively and efficiently to create better customer value. These vary widely depending on the scale of growth ambition, the extent of the capability issues and the scope of available resources.

Some companies opt for fully dedicated in-house teams staffed with experienced Marketing executives, working with a range of external marketing and learning experts. At the other end of the spectrum, the task can be the responsibility of a single Learning & Development manager striving to drive change as one part of their broad cross-functional learning remit.

Let's begin by looking in depth at how marketing capability development is handled at Unilever, a global consumer packaged goods company renowned for its commitment to marketing excellence.

 Unilever's Growth Ambition

Outlining his strategy for growth in a speech to the AGM in 2010, Paul Polman, CEO Unilever, referenced growth over 25 times. Growth has been at the heart of Unilever's strategy for many years, but in the fast moving markets in which it operates, and with highly active competitors, it is not easy to sustain. Yet in 2009 Unilever finished the year with two-thirds of its total business growing, leading to a 50% growth in its share price. Unilever's total shareholder return reached the top third of its peer group, at around 20%.

Back in the late 1990s, Unilever moved away from a decentralized approach to market and brand development, driven by the need to increase its impact, enhance efficiency and reduce costs by better leveraging its brand assets globally. This change led to a new organizational requirement to build and align marketing capabilities internationally to create a system capable of collaborating across international boundaries and driving growth on a global scale.

The Unilever Marketing Academy

The Unilever Marketing Academy was set up in 1998 to help drive this process. More than 10 years on, it remains an example of leading marketing capability practice. The unit has evolved, both in terms of role and structure. Today it comprises a team of 25 people led by a Marketing VP and supported by a network of regional champions, consultants and agencies, but its contribution in pioneering new thinking and building the marketing capabilities to drive Unilever's growth remains as important as ever.

In the years prior to its creation, Unilever had operated with a head office *Marketing Projects Group* (MPG), whose role was to support the global network with leading edge knowledge development and experimentation. However, as MPG itself identified, Unilever needed a more effective means of transferring and embedding learning throughout its global Marketing community. At the same time, the senior leaders in Unilever's global category teams had started an ambitious rethink about the capabilities needed to build global brands more effectively.

So, in 1998 the Unilever Marketing Academy was set up and Andy Bird was commissioned to build a team to develop and sustain global marketing capabilities to support the strategic and operational growth agenda of the business. It was this team that Mhairi McEwan was invited to join and where we, the co-authors first met (see Introduction – Our Story).

Mobilizing resources to build marketing capabilities

The commitment and resource devoted by many global organizations such as Unilever, P&G, Diageo, AstraZeneca and others to building their marketing capabilities over the years has been very significant and we will explore some of the main lessons and practical insights from their experience throughout this chapter.

But regardless of whether the scale of investment is in the millions or is far more modest in its scope and ambition, we have found that the key principles behind the successful mobilization of resources for marketing capability development remain the same.

The Five Building Blocks

To summarize these insights, we believe that there are *five building blocks* (see Figure 9.1) that describe how companies should approach the mobilization of resources to build marketing capabilities.

Let's look at each of these *five building blocks* in turn, sharing insights and practical examples of how marketing capability resources have been mobilized in a wide range of organizations.

Building block 1 – Establish clear leadership and governance

As we have emphasized throughout *The Growth Drivers*, if there is one factor that makes the most difference to the success of a marketing capability development initiative, it is securing the alignment, commitment and engagement of the senior business and Marketing leaders. There is general consensus that this is vital to ensure that marketing capability development is focused directly

1. Establish clear leadership and governance

2. Define the role of the Marketing Capability Team

3. Build a specialist Team of respected Marketing and HR executives

4. Engage and align with operational Marketing teams

5. Set up resources to drive embedding

Figure 9.1: *Mobilizing capability resources – five building blocks*

on meeting the business objectives and strategy, to ensure clear decision making and alignment, and to release the necessary resources – people, time and budget.

 Unilever Marketing Council

In the months leading up to the creation of the Unilever Marketing Academy, a senior group of thought leaders from Unilever's global businesses were given the challenge of developing a strategy to *"reinvigorate Unilever's traditionally strong approach to marketing training and development"*.

This group created the initial agenda for change, but it was clear that to make a real impact on the business, the leadership needed to reside with senior Marketers tied in directly to Unilever's functional reporting lines.

A new steering group was formed called the "Marketing Council" to ensure the Marketing Academy's work was linked directly to the needs of the business and had the commitment in terms of both management time and budgets. The Council was made up of Marketing leaders from each Regional Business Group, from each Global Category Team, and by HR leaders.

"The single most important factor is senior management sponsorship and working with the grain of the business. When I look at what has got traction in our business, made an impact, built our reputation – it's where we are really delivering against the change agenda of the business. **"**

Helen Lewis, *Consumer Insight & Marketing*
Strategy Director, Unilever Marketing Academy

Sponsorship

The crucial factor behind the early success of both the Marketing Council and the Marketing Academy was the work done to build support and alignment across Unilever's top management. Two sponsors led the charge: Keith Weed, now Unilever's Chief Marketing and Communications Officer (then an Academy sponsor as chairman of Unilever's Elida Faberge division) and Fergus Balfour, then Head of Corporate HR (previously a senior Marketer in Unilever's detergents business). They personally visited each member of Unilever's board and each Regional Business Group president to seek their input and win their active endorsement to establish the new organizational arrangements.

The "Marketing Council" had the authority to make decisions on behalf of all the divisions in Unilever's business. The group also had the authority to commit to the launch and implementation of initiatives and to the investment of time and money.

Today, the Marketing Academy's steering group combines the top regional executive vice presidents (EVPs) with the top category EVPs – evolving as the business itself has evolved.

"We continue to liaise very closely with the most senior Marketers across Unilever to ensure our agenda is aligned with the priorities of the business. **"**

Ros Walker, *VP Marketing Capability, Unilever*

CEO sponsorship and commitment

Given the value of effective marketing as a way to create better customer value and drive sustainable, profitable growth, CEOs often take personal responsibility for inspiring and sponsoring marketing capability development.

 CEO Support

Niall FitzGerald, then Unilever's chairman, personally launched the Unilever Marketing Academy by inviting every Unilever Marketer to visit the new Academy intranet site with an email. The message from him had the title *"Salary Increase"*, but once opened it said *"Gotcha. I thought that would get your attention!"* Niall went on to explain that while he was not actually increasing everyone's salary, Unilever was investing in a major new programme to build their professional marketing skills. His approach certainly cut through!

Leadership team role

Active ongoing commitment and involvement from business leaders is critical for genuine change to be delivered within an organization. However, the leaders of the Marketing function also need to play a central role in prioritizing marketing capability needs and in actively shaping the strategic programme of activity to address them.

Once the capability strategy has been defined (i.e. vision, goals, scope, plan), the leadership team will need to meet regularly to inspire, align, steer and make decisions. These will include alignment on "common ways of working" and any mandated tools, as well as to debate, sign off and

" When we announced our Q3 results, for the very first time ever, marketing was identified as a core strength of Aviva and that was on record and identified as one of the core capabilities that is going to help Aviva grow in future. So for me the fact that the chief executive is prepared to make such a statement is evidence that Marketing is seen as a key driver of future growth."

Amanda Mackenzie,
Chief Marketing Officer, Aviva

plan for the necessary resources. They will also need to commit to contribute to best practice – ideas, knowledge and case studies as well as people and budget to implement the agreed capability plan.

Most importantly, Marketing leaders need to actively champion marketing excellence in *everything* they do. This includes being role models for new ways of working, coaching and inspiring their teams to both contribute and benefit from best practice. They also need to sponsor and role model participation in capability programmes and initiatives – which in the case of initiatives leveraging digital and social technologies, may be highly challenging.

Finally, the leadership team should meet often to review programme effectiveness against agreed KPIs, to elicit business feedback and to provide ongoing challenge to help keep thinking current, sustain momentum and build competitive edge.

> *"[Our CEO] could see the role that Marketing needed to play to deliver our business objectives and the mismatch with where we were. He recognized that without strategic marketing thinking we wouldn't win."*
>
> Kerris Bright,
> former CMO, AkzoNobel
> (now CMO, Ideal Standard)

Marketing Leadership Team – role in driving capability initiatives

- Align the marketing capability strategy with priority business needs.
- Allocate the right people, support resources and financial resources.
- Shape and approve any new process principles and tools.
- Actively participate in key learning programmes and events (*not just the opening speech!*).
- Champion and inspire application in day-to-day operations.
- Review progress and shape future strategy development.

In many organizations, a marketing capability leadership team already exists to plan and integrate marketing strategy, activities and to manage people. The capability agenda fits naturally into the topics these groups discuss. However, in others, such leadership teams may either not exist or be a relatively recent development. The need to drive a corporate marketing capability development agenda may often be the catalyst to form global or cross-division Marketing leadership teams for the first time.

Throughout *The Growth Drivers*, we have reinforced the point that world-class approaches to marketing capability development take a *holistic* approach. They leverage all the core capability drivers described in *The Brand Learning Wheel* including those in the "bottom half" of the wheel typically managed by HR, i.e. the *Organization, People* and *Culture Drivers* of capability.

By engaging HR in the leadership team, strategy in these areas can be seamlessly integrated with other initiatives in the *Process* and *Skill Drivers*. HR leaders can also play a crucial role in engaging the rest of the organization and in planning and supporting the implementation of learning programmes.

One important responsibility of the leadership team is to be aware of initiatives being pioneered across the business to spot the ideas with potential to be shared more broadly.

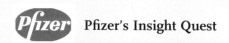 Pfizer's Insight Quest

Pfizer's "Insight Quest" capability programme, designed to transform the approach of its brand teams to generating and applying customer insight, was not a "top down" initiative. The initial impetus came from innovative work done by one brand team which was then rolled out internationally.

As Craig Scott, former Head of Speciality Analytics for Pfizer Europe, describes, "we explained what insight really meant, showed some examples, and demonstrated how it could not only transform a brand, it could also transform a 'brand team' in terms of it providing the rocket fuel of enthusiasm and belief".

The senior leadership within Pfizer responded extremely positively, and recognized the traditional approach to training across the organization would not be sufficient. *"The typical way of rolling out new initiatives was to do a sheep dip, train people over a couple of days and then send them back to their desks expecting the world to change"*, explains Scott. *"In this case, we needed to do things differently. We wanted to make it more of a 'movement', a cult that would start small but get bigger and bigger."*

Craig Scott remembers the moment when top level support was achieved for the new initiative. *"It was one of those full-on boardroom experiences with a guy who is in charge of a $16 billion division. I was on my feet, 'pom poms' out, explaining the insight hook on which our brand strategy will be hung and how we discovered it. They loved it and that was when we got the approval and support we needed to roll things out globally."*

Building block 2 – Define the role of the marketing capability team

Once the leadership for marketing capability development has been established, the next mobilization challenge is to determine the role and make-up of the operational resources needed to develop and deliver marketing capability programmes in practice.

 Unilever Marketing Academy

Initially, the idea at the heart of the Unilever Marketing Academy's role was to provide *marketing fuel injection* to enhance the performance of Unilever's business. Its long-term vision was *"to equip Unilever's marketers with the skills they need to achieve outstanding performance at each stage of their careers."* Today its purpose remains *"giving marketers the capability and confidence to outperform."*

When first established, the Academy's immediate focus was on two strategic priorities. The first was the launch, rollout and embedding of consistent, advanced ways of working in brand positioning and brand communication throughout the global Marketing organization. The other was to define a tailored, comprehensive marketing curriculum and establish a consistent global Marketing Foundation Programme for all new graduate recruits joining Unilever around the world.

The Academy's role

The role of the Unilever Marketing Academy was designed to be that of an "engine", driving forward the capabilities and performance of Unilever's Marketers over time and specifically:

- To seek out and capture best practice marketing processes, tools, techniques and case studies, both internally and externally.
- To translate this knowledge into accessible, relevant and practical support for Unilever's Marketing community.
- To share learning and embed new ways of working in Marketers' everyday activities and behaviour.

Defining marketing capability team leadership

The sponsorship for most marketing capability teams is usually the Chief Marketing Officer, or another senior and influential member of the Marketing leadership team. To make change happen, they often appoint a respected, senior Marketing leader with both experience and expertise within the organization to lead marketing capability development on a *dedicated* basis – often called a Marketing Capability Director, Marketing Excellence Director or VP Marketing Capability.

❝Things definitely need to be steered by senior Marketers as they are much closer to the business agenda, but you also need dedicated people to develop and drive the implementation of capability programmes systematically across the business.❞

Karen Jeffery, *Global Marketing Capability Leader, AkzoNobel*

Marketing capability team responsibilities

The extent to which companies have dedicated teams working on marketing capability development varies widely. The main influencing factor is the scope of the marketing capability strategy and plan agreed in the *Define Strategy* stage (see Chapter 4).

To determine the right approach, the first step is to review and agree the responsibilities of the team by reference to the core drivers of capability outlined in *The Brand Learning Wheel* (see Figure 9.2).

It is important to emphasize that not every marketing capability team takes on all of the tasks identified here: some are a more important part of their role than others. Some tasks may be led by HR, some may be part of cross-functional initiatives and others will be led by separate dedicated working groups. But it is essential to create mechanisms for senior Marketers to influence all these activities to ensure an integrated, holistic approach.

Marketing capability team models

Looking at the approaches being used across a wide range of different organizations, we have identified two broad models for marketing capability teams:

Figure 9.2: *Marketing capability team – Potential responsibilities*

1. Dedicated capability teams

Led by a Marketing Capability VP/Director (or Marketing Excellence Director) these teams may have several members (5–25) and are appointed to drive the overall functional capability agenda. Their role is to liaise with general managers, Marketing and HR leaders on strategy development and to coordinate and support the work of operational teams to develop and deliver initiatives. They also draw on the support of specialist external agencies, specialist consultancies, business schools etc. who provide focused resource on pioneering new marketing and learning ideas and for the cascade and embedding of change initiatives.

2. Extended capability teams

In this model, the dedicated team of marketing capability specialists is smaller (1–5 people). In some cases the team might consist of just one leader backed up with some administrative support staff. The responsibility for capability development is allocated across a group of line managers alongside their normal operational responsibilities. More extensive use tends to be made of third party consultants and suppliers to contribute to the strategy, provide external best practice knowledge, develop content and provide expert resources for facilitation and embedding.

 AkzoNobel Marketing Academy

AkzoNobel's Marketing Academy team works alongside or supports functional leaders in the development of new processes and tools, but takes the lead in introducing these to the wider community. In AkzoNobel's case, the "skills leaders" are all in line management roles and supporting capability work as just one part of their responsibilities.

❝ *I lead the Academy reporting to the CMO, but I have regular dialogues with the Regional Marketing Directors to ensure we are addressing their issues. We also have a number of functional skill leaders who we support in developing any new processes or tools.* **❞**

Karen Jeffery, *Global Marketing Capability Leader, AkzoNobel*

Building block 3 – Build a specialist team of respected Marketing and HR executives

Once the role of the marketing capability team has been agreed, a critical success factor in setting it up effectively is to staff it with the right team members. A blend of skills and experience is needed, including experienced Marketers, HR/Learning experts and efficient administrative support staff.

Based on our experience, having an effective Marketing leader is critical and the characteristics they need are outlined below:

Marketing Capability Leader and Team – Ideal Profile

- Significant commercial marketing experience – they appreciate what excellent marketing is and how it works in practice; with the gravitas to engage top Marketing, HR and other business leaders with confidence, credibility and respect.

- Passion for learning – they understand the power of learning and the impact capability development can have in driving changes in the ways people, teams and organizations work in practice.

- Strong conceptual skills – they can simplify and distil complex information, models and frameworks into practical tools and learning solutions.

- Excellent company knowledge – they understand how the organization works, how decisions get taken, and how to leverage the drivers of capability and of business growth.

- Strong influencing skills – they can network, engage and influence people across the business, gain the trust of Marketing leaders and the respect of operational Marketers.

When recruiting for a marketing capability role internally, a possible obstacle to overcome is that sometimes these jobs can be perceived as being of lower career value than more operational marketing roles. Positive factors to emphasize include the opportunities to extend the depth and breadth of marketing expertise, access to marketing best practice and playing to personal strengths and passions.

❝I enjoy it because when you do a brand job, you're so busy and focused on your own brand you don't get a chance to step out. Doing this job, I have learnt such a lot and when I go back to a brand I know I will be able to do a much better job.❞

Tim Bailey, *Head of Marketing Academy, AstraZeneca*

Marketing capability development leaders who are dedicated to this role (as opposed to a shared role) can give it much greater focus, create greater momentum and enable the business to build its expertise and experience in sustainable marketing capability development. They also play an important role in integrating different project work streams, in aligning marketing language, tools and techniques and in phasing workloads and implementation timetables.

"The corporate business deliverables are obviously essential, but for me the real joy is seeing people come out of a workshop session feeling energized about what they've learned and what they can now achieve."

Karen Jeffery, *Global Marketing Capability Leader, AkzoNobel*

Building block 4 – Engage and align with operational Marketing teams

One of the main functions of a marketing capability team is to plan the implementation and embedding of new ways of working across the company. Although they will also play a central role in its delivery, the likelihood is that other executives will have to be heavily involved to enable full-scale programme rollout.

As covered in Chapter 7, *Driving Embedding* includes activities such as the cascade of new processes and tools, internal communication about a restructured organization, the launch of new recruitment campaigns, the introduction of intranet-based e-learning and the ongoing implementation of marketing capability programmes to change behaviours or build skills. The type of activities will obviously depend on the strategy and scope of the programme and each will require different types of resources, including support from other functions such as HR and IT.

One key success factor for effective marketing capability teams is the focus on connecting the marketing capability team with operational Marketing teams in different departments, business units, or geographies. This usually works best as a cascade led by the global/regional/local Marketing leadership teams. In larger organizations, the support of a network of marketing capabil-

ity champions, set up across business units, divisions and operating companies, can be important in helping to manage the cascade and champion new
ways of working.

In effect, these capability champions form an extended internal network
of the central marketing capability team. They are not necessarily full-time
roles, but without them it is very difficult for a Marketing Academy or
Marketing Excellence Team to deliver a programme to embed tangible
changes in marketing ways of working throughout the organization.

Capability champions

The roles that local/business unit capability champions can perform
include:

- Communicating and championing marketing capability programme
  strategy and plans (in partnership with the local/business unit
  leader).

- Pulling together capability development programme embedding plans
  based on the needs of the business unit.

- Giving ongoing feedback to enhance best practice and share knowledge based on experience of using processes and tools in practice.

- Providing relevant local insight, case studies and competitor perspectives for use in capability development programmes.

- Identifying and briefing internal and external facilitators and sponsors
  to support embedding, e.g. at workshops and events, online, etc.

- Setting up experiential learning activities with external experts and
  advisors, e.g. specialist consultancies and agencies.

- Assessing programme effectiveness and future development needs.

Pfizer's Insight Champions

To support Pfizer's "Insight Quest", a team of carefully chosen "insight champions" was appointed across different brand teams to drive the programme's implementation throughout the company.

❝Insight champions have been selected who have an insightful approach to life, rather than on the basis of their position or level in the organization. They were hand-picked to help spread the word. They were engaged, enthusiastic and absolutely on board in terms of creating a new approach to marketing. It was a big ask in terms of time commitment. The champions have done a great job. Literally every brand team is doing an 'Insight Quest' in Europe, North America and Asia Pacific.**❞**

Craig Scott, *former Head of Speciality Analytics, Pfizer Europe*

Building block 5 – Set up resources to drive embedding

Once the leadership team is established, the marketing capability team set up and, if appropriate, a network of champions is in place, the next consideration is to confirm the resources needed to manage the launch and embedding of new processes, skills and behaviours.

The *Develop Solutions* stage of capability development is a major task for the marketing capability team, even with the support of subject matter experts and external specialists and agencies. But an even more difficult challenge, as covered in Chapter 7, is that of *Driving Embedding* of new ways of working to accelerate brand and business growth. This is where managers

❝*If we are initiating something big and we are engaging our Marketing counterparts, we can't assume their bosses will know and so we are finding we have to manage stakeholders in many directions.***❞**

Fiona McAnena, *Global Brand Director, Bupa*

across the organization need to be actively engaged to plan, implement and sustain a full-scale programme rollout and follow-up, to ensure changes get implemented in practice.

Embedding models

The resources required for *Driving Embedding* largely depend on the embedding channels identified in the marketing capability strategy and plan (see Define Strategy – Chapter 4). In planning these resources, organizations have tended to choose between one of two models, with most preferring a hybrid between the two.

In one model, a network of *internal* facilitators is developed to play a core role in learning delivery. Support comes from specialist marketing learning experts, whose contribution is to provide expert learning session design, learning and coaching techniques, facilitation support, support with delivery cascade, coordination of events and logistics and specialist e-learning support in the form of e-tutorials, portals and virtual classrooms.

> *Leader-led learning increases the chances of implementation because the leaders are directly involved in the thinking and rollout within the business. Secondly, it also demonstrates to everyone the cultural importance of learning and capability development.*
>
> Ros Walker, *VP Marketing Capability and Academy, Unilever*

However, many organizations do not have either the operational capacity or the inclination to divert their most experienced Marketers from operational line roles to intensive internal capability development. In the second model, a much smaller internal team directs a network of external experts, agencies, consultancies and third party strategic partners in an outsourced approach to capability development. A small central team plays a coordinating role across other agencies to manage the overall programme and facilitate face-to-face and virtual learning sessions.

In this model, active coaching and support is given to internal line managers and subject matter experts with the emphasis being to *coach and embed* new ways of working on the job, rather than manage the launch phase. Again in this model, a blend of e-learning solutions is usually developed and maintained centrally.

Most organizations adopt a hybrid of the two models, leveraging the internal knowledge and experience of senior line managers and a core team of capability champions and subject matter experts, together with the wider perspective and facilitation expertise of specialist external marketing, learning and capability experts.

As the blend of available learning channels fragments and becomes more specialist, external perspective and a wide network of resources is valuable to help organizations keep pace with the breathtaking pace of change.

Mobilizing to drive growth sustainably

One of the most important characteristics of *The 3D Approach* to marketing capability development is to emphasize that marketing capability development is not a one-off activity and requires a sustained, ongoing *organizational commitment.*

As we have demonstrated throughout *The Growth Drivers*, building marketing capabilities is about far more than "training". Its remit extends far beyond setting up marketing conferences, events, workshops or a "marketing university". And it should never be an isolated HR or learning and development initiative disconnected from the goals of the senior Marketing practitioners.

What marketing capability development does require is a deep understanding of, and respect for, the *marketing growth drivers* – those core marketing activities captured in *The Growth Propeller*. Success is dependent on the momentum and direction they bring to help *Marketers* be more effective at *marketing*, and to engage the rest of the organization in creating better customer value to drive demand-led growth.

To build and sustain the world-class marketing capabilities needed to drive that growth requires an ongoing, holistic focus that leverages all the core drivers of marketing capability, i.e. *Processes, Skills, Organization, People and Culture*. It also requires a systematic approach throughout the 3D's of capability development to create ongoing and tangible changes in the way Marketers work in practice.

At its heart, marketing capability development is the ongoing process of creating sustainable changes in the attitudes, skills and behaviours of Marketers, of Marketing teams and of organizations as a whole, to enable and equip them to create better customer value and drive growth. Ultimately – it's not a destination but an ongoing growth journey.

In the words of CMO Kerris Bright, with her extensive global marketing experience across organizations as diverse as Unilever, ICI Paints, AkzoNobel, British Airways and Ideal Standard, "The capability journey's been really exciting, but really challenging too. It has been a life of big highs and some real lows that you have to get yourself through, so I think it is for the resilient and not for the faint-hearted. But when you start to see an organization shift and you see that you're solving issues that you've seen alive in the organization, it's really, really rewarding."

CHAPTER 9 – AT A GLANCE

- Driving growth is an *ongoing* imperative not a one-off task. One of the best ways to drive demand-led growth is mobilizing resources to build, embed and drive improvements in marketing capabilities.

- There are many ways to organize resources to build marketing capabilities, depending on the scale of growth ambition, the extent of the capability issues and the scope of resources available.

- The five key building blocks to systematically build marketing capabilities are: clear leadership and governance, a well-defined marketing capability team role, respected team members, engagement with operational teams and the right resource levels to drive embedding.

- Marketing capability development is most effective when CEOs take personal responsibility for inspiring and sponsoring capability initiatives to drive growth.

- A Marketing leadership team representing the function is an essential prerequisite for alignment on the capability strategy and to champion its implementation in the business.

- Effective marketing capability development needs a respected Marketing leader with commercial marketing experience, the gravitas to engage Marketing leaders, a passion for marketing and for learning, strong conceptual skills, excellent corporate awareness and strong influencing skills.

- There is a growing trend towards the creation of empowered, dedicated marketing capability teams, often referred to as marketing excellence or academy teams.

- The organization needs to create an active network of local/business unit leaders, capability experts, internal and external specialists, subject matter experts, champions, facilitators and logistics support to effectively drive embedding.

- Marketing capability development is not a one-off activity but needs to be sustained over time to enable Marketers to create better customer value and engage the rest of the organization to drive sustainable, profitable, demand-led growth.

- Ultimately, marketing capability development is not a destination...it's an ongoing journey towards sustained growth.

Chapter 10

As we have reinforced throughout *The Growth Drivers*, there has never been a more challenging time to be a Marketer – nor, one could argue, a more exciting time. The advent of social media and the breathtaking pace of technological advances have brought about a seismic shift towards "people power" in a way unprecedented in previous generations. The full impact of this shift remains to be seen, but it is already transforming, not just business and other organizations, but the political, social, environmental and economic fabric of nations across the globe.

A World of Astounding Change

Organizations everywhere are grappling to keep pace with the immense challenges posed by the digital revolution, by the drive for global efficiencies and scale, and by the extreme urgency of delivering enhanced environmental sustainability.

As these macro factors play out, the relationships and dynamics between organizations and their customers are also undergoing a parallel transformation. Challenges include the complexity of coherent brand communication through fragmented social and digital channels; the extraordinary pace with which customers can communicate with each other; the necessity of collaboration to secure the best ideas, the fastest solutions and the greatest economies of scale.

Factors that could once be reasonably controlled like data security, confidentiality and privacy are becoming risk factors of significant proportions. The "mind race" between providers, competitors and sophisticated hackers is a fierce battle that will influence the lives of millions of people worldwide.

The Opportunities for Marketing

Yet, however challenging these developments, as in many earlier periods of revolution they are creating enormous growth opportunities for organizations to seize the moment and actively shape their future. And one imperative prevails · · · the organizations that win will be the ones that stick very close to the people who ultimately decide their future – their customers. So, the organizations that will thrive in these new surroundings will be those that constantly evolve to find new, innovative ways to create and sustain better customer value.

Because at their core, whatever the availability of technology, organizations are still financed and led by people, managed by people, staffed by people and they serve to deliver products, goods and services to *other* people. And people are not mechanical beings – they have physical, intellectual, emotional and spiritual needs. And when set free to make choices, people balance up competing offers and choose what best meets their needs at any point of time. They make choices based on their assessment of value – the extent to which products and services offer them the benefits they need or want for a price they are willing and able to pay.

For the world as a whole, people are increasingly asking if the price of environmental harm is worth paying for consumerism. As the balance starts to shift and the benefits of environmental safety and security become paramount, the value equation will change and customers will seek "value" in new benefits like mental and physical health or environmental sustainability that meet their needs and wants on new terms.

The organizations with the foresight to stay ahead of this curve by orienting their entire business around the search to provide enhanced customer value – ever changing, ever evolving – will be those who succeed in driving growth. And they will deserve it. The rest will be left behind.

Marketing is not a byword for consumerism. Marketing can also be philanthropic, it can be environmentally sensitive and it can lead to sustainable commercial decisions. To deride marketing and Marketers for being overly commercial or insensitive to wider considerations of sustainability risks sidelining a discipline of great value to the world in future. Marketing has an important role to play in helping to influence the products and services that are made available to people, as well as the attitudes and buying behaviours of customers.

Effective marketing is a discipline that can help any organization orient itself to the constant search to deliver better value to its customers, shareholders, employees and other key stakeholders, including society as a whole.

Sustaining the Engine to Drive Growth

So we believe now is the time for Marketers to step up and embrace their strategic role as *Growth Drivers*. They should work tirelessly to establish and sustain a compelling customer-focused vision for their organizations. They should inspire and engage people both inside and outside the organization to deliver that value and to constantly re-evaluate and assess their delivery of value as the external landscape changes.

To deliver momentum and growth they must first build the *engine* to drive that growth. The growth itself will come from effective marketing, but it is the capabilities needed to drive better marketing performance that will provide the energy and momentum for success. When the drive for growth is taking place in the context of the astounding pace of changes we have described, the building of marketing capabilities becomes not a "should do", but a "must do", for the very survival of an organization.

Getting Started

The Growth Drivers and the thoughts we have introduced in this book have been all about growth and the role that effective marketing and marketing capability development play in enabling organizations to drive that growth. Its focus has been on explaining what world-class marketing really is and how it works in practice, explaining the unique role played by *marketing*, by *marketers* and the role of *marketing capabilities*. We have also outlined in detail how *any* organization can build the marketing capabilities needed to deliver better customer value and thereby drive growth.

In closing, we will share one final tool to help readers make the first step towards a transformation in the marketing capabilities of their own organizations and to help define their growth driving agenda. This tool is just a simple springboard for CEOs, CMOs, Marketing and HR directors, or indeed anyone within an organization who wants to challenge the approach to capability building and bring about a growth transformation from within.

> *A journey of a thousand miles begins with a single step*
>
> Lao Tzu *(604 BC–531 BC)*

Fit for Growth tool

This *Fit for Growth* tool, with its 15 simple but far-reaching questions, has been developed to help readers probe the status of marketing and the quality of the marketing capability strategy and plan within their organization. Together with the guidance we have given throughout *The Growth Drivers*, this will also help business leaders identify how to create a more powerful strategic plan of action to build the marketing capabilities needed to create better customer value and drive sustainable, profitable demand-led growth.

Marketing Capability: Fit for Growth Tool

Allocate a score of between 1 and 5 to each of the following questions, based on a scale of 1 (Not at all) to 5 (Completely) and then refer to the scores and recommendations on page 286.

Stakeholders

Rating scale

Question 1: How well does the CEO/board understand the function of Marketing?

1   2   3   4   5

Is Marketing as a function well understood? Is there an understanding of the broader role of marketing and what it is capable of delivering to the organization in driving growth? Are the differences between Marketing with a big "M" (function) and marketing with a small "m" (whole organization) appreciated?

Question 2: How committed are the CEO and CMO to the need to build marketing capabilities to drive growth?

1   2   3   4   5

Is senior management commitment deep or superficial? Is it clear who the marketing capability development sponsors are? Is there broad functional, geographic, cross-business unit and cross-functional alignment to the needs for effective strategic marketing?

Vision

Question 3: How clear is the vision for the role of   I 2 3 4 5
Marketing in my organization?

Given the organization's overall objectives and strategy,
how clear is the vision for the role of Marketing in
driving growth? What specific role should Marketers
adopt in future to help drive profitable growth by
creating value for customers?

Question 4: How well defined is the scope of   I 2 3 4 5
marketing capability development?

Is it clear what is in and out of scope in terms of
marketing capability development? How holistic is the
focus? Are capability growth-driving initiatives operating
across the entire *Brand Learning Wheel* influencing
Processes, Organization, People, Skills and Culture, or is
attention focused in specific areas?

Situation analysis

Question 5: How strong is the organization overall
and in terms of each key driver of marketing
capability around *The Brand Learning Wheel*?

(a) Processes   I 2 3 4 5
(b) Skills   I 2 3 4 5
(c) People   I 2 3 4 5
(d) Organization   I 2 3 4 5
(e) Culture   I 2 3 4 5
(f) Overall integration around the "wheel"   I 2 3 4 5

What are the organization's strengths and weaknesses in each key driver of capability? What are the key drivers and barriers of success? Where is the greatest growth-driving challenge?

Question 6: Is there alignment on the priority issues and insights on which marketing capability development should focus?   1 2 3 4 5

Based on analysis and assessment of the current situation, what are the most important issues and opportunities that have most impact on marketing capabilities and commercial growth performance?

Objectives

Question 7: Is the overall goal of the marketing capability programme or initiative clear and linked to the business or organization's overall objectives?   1 2 3 4 5

What is the central purpose of the marketing capability development programme? How closely aligned is this goal to the overall growth objectives of the organization?

Question 8: How well defined are specific capability development objectives, KPIs and the approach to tracking results?   1 2 3 4 5

How is the success and progress of marketing capability development activities being measured over time?

Strategy

Question 9: How clear and focused is the strategy   1 2 3 4 5
and the guiding principles for the capability
programme's design?

What are the key assumptions and beliefs that underpin
the design of the programme? Which principles must be
taken into account to ensure the initiative builds the
capabilities needed to drive growth and fits the culture of
the organization?

Question 10: How clear are the main capability   1 2 3 4 5
programme elements and project streams required to
deliver the objectives?

What are the key deliverables, modules or work streams
at the heart of the capability development programme?
How will these be structured and integrated to make
sure the programme is focused, clear and coherent and
achieves its goals?

Question 11: Is the capability programme branding   1 2 3 4 5
hierarchy and communication clear, compelling and
aligned?

What names, logos, icons, positioning, graphic identity
and internal communication strategy are being used to
build awareness, involvement and commitment for the
programme within the business?

Plan

Question 12: Are the roles and capability development responsibilities of key stakeholders clear and understood?   1 2 3 4 5

Who is responsible for the leadership, development and delivery of the programme as a whole and for each specific project element?

Question 13: Are the resource requirements well defined in financial and people terms?   1 2 3 4 5

What financial budget is needed to fund the investment in marketing capabilities? What resources are required to work on the initiative? What is the commercial justification for allocating these resources to the programme?

Question 14: Is the overall time plan clear, realistic and achievable?   1 2 3 4 5

What are the key milestones in the development, delivery and review of the programme to ensure sustainable impact?

Question 15: Is my personal role clear in driving or sponsoring marketing capability development?   1 2 3 4 5

What is my personal interest here? Am I able to play a role as a leader of marketing excellence, a sponsor, a subject matter expert, a champion, a cross-functional team member or another role? How might I take this forward? How should I seek to engage?

Scores (maximum 100 points)

<40 – Behind the curve: It sounds as though marketing excellence is not yet high on your organization's agenda. The key priority is to make sure the CEO or CMO appreciates the importance of creating a marketing capability strategy and plan to help them drive their business growth ambitions for the organization. Without their sponsorship and active endorsement it will be impossible to deliver change.

40–60 – Average: Some of the foundations are in place but you still lack clarity in some fundamental areas that are essential for building marketing excellence. A stage of diagnosis, assessment and stakeholder interviews to help build alignment would be well advised to bring together the Marketing and HR leaders to define the strategy and agree on priorities and elements of the marketing capability programme.

60–70 – Good: This organization sounds like it has begun its journey towards marketing excellence but it would be advisable to focus on the areas that still lack clarity. The business may not yet be thinking or working in a holistic way across *The Brand Learning Wheel*. Or, a marketing capability development strategy may have been defined but not yet moved to the stage of having successfully developed solutions or driven the embedding of change. The business may need to re-evaluate its approach and look again at whether it is effectively driving changes in ways of working or has fallen into the *training trap*.

80+ – Very strong: You are clearly well on the way to building marketing excellence. Your focus should be on sustaining the momentum and keeping ahead of the curve. Focus on pioneering new thinking in new and priority marketing areas while working more effectively around *The Brand Learning Wheel* to ensure marketing capability development is holistic and integrated. Make sure you are at the forefront both of marketing and of learning innovation. Live-action learning and developing learning communities should be high on the agenda. Think also about how the Marketing department can play a stronger role in equipping and enabling the wider organization and executives in other functions to create better customer value to help drive more sustainable, profitable, demand-led growth.

For further information and useful resources, or if you would like to set up a consultation to discuss specific marketing capability development needs, visit www.brandlearning.com.

INDEX